THE
MIDDLEMAN
ECONOMY

THE
MIDDLEMAN ECONOMY

How Brokers, Agents, Dealers,
and Everyday Matchmakers
Create Value and Profit

Marina Krakovsky

palgrave
macmillan

First published in 2015 by
PALGRAVE MACMILLAN®
in the United States—a division of St. Martin's Press LLC,
175 Fifth Avenue, New York, NY 10010.

Where this book is distributed in the UK, Europe and the rest of the world,
this is by Palgrave Macmillan, a division of Macmillan Publishers Limited,
registered in England, company number 785998, of Houndmills,
Basingstoke, Hampshire RG21 6XS.

Palgrave Macmillan is the global academic imprint of the above companies
and has companies and representatives throughout the world.

Palgrave® and Macmillan® are registered trademarks in the United States,
the United Kingdom, Europe and other countries.

ISBN: 978–1–137–53019–6

Library of Congress Cataloging-in-Publication Data

Krakovsky, Marina.
    The middleman economy : how brokers, agents, dealers, and everyday
matchmakers create value and profit / Marina Krakovsky.
        pages cm
    Includes bibliographical references and index.
    ISBN 978–1–137–53019–6—
    ISBN 1–137–53019–7
        1. Brokers. 2. Distributors (Commerce) I. Title.
HF5422.K717 2015
381'.2—dc23   2015007978

A catalogue record of the book is available from the British Library.

Design by Newgen Knowledge Works (P) Ltd., Chennai, India.

First edition: September 2015

10 9 8 7 6 5 4 3 2 1

Printed in the United States of America.

To my family

CONTENTS

INTRODUCTION

NOBODY LIKES A MIDDLEMAN, BUT MOST OF US ARE MIDDLEMEN

IN JANUARY 2014, AFTER PRESIDENT OBAMA DELIVERED his annual State of the Union address to Congress, several Republican senators responded with predictable disappointment. One detractor, Mike Lee, the junior senator from Utah, focused his carefully prepared critique on what the government should do to make the American Dream a reality for more people. To show that the president had failed to keep his word about the problem of income inequality, Lee said that for the past five years, the president "has promised an economy for the middle class, but all he's delivered is an economy for the middlemen."[1]

It wasn't clear who these "middlemen" were—Lee didn't explain[2]—but his choice of words was shrewd. Though the divide between the country's rich and poor grows ever wider, many Americans continue to consider themselves part of the middle class, which is why "the middle class" dominates rhetoric across the political spectrum,[3] but few think of themselves as middlemen.[4] And why would they identify as middlemen when the word carries so much ugly baggage? In English, most uses of "middleman" are derogatory, suggesting either that middlemen create no value or, at best, are a necessary evil.[5]

If you look more closely, though, you see that a huge number of people are in middleman professions, even if they avoid the word. The US Bureau of Labor Statistics tracks the obvious middlemen, those professionals who connect buyers with sellers. These are the millions of people in jobs like sales rep, real estate agent, financial advisor, headhunter, and insurance or mortgage broker. What's more, many other jobs in our complex economy have a less obvious middleman component. Think of wedding planners, those stylish and ultra-organized women and men who orchestrate the big event and help keep the bride from becoming bridezilla; that doesn't sound like a middleman job—until you consider all the vendors (such as the florist, the baker, the wedding-gown maker) who must be carefully selected and, equally important, held to the highest standard of their professions. Lawyers, too, act as middlemen when they broker deals. Your family doctor is a middleman when she refers you to a specialist or, more often, prescribes one particular drug rather than another: if your health insurer is a middleman between you and your doctor, your doctor is a middleman between you and the drug maker. Even as a reporter, I often think of myself as a middleman between the many people who have information to offer and my readers, who count on me and my editors to deliver only information that is interesting, accurate, timely, and useful to them.

The middleman element in these jobs isn't always apparent to the person doing the work, but it can make the difference between doing a decent job and doing an excellent one. For jobs where the middleman element is the very essence of the job, the effect of playing the role well is even more stark: buyers and sellers have certain expectations of people in a middleman position, and not meeting those expectations can sour business relationships. People rarely express these expectations until things go wrong, but this book lays them out explicitly, identifying the roles middlemen serve and what buyers and sellers expect from each role.

Why Middlemen Are More Important Than Ever

In every age, a new technology seems to herald the end of the middleman: from railroad networks to air travel, from the telegraph to the Internet to social media, each technology brings with it the promise of direct trade. After all, the thinking goes, who needs middlemen when buyers and sellers can communicate directly? In the mid-1990s, no less a tech visionary than Bill Gates proclaimed that the Internet would bring us "friction-free capitalism," eliminating the sort of waste that comes when people must drive all around town comparing prices of TVs, for example. Gates expected that the Internet itself (or the "information superhighway," as we were calling it then) would become "the ultimate go-between, the universal middleman," such that "often the only humans involved in a transaction will be the actual buyer and seller."[6]

Why didn't things play out that way? A major reason is the need for trust. Because middlemen have more frequent interactions with buyers and sellers than those people would if doing business without a middleman, they have more opportunities to establish trust with both sides. In no place is this more visible than on eBay—where, despite the opportunity for buyers and sellers to transact directly, most of the trading flows through trusted middlemen, those sellers who have built up the best reputations over thousands of transactions. We see in eBay's early days, for example, the rise of brick-and-mortar services like AuctionDrop and iSoldIt; people trying to make a buck through eBay's virtual garage sale didn't list their old Beatles albums and Pez dispensers on eBay themselves but paid these intermediaries a commission of as much as 45 percent to do it for them. Now that eBay has been around for years, thousands of people make their living by buying specialty products and reselling them on the site, the preeminent among them enjoying over \$150,000 in sales *per month*. Even those in the second tier, the platinum-level power sellers, make monthly sales of at least \$25,000. These hugely successful sellers, one of whom you'll meet in this book, clearly aren't selling their own castoffs—they are wholesalers and retailers of other people's goods. Far from killing the middleman, eBay has generated a thriving new breed.

It's not just eBay. What's happened on eBay is very similar to what's happened on LinkedIn. It's all about middlemen. Even though hiring managers and prospective employees can find and contact each other through the site, the fact is that professional recruiters are the company's highest-revenue customers, paying more than do all of the job seekers on LinkedIn combined.[7] Likewise, instead of pushing aside real estate agents, sites like Trulia and Zillow (recently merged into one company) partner with the agents by charging them to advertise.[8] Even though real estate agents no longer have a lock on local listings, 91 percent of houses in the United States are still sold through an agent.[9] YouTube, through which anyone can post their own videos, build an audience, and get a share of the resulting ad sales, is the sort of site that suggests we can bypass cultural "gatekeepers"; indeed, it is a do-it-yourselfer's dream, and it has made micro-celebrities out of hundreds of niche performers (teen makeup mavens, quirky home cooks, surprisingly compelling housecats) who, talented or not, would have remained obscure without the Internet's low distribution costs. Yet, to reach new heights of fame and fortune, these newly minted celebrities have been signing with professional middlemen—the talent agents who scout YouTube for clients needing an advocate in negotiating TV deals and endorsement contracts.[10] Facebook, Twitter, and other social media make it easy to strike up conversations with strangers, but when big stars use Facebook and Twitter to engage with fans, it is typically through social media marketers, publicists, and other middlemen with the expertise to do the job better and more efficiently than the celebrities could on their own.[11] Finally, consider the workings of the so-called "peer-to-peer" or "sharing" economy—people selling bits of unused labor or other form of spare capacity—which wouldn't exist through buyers and sellers acting alone. Everywhere you look in the sharing economy, from Airbnb to TaskRabbit, Uber, and ZocDoc, right in the center is a middleman business.

So much for the end of middlemen. Of course, there is no question that the Internet has shaken up entire industries and caused the loss of many middleman jobs: think of the stockbroker who merely executes your trade or the travel agent who does nothing more than take your order. But on the whole, the web's growth has actually gone hand in hand with a rise in the middleman class, and economic statistics show that middlemen now make up a larger part of the economy than ever. Daniel Spulber, the Kellogg economist who's studied the matter more than anyone, calculated that back in 1999 middlemen contributed 25 percent to the gross domestic product (GDP) of the United States, already an impressive figure.[12] But by 2010, the last year for which enough data was available, the portion had grown to 34 percent: more than a third of the US economy was made up of the efforts of middlemen.[13]

What Do Middlemen Do, Exactly?

How is it possible that middlemen are still thriving? The simplest answer is that they provide value to buyers and sellers, and providing value is the surest way to staying relevant. Interestingly, and somewhat counterintuitively, the Internet has created new opportunities for middlemen to provide value. One such provider is Mike Maples Jr. the founding partner of the venture capital firm Floodgate, whose work we will look at later in this book. "One way to look at middlemen," Maples says, "is that because of the advent of the Internet, the world has become more 'inter-networked.'"[14] More people, companies, and products are connected than ever.

In this highly connected world, "things and entities that acceler-ate connections are going to be more valuable," Maples believes.[15] This idea is self-evident when you think of core Internet tech-nologies and social networking tools that speed up our personal connections; it is also true of middleman businesses Maples has backed, such as Chegg, Lyft, and TaskRabbit, that speed up con-nections between buyers and sellers. Perhaps more surprisingly, it is also true of many human middlemen, including venture capi-talists like Maples himself: great at spotting high-potential entre-preneurial ideas, effective venture capitalists (VCs) command the space between entrepreneurs and the limited partners (LPs) who entrust VCs with their capital. For the LPs, a venture capitalist connects their investment dollars with business ideas capable of generating high returns; for the entrepreneurs with these promis-ing ideas, the venture capitalist channels the LPs' dollars toward the ideas and also helps entrepreneurs quickly form other important connections—to talent, to trusted advisors, and, if all goes well, all the way to the stock market.[16] The rest of us benefit, too, whenever we enjoy the products and services of innovative entrepreneurial ventures, because without the VCs, the most high-flying compa-nies might never get off the ground. "That's how I look at what a middleman does," Maples says. "They connect nodes on a network to increase the value of the network."

That is as simple and useful an explanation of a middleman's job as you're likely to hear. But for someone looking to become such a middleman, that job description raises new questions. What kind of networks most benefit from the addition of a middleman? Which nodes should middlemen focus on connecting? How do they form those connections, and what can they do to strengthen them? In answering such questions, I contend that middlemen provide value by playing some combination of six roles and that the most successful middlemen are those who play those roles best.[17] Each role solves a particular problem—reduces a specific friction, a specific transaction cost—that, without the middleman, would inhibit or prevent mutually beneficial deals:

- The Bridge promotes trade by reducing physical, social, or temporal distance.
- The Certifier separates the wheat from the chaff and gives buyers reassuring information about the seller's underlying quality.
- The Enforcer makes sure buyers and sellers put forth full effort, cooperate, and stay honest.
- The Risk Bearer reduces fluctuations and other forms of uncertainty, especially for risk-averse trading partners.
- The Concierge reduces hassles and helps clients make good decisions in the face of information overload.
- The Insulator helps clients get what they want without the stigma of being thought too greedy, self-promotional, or confrontational.

In reality, of course, the roles overlap and interact: for example, in the course of even a single phone conversation, a successful middleman might move between playing an Enforcer and an Insulator without even noticing it. But to clarify these roles, we look at them one at a time, through a chapter devoted to each, showing how each role is played by some of the most skilled middlemen around. You will learn the mindsets and skill sets of value-creating middlemen, the nonobvious common denominators across industries that will enable eBay sellers (for example) to learn from successful talent agents, investment advisors to learn from travel agents, lawyers to learn from headhunters, and any middleman to learn something from all of them.

Notice how this approach differs from that of people who predicted that electronic commerce would lead to the end of middlemen. Proponents of that idea, which has been called the "threatened intermediaries hypothesis," began their argument with the premise that middlemen have traditionally been necessary to reduce the high transaction costs of the brick-and-mortar world. So far so good. But the rest of the argument was flawed: they reasoned that if the Internet reduced transaction costs, middlemen would become less necessary. The big flaw is to view all middlemen as providing just one service.[18] But reducing transaction costs covers a large mix of services that don't necessarily come in one bundle.[19] If the Internet lowers transaction costs, it could actually create more demand for middlemen. After all, the Internet reduces costs for everyone—and when it reduces a middleman's costs more than it does someone else's, buyers and sellers prefer to keep doing business through the middleman.[20] That's why, despite the obsolescence of many travel agency jobs, for example, a certain class of travel agent is still thriving.[21] Ellison Poe, owner of Poe Travel in Little Rock, Arkansas, is a perfect example, and after you meet her in a later chapter, you will understand why she says the Internet has had no downside whatsoever for her and why, on the contrary, it has been "a total pro, a great thing, a positive force in the world."[22] As some middlemen disappear, others will become more successful. As the journalist Thomas Petzinger Jr. astutely pointed out during the dot-com era, "The same communication and information technology by which Wal-Mart wiped out small-time retailers permits a small-time industrial distributor to compete with General Electric."[23]

Out with the Parasite, In with the Partner

I've said that the most successful middlemen provide value for buyers and sellers; this is true, but it is not the whole story. The missing piece is that it is not enough to create value: you must also be able to capture some of the value you have created. The middleman who creates $100 worth of value per transaction but incurs $150 in costs to do so won't stay in business for long. Raising the price to better cover costs isn't the answer because it means charging more than the value you create. A constant challenge for every middleman is to do the work at lower cost (more efficiently) than buyers or sellers could on their own and more efficiently than competing middlemen; only then can the middleman be seen as a good deal for both sides.

In thinking through the sorts of middlemen I want to hold up as exemplars, I have used a simple two-by-two matrix, based on an elegant model developed by the psychologist Susan Fiske and her colleagues to explain how we respond to individuals, groups, and even brands[24] (see Figure 1).

The worst type, combining low warmth and low competence, is the Parasite. Leeches, bloodsuckers, and scum—all these hateful words reveal a view of the middleman not only as subhuman but also as not capable of productive activity.[25] By prospering at the expense of others, such people evoke disgust or contempt, hence the impulse to avoid or root out the parasite, to "cut out the middleman."[26] When I began my research, I thought that those who thought of middlemen as parasites weren't giving middlemen proper credit. As the late economist Robert L. Steiner once wrote, "Society honors those who build better mousetraps but suspects those who market mousetraps better."[27] I reasoned, as Steiner did, that any contempt toward middlemen came from ignorance of the

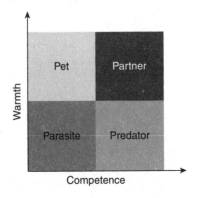

Figure 1 Each quadrant represents a unique combination of warmth and competence. The Partner, combining warmth and competence, inspires admiration. Its opposite, the Parasite, inspires contempt or disgust. The Predator and Pet inspire ambivalent feelings: the cold and competent Predator breeds resentment, while the warm and incompetent Pet inspires pity.

sometimes hard-to-see value middlemen provide: compared to the concrete and well-defined work of most producers, what middlemen do is abstract, intangible, and often nebulous. It is, after all, much easier to see the value of the farmer who sweats in the fields or of the painter who transforms a blank canvas into a work of art than it is to appreciate the value of the merchant or the gallerist, people who "merely" bring these products to market. It has not helped matters that scorn toward middlemen has historically been wrapped up with ethnic hatred toward middleman minorities, such as Jewish financiers and Korean shopkeepers. To my mind, nasty characterizations of middleman minorities as unwelcome guests feeding off their hosts further discredited the notion that middlemen are parasites.[28]

I am still convinced that the general *stereotype* of the parasitic middleman is wrong—as all stereotypes are—but the more reporting I did, the harder it was to deny that in many *specific* cases, individual middlemen or organized groups of them do act like free riders, causing more harm than good. That's how many of us regard Goldman Sachs, the Wall Street giant that the journalist Matt Taibbi famously, and to great applause, called "a great vampire squid wrapped around the face of humanity, relentlessly jamming its blood funnel into anything that smells like money."[29] Indeed, a study of brand perceptions showed that people's ratings of Goldman Sachs put the company squarely in the cold-incompetent quadrant.[30]

It's not just Goldman Sachs that can evoke contempt, of course. Consider today's typical money managers: whether they are personal financial advisors or pros managing multibillion-dollar mutual funds, most fail to beat the market—and when you take management fees into account, most actually underperform cheaper alternatives, such as index funds.[31] What's more, although there may be value to having an expert tailor a portfolio of investments right for your age and risk preferences, recent evidence suggests that financial advisors tend to create one-size-fits-all portfolios for their clients, providing off-the-rack services for bespoke-level fees.[32] So when people say, as PBS economics correspondent Paul Solman has, that "most money management firms are parasites who live handsomely off innocent investors," their strong feelings have a basis in reality.[33] Consider, too, the primary middlemen in car sales in the United States: although many new-car dealers are probably skilled, honest, and customer-oriented, their trade groups are another story: the National Automobile Dealers Association and its state and local counterparts seem most concerned with lobbying for protectionist laws that benefit neither car buyers nor manufacturers.[34] Middlemen who are seen as both cold (interested only in their own gain) and incompetent (creating more cost than value) will evoke contempt,[35] and for them, the Parasite label is harsh but more or less apt.

Being seen as a Predator is somewhat better: Predators are at least good at what they do. But a Predator is far from an ideal partner because he is really looking out for number one. Like some of the comically greedy investment tycoons on the TV show *Shark Tank*, or any bully of a middleman, Predators are competent but cold, capturing an outsize share of any value they create. The Fair Trade movement has tried to protect smallholder farmers in the developing world from precisely such middlemen,[36] who in Latin American countries are known by the wolfish moniker "coyotes."[37] Middlemen can prey on unsuspecting buyers, too, as when some retailers in the Fair Trade supply chain take advantage of the naiveté of Western consumers by charging markups for the fair trade label that are far higher than what growers receive.[38] In general, anyone who preys on the vulnerable or ill-informed fits the bill: in banking, it's lenders to the desperate, from mafia-style loan sharks to the predatory lenders who exploit the elderly and the disabled.[39] In high tech, it's patent aggregators, also known as patent trolls—companies that build up portfolios of patents not to ease patent licensing to firms that create products but to threaten alleged infringers with costly lawsuits.[40] In academia, it's predatory publishers, those with no scholarly credentials masquerading as distributors of legitimate journals.[41] A snake in the grass is still a snake, and a wolf in sheep's clothing is still a wolf—only more dangerous. For any two-faced middleman, the Predator label is apt.

There's another class of middlemen who, by dint of high skill and low morals, fit the Predator mold. This is the middleman who causes harm to the larger society, creating what economists call "negative externalities." Pimps and drug dealers, for example, may be great at what they do, but most of us wouldn't call them good, even if they do provide value for one side or the other. Similarly, middlemen who abet insider traders, thieves, and other law-breakers can be perfectly competent insulators, but they won't be seen by most of us as warm. (Parasites harm society, too, but they are worse because they harm even the buyers and sellers.) In general, people seen as cold and competent can do quite well for themselves, but they inspire resentment and a desire for retaliation against the harm they cause.[42] The Predator is fearsome but makes so many enemies that he is always at risk of being toppled or pushed aside either by government action or by warmer competitors, those who offer more favorable deals.

The opposite of the Predator is what I call the Pet—the small class of middlemen who mean well but lack the skill to deliver on their good intentions. The prototype is your ten-year-old neighbor selling Girl Scout cookies to raise money for her troop: she means well, and the cookies are pretty tasty, but would you prepay $5 per box if they weren't for a good cause? Some mom-and-pop shops are in the same boat. We buy from local merchants for a variety of reasons, including convenience, but sometimes we choose such stores only for sentimental reasons and despite inconvenience and high prices. Picture, for example, a shopkeeper who might have done well in an earlier era but is struggling to adapt to modern times: he truly wants to serve you when he offers to place a special order for an item that's not in stock, but if you can get it online more quickly and at a lower price, you probably feel at least a little ambivalent about buying from him. Sentimentality goes only so far: if the price gap reaches a certain point, you may well switch loyalties. This warm and incompetent type inspires pity and a desire to help, which sounds nicer than the Predator. But as a middleman, you don't want to be the Pet type, who, like a lost puppy, relies for survival on the kindness of strangers.

My focus in this book is on the best combination, the Partner: those middlemen who are good at what they do and good to us. Psychologists tell us that to be admired, a person has to be seen as both *warm* (having cooperative intentions, like a friend or ally would) and *competent* (able to deliver on those good intentions). Admirable middlemen needn't be selfless; rather, they are interested in mutual benefits, win-win deals. If by helping buyers and sellers, they also benefit the larger society—creating, as risk-bearing VCs do, positive externalities—these middlemen are golden. With middlemen like that, everybody wins.

A Course on Middlemen

The most admirable middlemen never got a formal education in being a middleman because no such classes exist. Yet there's plenty of material for such an education because lots of social scientists have studied, from one angle or another, the questions of how middlemen provide value and profit from their roles between buyers and sellers. For example, economic theory has much to say about transaction-cost economics, two-sided markets, and intermediaries' ability to reduce information asymmetries between buyers and sellers. In particular, game theory informs our understanding of repeated interactions, reputations, shirking and cheating, and third-party enforcement. Social psychology and experimental economics show how acting on behalf of others affects people's behavior and impressions. And sociology offers insights into the ways the structures of social networks create opportunities for middlemen. This book reports on fascinating research from these and other fields, revealing the ways in which the scientific findings illuminate and reinforce the lessons that top middlemen have picked up on the job.

Conventional wisdom says that middlemen take a cut of every deal, so they raise buyer costs and reduce seller profits. In reality, by facilitating transactions that would otherwise not happen at all, good middlemen enlarge the size of the pie, making all parties better off. Many people assume that middlemen's work is easy because they don't actually create anything. But to create value, as we'll see, good middlemen must cultivate distinct skills and practices, which they deploy in work that, until now, has been largely hidden from public view. This book pulls the veil off these hidden traits and shows how you can cultivate them, too.

There are other myths this book dispels. Many of us believe that when buyers and sellers already know each other, they should deal with each other directly. Underlying this belief is the assumption that a middleman's only purpose is to bring buyers and sellers together. In fact, it turns out that sometimes everyone is better off when buyers and sellers keep their distance. Some of the most successful middlemen are masters at insulating their clients from the problems of being too close to the other party.

Instead of the demise of the middleman, we are seeing the rise of the middleman. In fact, ours is more than ever a middleman economy. You are surrounded by middlemen in ways you never realized. You may be a middleman in ways you never understood. If so, this book will help you be better in fulfilling your role by explaining why and how the very best are so successful and showing what to do to reach their level. If you're truly not a middleman, this book will not only teach you what to expect from the middlemen all around you, but will open your eyes to a set of opportunities for making a living that you never imagined.

1

THE BRIDGE

Spanning the Chasm

THE ROLE: *The Bridge promotes trade by reducing physical, social, or temporal distance. The most effective ones spot opportunities between disconnected individuals and groups. Bridges also understand that they must have something to offer each side from the get-go.*

Trading Between the Bungalows

Early in World War II, the Germans captured a young British soldier named R. A. Radford and sent him to an Italian Oflag, a prisoner of war camp for officers. The camp, like other Oflags, was run in accord with the Geneva Convention, which meant, among other things, that the prisoners didn't have to work to earn their keep. The captors took care of the prisoners' basic needs, and in addition the captives received occasional parcels from the Red Cross—packages consisting of canned beef and salmon, milk and butter and cheese, even small luxuries like cigarettes and chocolate. A few lucky prisoners received private care packages as well.

Like kids at home after trick-or-treating, officers began trading their rations. Some of the soldiers, for example, were Sikhs and didn't eat meat, so they would gladly exchange a tin of beef for some jam and margarine. Nonsmokers readily traded cigarettes for food. And just about everybody, including smokers without dietary restrictions, had varied personal preferences that created gains from trade: whenever two people wanted to trade, both would be better off.

This makeshift economy was the picture of cooperation. Before long, though, middlemen entered the picture. There was, for example, the Urdu speaker who capitalized on his knowledge of the language to buy beef from the Sikhs and resell it to others. And there was a story going around about a priest who wandered from bungalow to bungalow, trading this for that, until at the end of the day he had managed to turn a tin of cheese and five cigarettes into a complete parcel *in addition* to his original cheese and cigarettes. There's a perverse echo of the biblical loaves and fishes story here—as if the priest performed a miracle, not to feed the multitudes but to fatten himself.

It makes sense that the anecdote of the itinerant priest spread through the camp like a legend. Since he didn't produce any new goods, many people can't see where the surplus came from—so it looked to many as if something untoward was going on. To those used to zero-sum thinking, as many of us are, it looks as if the priest stole something or conjured it through black magic instead of earning it fair and square.[1]

We know all this because R. A. Radford was not only a soldier and a POW but also a trained economist. After his release, he wrote about his camp experiences in an academic paper that's become a classic in the economics literature and required reading in many an econ course.[2] Radford was interested in several aspects of life in the camp's simple, enclosed society—from the emergence of commerce without labor to the rise of cigarettes as the coin of the realm. But you sense, reading his paper, that he was particularly intrigued by the middlemen, who aroused curiosity but did not quench it: probably sensing the public's hostility toward them, the middlemen tried to keep a low profile.[3]

There is something iconic and deeply true about the story of the itinerant priest even if its repeated retelling distorted some of the details. The story conveys the essence of the middleman I call the Bridge. First and most important, the Bridge connects one island of people to another, spanning otherwise disconnected social networks. Radford, who had experience in several POW camps, explains that a typical Oflag—consisting of 1,000 to 2,500 prisoners—was divided into a bunch of bungalows, each with about 200 residents. In the camp with the trading priest, he writes, "we did not visit other bungalows very much and prices varied from place to place." In moving from bungalow to bungalow, then, the middleman could engage in a simple arbitrage, shrewdly exploiting the price differences across barracks.

Contrast this lively trade with the absence of a middleman: if people could trade only with their own bunkmates, they'd limit their market and fail to capture their goods' full value. Think of a bungalow with only vegetarians, for example, where dozens of tins of beef go to waste. By bridging the various bungalows, the middleman dramatically reduced such inefficiencies. Helping the captives get more of what they wanted for what they didn't want as much, the middleman created value and profited personally by capturing some of the value he created.

The world of the bungalows is so artificial that it may appear to have nothing to do with the real world of business. Yet its lessons apply all around us because versions of these bungalows are everywhere: in theory, of course, we are usually free to trade with anyone and everyone we want, but in practice our choice of direct trading partners is quite limited.

Most obviously, we are separated from others by geography, which has always held potential for great gains from trade and posed substantial trade barriers. The potential is great because two starkly different lands have quite different things to offer each other. Think, for example, of the frozen ponds of New England, where ice is so abundant it can be had almost for free, and the arid cities of India, where before refrigeration ice was so scarce that only royalty had ever seen it. The potential for profit was immense, but so were the impediments, the great distance raising the risk that much of the ice will melt on the long journey, thus evaporating any profit. It took a bold merchant, the "Ice King" Frederic Tudor, to bridge the divide. Think, too, of the silk traders and spice merchants who traveled across vast distances along the Silk Road to bring exotic goods from East to West. Within a single nation, too, geographic differences have always created gaps that were best filled by middlemen: it was middlemen who brought grains and fruits and vegetables from farms to cities and middlemen who took factory goods in the opposite direction.

The frictions of space have shrunk over the centuries—technologies like railroads, canals, container ships, and airplanes have made travel faster, cheaper, and safer. Physical distance is still important, but even more important is social distance, those gaps that separate people even when they live just a few miles apart.

Social Distance: Between Founders and Funders

When Drew Houston, one of the wunderkind founders of cloud-based file storage company Dropbox, tells the way he obtained venture funding for his start-up from Sequoia Capital, he credits a man named Pejman Nozad. Nozad, a highly successful rug salesman in Palo Alto when he met Dropbox's founders in 2008, had managed the unlikely feat of parlaying his position in the rug business into a far more lucrative one as a bridge between company founders and prospective funders. "Basically he was our pimp," Houston told Forbes magazine.[4]

Nozad, who thinks of the people in his large personal network as his friends—and of the introductions he makes as favors that need not be repaid—would prefer a less mercenary metaphor for his bridging role. But there's no arguing with the essence of what he accomplished: he connected a pair of hungry entrepreneurs with a team of deep-pocketed, experienced investors, simultaneously helping both sides and, indirectly, himself. Sequoia's willingness to bet several million dollars on Dropbox confirmed Nozad's hunch that the start-up had a bright future and cemented his decision to invest his own money. In the next several years, as Dropbox's valuation has soared, so has Nozad's personal fortune. His stake in the company is now valued at tens of millions of dollars; perhaps most important, his association with Dropbox also burnished Nozad's name as someone whom investors and entrepreneurs should take seriously, enabling him to go from angel investor to founding partner in his own VC firm, Pejman Mar Ventures, thus formalizing his middleman role between young entrepreneurs and people with funds to invest.

Pejman Mar Ventures is currently housed in an airy loft in downtown Palo Alto, just a few blocks from the Medallion Rug Gallery, where Nozad began building his network. The decor inside—spare, hip, and modern, with no Persian rug in sight—perfectly matches the youthful "lean start-up" set to which the firm caters. In some ways, of course, Pejman Mar is just like any venture capital firm, pooling money from investors, called limited partners, and divvying it up among the start-up companies in its portfolio. When a portfolio company does well, going public or getting acquired for a large sum, the venture firm and its LPs share in the profits. If a start-up flops—as even the most promising ones often do—everybody loses his or her share of the investment.

Mar moved from rug sales to high-tech investing at an auspicious time. The cost of starting a tech company has plunged in recent years, thanks to free and low-cost development tools and an distribution methods. Anybody with an idea, a laptop, and an Internet connection can give it a go, and many do, leading to an abundance of entrants, many of them still living in college dorm rooms. Although these founders do eventually need to raise money to fuel growth, they have many more sources of funding beyond the big firms with posh offices along Menlo Park's Sand Hill Road. Some need expert guidance and trusted connections as much as they need capital. VC firms have always provided a combination of all these services, but these services are increasingly becoming unbundled: as the competition among investors to back the next Facebook or Dropbox has intensified, the most promising entrepreneurs can pick and choose what they most want in an investor. As a result of these developments, even the most prestigious VC firms, like Sequoia, can no longer sit back and wait for the pitches to roll in.[5] Nozad saw that he could provide value to these VCs by connecting them to investment opportunities they might not otherwise have known about.

Now that he is running his own VC firm, Nozad offers budding entrepreneurs what few others currently do: free office space and access to his extensive network with no strings attached. This generous, nontransactional approach has worked for him before he became a VC. "I started making these introductions without any expectation that these favors would be returned," Nozad says. He points out, for example, that he likes to help entrepreneurs even if he's not a shareholder of their company. His relationship with Dropbox, which started at an event at the start-up accelerator Y Combinator and began to blossom over Persian tea at the rug gallery, was never transactional, either. "It's not like an agency—'I'll introduce you to these Hollywood producers, and if you raise money, I'll get five percent of the profit you make at the end of the day'—it never was like that."[6] At one point, as I began posing a question about "deal flow," a piece of VC jargon that had slipped from his lips, he interrupted to make sure I didn't get the wrong idea. "A lot of people look at deal flow," he said, "but these are all human beings, and we try not to call companies 'deals' or 'deal flow.'" Similarly, when I wondered whether he's thought about what his network looks like, he cut me off, as if objecting to the instrumental implication of the question.

"I don't look at it as tools, I look at it as my friends," he said. "In my mind everyone is a friend. I don't look at Doug Leone [his friend at Sequoia] as a tool to get to a company, or the executive at Google to get richer and do this thing," he said. He makes no distinction between his personal and professional connections, either: his colleagues, his business associates, the people he knows from his life as a soccer buff—they are all just friends, and friends help each other.

Recent psychological research suggests that this outlook might help would-be Bridges overcome awkward feelings that tend to arise from networking for professional gain. Many people feel uncomfortable engaging in professional networking. (One clever experiment showed that participants who thought about the prospect of going to a networking event to make professional connections actually expressed a greater urge to use cleaning products afterward, as if contemplating networking activities made them feel physically dirty.[7]) These feelings are especially acute if the networking is deliberate and calculated, rather than spontaneously arising out of working together. We don't get these icky feelings when we go out to make friends. Friendship is a two-way street, as concerned with the other person as with yourself, whereas professional networking often involves cultivating a relationship with the ultimate goal of personal gain, and most of us hate feeling that we're being selfish, let alone using another person. These unpleasant feelings deter us from networking more often. How do you overcome this psychological obstacle? The research suggests that one way is to think of your networking efforts as a way to help friends.

If that sounds like blurring the lines between business and friendship, that's because it is—in a good way. Problems in mixing business and friendship tend to arise when people do it backwards, tainting the friendship by exploiting it for business gain.[8] That's why few of us enjoy attending Tupperware-style home sales parties, which pressure us to buy from the host; these are business events under the guise of a social occasion. It's also what's so annoying about people who use Facebook to shill for their business—these are the people you want to "unfriend."

That's the opposite of Nozad's networking style: instead of looking for ways to use his friendships for business gain, which frays these personal ties, he is always looking for ways to help his friends and would-be friends, a pattern of behavior that tends to strengthen social bonds. In fact, this helpful attitude is the number one networking "secret" he offered in a list to accompany a *Forbes* magazine profile of him: with no expectation of anything in return, you should always be willing to help others with an introduction or a bit of your time, he told the magazine.[9] "If you do that for long, you create a reputation," he explained to me. "Silicon Valley is a small town—everybody knows each other."[10]

It is certainly true that reputational information travels quickly through small, tight-knit networks. In fact, that's why such networks can sustain a high level of cooperation: when people know there's a good chance that their honesty, kindness, and generosity will become well known to others (and potentially reciprocated), they're much more likely to engage in such altruistic behavior.[11] In a vast, sparsely connected environment like a big city or, worse, an anonymous online forum, Nozad's advice to always be willing to help others would actually backfire, making you a chump who always bears the costs of helping without a chance to reap the benefits. It is not all about the size or density of a network: in well-run online communities, in which users must go by their real names and can see each other's behavior, individuals can build a reputation, which promotes helping and deters incivility even on a massive network like LinkedIn. Typically, though, that is because a middleman Enforcer—a role we will get to in another chapter—plays an active part.

In reality, Silicon Valley is both a small town and a big city: not everybody in the Valley knows each other, of course—especially at times like these, when new players are emerging every day. This truth is evident from Nozad's own experience: if everyone actually knew each other, there'd be no need for Nozad's introductions. But there is a need, even though the people he is introducing might be living within five or ten miles of one another. Nozad's story shows that social distance, much like geographic distance, creates opportunities for Bridges.

To see what I mean, think of people as points on a piece of paper and think of the relationships between them as lines that connect those dots. Nozad might balk at this abstract, overly mathematical depiction of the ties between people, but it's a common way to look at human connections, especially in our Web 2.0 era. When Mark Zuckerberg or Jeff Weiner talk about the "social graph," this is what they mean, except they're referring to users of Facebook or LinkedIn. The points, or nodes, represent individual people, while the lines or links represent the social ties between the individuals.[12] Our social graphs from the online world are often a crude replica of our actual social networks. Just think of the people you may be close to who don't use social media. (Some of your close relatives, whom you talk to by phone, may not be on Facebook at all, and your own kids might be following half their classmates on Instagram, but not you.) Conversely, think of all your LinkedIn connections whom you last saw two jobs ago, if at all. Your social graphs online certainly overlap with your real-world network, but they aren't the same thing.

When sociologists plot out people's social networks, on the other hand, they look at actual interactions, whether online or off: who do you talk to most often? Whom do you e-mail every day, and who e-mails you back?[13] These sorts of interactions are the real clues to where the lines in the network diagram should lie: the more frequent and reciprocal the contact, the stronger the social tie. Social scientists have been constructing such diagrams[14] for decades for all kinds of social groups, from students at a suburban high school to members of a criminal gang.[15] And no matter what community you look at—the students, the criminals, employees of a company, residents of a city, members of a congregation, or far-flung colleagues in a professional association—the dots and lines in social networks aren't scattered randomly. Instead, people tend to form clusters: often by predictable groupings like age, gender, occupation, and so on.[16] If you work in a marketing department of a large company, for example, you're much more likely to have ties with other marketers than with people from accounting or product development. You might know one or two people in these other departments, and maybe more, but not nearly as many as you know from your own group. Likewise, the accountants form their own cluster, engineers their own cluster, and so on. The social distance within a cluster is much shorter than across clusters: interactions are less frequent, and information travels more slowly, if at all. When managers in a large organization bemoan the "silos" that make it hard to get anything done across departmental lines, they're talking about the downside of disconnected clusters.

But these silos and clusters can create a common way of talking and thinking about recurring situations, which makes it easier and faster to communicate and get things done within the cluster. And, as we've said, a close-knit cluster promotes trust. Clusters are efficient.

But the downside is a closedness to information and opportunities from outside the cluster, since people in a cluster tend to have the same information as others in the same cluster. Getting new information often requires looking outside the cluster, as the sociologist Mark Granovetter famously showed in his study of how men in the Boston suburb of Newton had gotten their jobs.[17] The job seekers in Granovetter's study, conducted in the 1970s, learned about job openings not from their inner circle (their own cluster) but from their "weak ties," such as people they knew from a previous job but rarely spoke with. Because of the flow of redundant information, clusters can become echo chambers, in which the same ideas actually get amplified over time, drowning out new, potentially better ideas.

So why don't we go outside our own clusters more often? Because doing so is costly. Look at Twitter, for example, where you can easily decide to follow anyone you want, even if they aren't following you. If you follow someone your friends don't follow—a specialist in medieval choral music, say, or a birdwatcher in Ireland—you may well hear an interesting and relevant new tidbit before your friends do, but you will also have to scroll through a lot of tweets that are irrelevant to you and your friends. If that signal-to-noise ratio falls too low, you'll want to stop following the outsider and stick with your existing cluster. The cost of maintaining a multitude of diverse connections, even in such a low-cost medium as Twitter, can be too high. In deciding how diverse to make our networks, we constantly face a trade-off between the novelty of going outside the cluster and the efficiency of sticking with our own kind. We make these trade-offs all the time, even if we aren't thinking of our online activity that way.

Because people tend to stay in their own cluster, the network structure has gaps between clusters—what the sociologist Ron Burt calls "structural holes."[18] A structural hole, which Burt describes as a boundary between two sides of a division of labor, keeps information from flowing from one cluster to another, much as physical chasms between countries make it more difficult for those countries to trade with one another. But whenever information from one group is valuable to people in another, anyone who can step in to bridge that divide—who can fill the structural hole—can provide value to one or both groups, and can enjoy various forms of profit. This special person is who I call the Bridge.[19]

Where do Bridges come in? They are the people directly connected to more than one cluster; often they belong to one of the clusters but have at least one close tie to another. For example, an engineer with a close friend in the accounting department can learn information to bring back to the engineering group. Bridges specialize in talking across groups and know what is most relevant for each. In so doing, Bridges help us obtain novel information without paying a high price for it. In fact, Burt has found that people who bridge structural holes are more likely to have their ideas judged as valuable.[20]

Understanding network patterns creates opportunities to bridge the gaps. That's true for all kinds of social networks, but it's especially clear in our founders-and-funders example, where Pejman Nozad acts as a Bridge. VCs certainly know the founders of the companies they've invested in, and those founders often go on to become VCs themselves. Still, the worlds of early-stage founders and those of established VCs are largely separate: even if the two groups live within five or ten miles of one another, VCs are more likely to know other VCs (and founders to know other founders) than for VCs and founders to know each other. This is the key divide in the social structure of the tech business, and there are at least two major reasons for it. First, one group is older and far wealthier than the other: 50-year-old multimillionaire VCs travel in different social circles than scrappy engineers fresh out of Stanford or MIT. Any two seasoned VCs are likely to have worked together, sat on the same corporate or nonprofit board, invested in some of the same companies, or have at least heard of each other through colleagues. They might have crossed paths with each other in personal life as well, running into each other at an elite club, restaurant, or fundraiser. These are just some of the ways, business and strictly social, through which they become enmeshed in roughly the same network cluster—a cluster young founders aren't a part of.

Even when funders and founders do find themselves at the same gathering—such as the parties Nozad has become known for—the groups don't mix naturally on their own: people feel much more comfortable with those who look like themselves, especially in unfamiliar environments. This is the other reason for a natural divide between funders and founders. For example, at a cocktail party to which Nozad had invited some young entrepreneurs, *Forbes* magazine reporter Victoria Barret observed that "Nozad's scruffy-looking crew sticks together like a high-school clique even though most barely know one another."[21] Having come to a networking event, they're avoiding the older men they might very much like to meet. That cliquishness, in turn, makes it all the less likely for a VC to approach them. The differences between the two groups, superficial and otherwise, make it hard for them to connect, let alone to see if there's potential for a mutually beneficial relationship. So even in close proximity, social distance creates a need for a Bridge.

In coming up with the idea of structural holes, Burt, now a professor at the University of Chicago Booth School of Business, was extending the observation of "weak ties" from Granovetter's study of how people find jobs; Burt saw the structural hole as the key to the patterns of information sharing. Bridges always have ties with members of each group, but these ties don't have to be weak. "Whether a relationship [spanning a structural hole] is strong or weak," Burt wrote in his seminal book, "it generates information benefits when it is a bridge over a structural hole."[22] Bridges, in other words, are ideally positioned to carry valuable information across clusters—and as Burt's research has shown, to profit from playing this bridging role.[23] Excellent networkers seem to understand this intuitively; for example, Reid Hoffman, the LinkedIn founder who is also known for his off-line networking skills, offers this piece of advice: "Introduce two people who do not know each other but ought to."[24] Doing this requires that you think about the people you know with an eye to how you can help them. That's what the Bridge does on a broader scale.

A Bridge to Somewhere

Burt's findings have led him to conclusions quite different from many people's intuitions about how networking works. Many of the MBA students he teaches, for example, are "looking to get connected to well-connected people," he says.[25] They try to ingratiate themselves with these powerful individuals, or they show off how clever they are—all in the hope that their new-found connections will somehow lead to an easy, high-paying job. It's a natural mistake to make: when we look around and see successful people, we notice that they have relationships with well-connected colleagues, leading some of us to assume that those connections helped them become successful. But a snapshot of a network at a single moment in time can't answer questions of what came first and which caused what, the connections or the superior performance.

Burt's research, though, does answer such questions, and shows that many people's intuitions about networking are wrong. Successful people aren't successful because of their ties to well-connected others; rather, they were able to develop ties with well-connected others because they themselves had something to offer.[26] Drawing on this research, Burt sets his students straight, often quoting from a teaching of Confucius: "Don't worry about whether you're known, worry about whether you're worth knowing." In other words, come up with great ideas, be well-connected yourself, and then people who *are* well-connected will want to be connected with you.

The advice to become worth knowing applies to anyone. It is about becoming excellent at what you do, whatever your profession. People who are good at what they do naturally build up a network of peers who respect them—fellow practitioners, customers, suppliers, and friends. By and large, the better we are at what we do, the better are the other people in our network: more capable and more respected themselves. It's the old birds-of-a-feather effect. But to become a Bridge, it is not enough to be at the center of your own network, no matter how good that network may be. (By definition, we are each at the center of our own network.) A Bridge must have substance and must *do* something.

This is wisdom Nozad seemed to have intuited all along. His job as a salesman at the Medallion Rug Gallery certainly gave him extraordinary access to well-connected individuals—think of not only the VCs, but CEOs and other rich and powerful locals who came into the store. But if he had stopped there, he would never have been able to be more than a rug seller to them, no matter how good he was at his job. Any bridge he was building would be a bridge to nowhere except maybe the rug bazaars of Iran and Pakistan. To offer something more valuable, he had to venture out and connect with entrepreneurs. That's when he began attending talks and conferences where such people flock and eventually hosted networking events himself, such as the Friday afternoon meet-and-greets at the rug gallery, bringing in speakers and serving cocktails. As he came to know more and more people, he was able to create more and more connections, and, in the process, to attract attention to the rug store and to himself.

Nozad's story is a lovely illustration of how a Bridge profits from helping both sides, but Nozad's experience is actually not typical of how a Bridge tends to arise. That is because Nozad didn't start out as a member of either group: he was neither a founder nor a funder. He wasn't exactly starting from nothing since he was able to forge some of his connections in the course of selling rugs, but he had to expend extraordinary effort to earn the trust of so many people in industries outside of his own; he also had to go out on a limb since he couldn't be sure that any of his efforts would ever pay off. Normally, it is much easier for a Bridge to emerge out of one cluster or another. If the Bridge is an outsider to both groups, then people tend to regard the person with suspicion. Burt says that when he presents his research on structural holes and asks students where in their organization they'd put in a bridging tie to improve operations, "they inevitably put a dot that links up stuff." That placement of the Bridge isn't likely to work. "Why would anybody buy into this person?" Burt asks. People are strapped for time, so they don't want to bother with an interloper even if that outsider might help them in the end.

Therefore, it is wiser to "go for bridges that pay for themselves right away," Burt says. "If you don't, then bridging merely adds costs, and nobody is for that." The best way to get a Bridge to "pay its own freight," as Burt puts it, is for the Bridge to already know the problems of one group, so as to be able to quickly start solving those through the resources of the other group. Often, the best way for the Bridge to do that is to emerge from one of the groups.

A Bridge Across Time

But what if you don't seem to have anything of value to offer, such as access to a wealthy clientele or a beautiful rug gallery to hold parties? What if you don't have a profession that embeds you in a network of valuable contacts? Is there any chance of becoming a Bridge then? The story of LaJuan Stoxstill-Diggs,[27] a man who makes his living buying and selling appliances on Craigslist, shows that there is. His opportunities to profit are constrained by what he knows and whom he knows—as they are for all of us—but his knack at spotting middleman opportunities has propelled him well above others with a similar background.

In talking about how he got to where he is, Stoxstill-Diggs usually starts with the story of his first sale, in 2004, when he was an out-of-work 21-year-old father of three, broke, and rather desperate. Months earlier, when the insurance company he was working for shrank its Nashville office, he lost his job processing medical claims. His wife was going to school and taking care of their young children, so the breadwinner role fell to him, and when his unemployment insurance ran out, he tried to make ends meet by helping out his brother in his moving business. That business wasn't thriving, either. His brother didn't even own a moving truck: when he got a gig, he'd rent a U-Haul, and when he needed an extra pair of arms, he'd hire Stoxstill-Diggs, paying him $100 a day. For Stoxstill-Diggs, these opportunities for day labor would pop up once or twice a week, not nearly enough to support a family of five. But the moving business had its perks. Clients often gave away their old furniture or appliances before the move, and one day his brother passed a washing machine on to Stoxstill-Diggs. Their deal was simple: if Stoxstill-Diggs sold the washer, the brothers would split the proceeds.

That day, Stoxstill-Diggs called a few people who might know someone who needed a washing machine, but got no takers. Seeing no other options, he turned to Craigslist, where he posted a couple of pictures and a description of the appliance. To his surprise and delight, he found his buyer within two hours and sold the used washer for $125. For someone in his position, this was a windfall—and more important, the first step on a path he's still following today. Instead of waiting for someone to hand him a washer or dryer, as his brother had done for him, he buys used ones on Craigslist, often for as little as $50 or $100, and turns around and resells them, again through Craigslist, for $150 or more. He calls this business of flipping the "Craigslist Hustle." Most weeks he earns $1,200 to $1,500, and he has built a solid middle-class life for his family: they've since bought a house and cars, taken vacations, gotten insurance coverage, and begun a savings plan.

All that is a long way from where he was right after his first Craigslist sale, when he sensed that flipping appliances was a good venture but lacked enough money to buy another appliance to resell. He decided to sell off some of his own possessions to scrounge up the cash. "I just went through my house finding items I knew I could replace—like a chair, an end table, some computer hardware—and just scraped together as much as I could at the time so I could purchase something I could make a profit on." Selling your possessions to invest in items you hoped to flip for profit may sound dicey, but Stoxstill-Diggs wasn't that scared because he had so little to lose. "In the beginning, I was already at the bottom, so it didn't hurt me to sell things I didn't need at the moment," he explains. "I was thinking of surviving day by day, so I really didn't have time to think about it." Later, he would have time to think, but after four or five of these flips, he could see that what he was doing was working, so he felt completely comfortable.

You might say he had a leg up on the middleman livelihood. Stoxstill-Diggs, who today is the kind of person who ends his conversations by telling you to "have a blessed day," narrowly managed to escape his rough East Nashville neighborhood without a rap sheet, but not because he was squeaky-clean. "I did a lot of illegal activities that I never got arrested for"—mainly street narcotics, he says—"so I have the mindset of a hustler." Dealing drugs was dumb, he now realizes, since friends of his have landed in jail. But it was a quick way to make a buck, better than other options open to him at the time, and it taught him a basic lesson in being a middleman. "As youngsters we learned the value of buying low and selling high," he says. He believes Craigslist is full of similar opportunities for hardworking people who have trouble finding a regular job. Anyone can buy and sell on Craigslist, even people with a criminal record, whom most employers avoid hiring.

This openness has been both a blessing and a curse for the site and its casual users: a market with easy entry attracts lots of buyers and sellers, which creates lots of chances for trade. Yet it also invites spammers, scammers, and worse, as several well-publicized Craigslist murders made painfully clear.[28] For people like Stoxstill-Diggs, though, the site's openness is mainly a blessing, enabling him to reach both buyers and sellers without spending money on advertising. In fact, by letting people post their ads for free, Craigslist has diverted hundreds of millions of dollars a year in classified ad revenue away from local newspapers, who are the big losers in this development.[29]

Most people who hear the story of Stoxstill-Diggs are impressed by the way he bootstrapped his family out of poverty; in fact, friends urged him to write a book to tell others what's he done, and to teach them to do the same. He's done this in his e-book, *The Craigslist*

Hustle, which he says has sold several thousand copies.[30] What interested me most about Stoxstill-Diggs, though, is that he found a middleman opportunity in a free online marketplace. Millions of people in each market where Craigslist operates flock to it when they've got something to buy or to sell. So why would someone sell a washer or dryer to Stoxstill-Diggs on Craigslist for $50, instead of selling it for the $150 Stoxstill-Diggs can ultimately get for it? Why do buyers pay $350 for a pair of appliances if they can get the same used pair for the $100 or $150 Stoxstill-Diggs pays? Put another way, if Craigslist is a marketplace open to anyone, why is there room for a middleman and his markup?

I put this question to a finance professor, Jim Angel of Georgetown University, because I had a hunch that what Stoxstill-Diggs was doing on Craigslist wasn't so different from what a certain class of professionals do on Wall Street. These people, broadly called "market makers," sometimes go by other names: on the New York Stock Exchange, they're called specialists; on NASDAQ, a purely electronic market, they're called dealers. But wherever they operate—and this could include the Dojima Rice Exchange in Osaka or the Chicago Board of Trade or any of a number of securities exchanges around the world—market makers are just "a bunch of people who do exactly the same thing," Angel says.[31] All these market makers provide *liquidity* by being willing to buy what other people want to sell, and sell what other people want to buy, without actually using that inventory: they take that inventory as soon as the seller wants to get rid of it, holding on to it in the hope of profiting from a higher price later.

Why does Craigslist need market makers? The same reason the NYSE does: without them, you might not find a willing buyer just when you want to sell. And even if on Craigslist you were willing to wait a day or two to find the right buyer, you can't be sure the buyer will be there then, either. Angel explains it this way: "Craigslist will tell you who's in the market right now, it'll tell you a little about who was in the market earlier, but it doesn't tell you anything about who will be in the market [at some point in the future]." This is where the professional middleman comes in: "Someone who's more familiar with the market, who understands its ebbs and flows, will have a much better sense of what the market will look like when they go to off-load their inventory," Angel says, using the appliance example to explain how this model works for Stoxstill-Diggs. "Let's say I want to get rid of my old Kenmore washer and dryer. I stick an ad on Craigslist, and I sell it for a song, and I'm just grateful that they hauled it away. I could go through the old Craigslist ads to see what similar washer-dryers were advertised for, but I don't know how many were actually sold, and I don't know what kind of people were buying them: I don't know what kind of response the previous ads got. So even though there's a lot of information on Craigslist, it's painful to wade through." Someone who's constantly scanning Craigslist posts, and doing this day after day and month after month, has already done that. Stoxstill-Diggs knows with a high degree of certainty what that Kenmore washer and dryer will sell for, or how long he has to wait in the middle of the summer to sell a three-year-old Maytag washer for $350. "There's a lot of experience in the middleman," Angel says.

Indeed, the day I spoke with Stoxstill-Diggs, he started our conversation by pointing out a pattern that most people without his experience wouldn't have known. It had been a good morning, he said, "because the weather is warming up, and it's the end of the month, when lots of people are used to moving." That particular end of the month happened to fall on the weekend, another busy time for moves, so Stoxstill-Diggs knew there'd be a lot of great bargains over the next two or three days. Although he resells 70 percent of his appliances on the first day, and never takes longer than three days to flip an appliance unless he's going out of town, he can fit up to fifteen washer-and-dryer sets in his garage, so if he wanted to take full advantage of the weekend's bargains, he could stock up over the weekend, and then spend the coming days only on selling them.

Understanding these cycles helps Stoxstill-Diggs provide a service to sellers, who either don't know that they could charge a higher price or just don't want to wait to turn their old appliance into cash. Some of his sellers are either moving or upgrading to newer appliances—but most, he says, are in desperate straits: they're facing divorce, foreclosure, and bills that need to be paid right away. They are liquidating their assets, and Stoxstill-Diggs is sitting by to give them that liquidity. If he weren't there, they'd have to sell directly to the next user of that appliance, which means waiting for that person to come along. Of course, both occasional sellers and professional middlemen would like to get the highest price with the minimum waiting—but when they have to choose one or the other, they reveal their true preferences. Professionals are usually willing to wait a little longer to sell something at the right price, in part because they know what the target price should be and how long they will probably need to wait. Occasional sellers are usually less patient and are willing to sacrifice some money for time: they'll settle for $50 or $100 less if they can avoid having to wait days for the right buyer, field questions, and so on.

So it's easy to see how Stoxstill-Diggs provides value to sellers. What may be harder to grasp is the value Stoxstill-Diggs provides to buyers, who, after all, have to pay more than if they'd bought from the seller directly. Why would they want to do business with a middleman? But here's the thing: he's providing a degree of liquidity to them, too. Think of the person whose washing machine breaks down on a Tuesday. This would-be buyer goes to Craigslist in search of a replacement. Maybe he finds one, and maybe he doesn't; it all depends on the supply at that time. Without the middleman, the supply is uneven—quite high on weekends and month ends, for example, and too low at other times. The middleman evens out these peaks and valleys: because of the profit he stands to make from buying at times of abundant supply (and low prices) and selling at times of scarcity (and high prices), he makes it more likely that even midweek there'll be an appliance available for purchase. In this way, he provides liquidity to both sides, serving as a kind of bridge across time: in effect, he's connecting Saturday's seller to Monday's buyer.

By providing a valuable service to both buyers and sellers, this middleman becomes something of a two-way Bridge. And that creates a kind of synergy that neither a storage business nor the moving business can enjoy. I've already compared him to a market maker on Wall Street—but he is also like a bank, which doesn't just lend money but also takes deposits, able to operate more efficiently because of a synergy between the two activities.[32]

Becoming a Bridge: SitterCity

Another middleman who has profited from spotting a bridging opportunity is Genevieve Thiers. When I get Thiers on the phone from her home in Chicago, she's snowbound with her two-year-old twins. The weather outside is -3 degrees F (-16 degrees C), and nobody is going anywhere. The little boys are with their nanny; child care is not a problem, Thiers jokes because she knows I want to talk to her as the founder of SitterCity, an online service that matches parents with babysitters and nannies.[33]

SitterCity, which today is successful enough to have allowed Thiers to retire on a chunk of her founder's stock, struck me as remarkable for two reasons. First, the business started during the dot-com bust—not only before such online matching businesses as Uber, TaskRabbit, and Airbnb had begun to spring up everywhere, but even before the rise of social networking sites. Facebook, LinkedIn, and even now-defunct Friendster did not yet exist in 2000. The other surprise about SitterCity: Thiers is no tech whiz, and she hadn't taken a single business class; when she conceived of the idea, she was studying opera as a music major at Boston College.

The idea for the service came to her when she saw a heavily pregnant woman who had come to the college to post fliers in search of a babysitter, and Thiers couldn't believe the absurdity of the situation. There had to be an easier way for parents to find child care, she thought, especially in a region so full of students looking for part-time work. The Boston area is home to 33 colleges—not just Harvard and MIT and Thiers's own Boston College, but also Tufts, Brandeis, Babson, Northeastern, Boston University, Wellesley, Simmons, the Berklee College of Music, and dozens of community colleges, trade schools, and other places to find students interested in babysitting. The demand side was strong, too: Boston's suburbs are home to hundreds of thousands of affluent families with young children. Yet the two groups didn't travel in the same circles. They were free to interact, of course, but for all the contact they had they might as well be POWs in their separate bungalows.

Parents did have some options for finding sitters in those days: they could turn to a pricey agency, which could pair them with a prescreened nanny. And they could use word-of-mouth referrals, fliers, and maybe a help-wanted ad or Craigslist. But there was nothing in between. "When I saw that mother posting fliers on campus," she once told a reporter, "I realized that there was this weird white space between paying $2,000 to join a nanny agency and trying to find child care yourself, so I set out to fill it."[34]

It was as if there were a chasm separating the sitters and the parents, with a pricey toll bridge on one end and a rickety footbridge on the other. One was fast, reliable, and expensive; the other cheap, slow, and dangerous. The huge space between those routes was begging for a wide, reasonably priced bridge, one that the vast majority of people would prefer to use. Thiers set out to build this bridge.

Bridges as Two-Sided Markets

Lacking both experience and theoretical knowledge, she didn't realize that the bridge she was trying to build had the interesting properties of what economists call a *two-sided market*. These days, two-sided markets (sometimes called two-sided networks or two-sided platforms) are everywhere because many of today's Internet start-ups are middlemen businesses of exactly this type: whether you're talking about connecting homeowners with guests (Airbnb) or drivers with fares (Lyft and Uber) workers with small jobs (TaskRabbit) restaurants with diners wanting take-out meals (GrubHub, Eat24) or doctors with patients (ZocDoc), you're describing a two-sided market. At the same time, and maybe not coincidentally, the study of two-sided markets has become a popular field among academics, with many opinions about what counts as a two-sided market. One researcher I talked to, economist Marc Rysman of Boston University, told me there have been so many papers proposing their own definitions that he was "almost embarrassed to have participated in that literature."[35]

Under some definitions, just about any market is two-sided, but such an inclusiveness makes the label useless. What can all researchers agree on? Media companies, such as magazines and TV networks and social media, are two-sided by any definition, since they match advertisers with relevant audiences. Online matching markets, including SitterCity and Match.com and many others, also count. What all these companies have in common, Rysman explains, is that an intermediary is setting prices for mediating between two distinct groups of users (the two sides of the market), and crucially, "there's a sense in which one side cares about what happens on the other side." On Match.com, for example, women looking to meet a man want to see how many and what sorts of men are using the service, and men feel the same way about the site's female users. Having lots of participants on both sides increases the odds of finding a good match. Because buyers usually want to be where sellers are, and sellers usually want to be where buyers are, a two-sided network with an abundance of participants on one side tends to attract more comers on the other side. In the language of economics—and increasingly of tech investors—two-sided markets usually create "indirect network effects."[36] As one side grows, the network becomes more attractive to the other side, and as the other side grows, it attracts more users who want to connect with that side. This positive feedback loop promotes rapid growth once you reach critical mass. That's why tech investors love network effects.

But this same growth curve means two-sided markets are extremely hard to get off the ground, as Thiers found out firsthand: how do you get a sitter to sign up for a service that doesn't have a single parent, and likewise, how do you get a parent to sign up for a service that has no sitters?[37] It's not that the service is untested—that would be a problem any new business must contend with. Rather, it's that without both sides on board, there is no service at all. If you want to open a gift shop—a middleman business that by most definitions is *not* a two-sided market—you lease your retail space, you buy some inventory from a wholesaler, and you're ready to roll: a wholesaler won't refuse your prepaid order because you have no customers yet. But if, on the other hand, your whole value proposition is access to your network, then if you have no network, you've got nothing. So how can you possibly begin?

The typical way out of this chicken-and-egg problem is for the middleman to subsidize one side, thus getting these initial users to sign up before there's anything on the other side. Even after a two-sided market takes off, with plenty of users on both sides and therefore the potential to charge both sets of users, middlemen usually continue to offer the service for free to one side while making all their money from charging the other side for access, relying on these cross-subsidies for continued growth and profit. As Chris Anderson put it in *Free*, "People are making lots of money charging nothing."[38] Some middleman businesses go so far as to *pay* one set of users to join the network, hoping that a large user base will attract enough paying users on the other side to more than justify the subsidy. Banks that issue credit cards, for example, can charge an annual fee to cardholders and transaction fees to merchants, and some do both. But many banks offer credit cards with no annual fee and further sweeten the deal by paying cash back or letting cardholders earn airline miles—all with the expectation that as more cardholders use the card, more merchant fees will pour in. Similarly, middleman businesses like GrubHub, in an attempt to attract paying restaurant partners, offer the service of convenient take-out ordering for free to diners and also hook diners with discount coupons. All these subsidies are an investment in building the network: the more active users the middleman has, the easier it will be to get paying participants on the other side.

Whether the middleman in a two-sided market pays one side to use the service or merely offers the service for free, the middleman bears considerable up-front costs—building the site, evangelizing the service to prospective users, answering customer questions, and so on—and must do so for some time before the business has any chance of taking off. There's another problem: once you see the wisdom of footing the bill for one side, it's not always clear which side should pay. For Thiers, who didn't even know to ask this question, the answer was a no-brainer since she and many people she knew had been sitters themselves. "I understood that none of us had any money, so I never charged the sitters," she says. In this case, she lucked out with the right choice; who pays is not always a simple matter of who has deeper pockets. Pricing strategy in two-sided markets is trickier than that since the decision must also consider each user's alternatives.[39]

Even the most calculating among us probably don't think of our personal social networks as markets, two-sided or otherwise, but the experiences of Pejman Nozad and Genevieve Thiers show that both the informal networker and the builder of a middleman business face the same problem and resort to the same solution: giving before taking. As the psychologist Adam Grant points out in *Give and Take*, the selfish types he calls "takers" (people like Enron's convicted CEO and Chairman Ken Lay) engage in giving as a way to pave the way to ask for a favor later, and do so only with people they believe have the power to return the favor.[40] Distasteful as that may sound, such strategic giving can actually work quite well, hence the success of many a narcissist, but the strategic giving of a taker fails to build as broad, diverse, and healthy a network as the network of a "giver," in Grant's terms. For one thing, other people are good at sniffing out ulterior motives, and nobody likes feeling manipulated. Much more admirable and effective is the giving of someone like Pejman Nozad, willing to grant a small favor to anyone who asks and without expectation of a return.

Everybody loves a giver, and this book skews toward them. In part this is because they make for more admirable middlemen, so they are already overrepresented in this group that I want to focus on; it is also because givers are more likely to grant interviews with no strings attached. When Genevieve Thiers was giving away the SitterCity service to babysitters, she was merely following the logic of two-sided markets, not proving she was generous; market norms don't make such moves appear manipulative at all.[41] In talking to me she was a giver through and through, going so far as to e-mail me articles and to suggest other middlemen I should talk to. Whether you are generous in a communal relationship or calculating in a market relationship, you need to give something to one side before you can expect to get something from the other side. Doing so solves the chicken-and-egg problem of two-sided markets, and it is also a way around the problem Ron Burt described: why would anybody buy into this person? To be accepted by both sides, a middleman must pay his own freight and must be lucrative to each side right away.

Even with sitters on board, getting parents to sign up required tireless effort. Thiers describes chasing moms in supermarkets, sneaking into college dorms to paper them top to bottom with flyers, handing out candy on college campuses, buying pizza, babysitting kids for free, and on and on. "I did this over and over, nonstop, for two years," she says. "There's an education component in these middleman businesses that is vast." At the same time, she was also learning from her prospective users. At one point, she got herself invited to a meeting of moms in Newton, coincidentally the same suburb Mark Granovetter had used decades earlier as the setting of his job-seeking study. There she conducted a focus group, asking how much the women would be willing to pay for the SitterCity service. Some said they wouldn't pay at all, some said $100/year, and one person said $1,000/year. Thiers averaged out the answers to settle on a fee of $40/year.

She actually got a kick out of the sales part of her job, especially some of her guerrilla tactics, a valuable skill she chalks up to her opera training. "You can't be afraid to get right in front of people and tell them about what you're doing and talk them into doing it," she says. As a result, many people are ill-suited to doing this kind of work, getting knocked out of the running after a few meetings. Put another way, Thiers's outgoing personality and stage experience lowers her cost of doing Bridge work; much the same is true for Nozad, whose view of everyone as a friend he can help made it easier for him to engage in networking that many people find uncomfortable.

Still, starting SitterCity was expensive, and not only because of all those flyers and pizza. Since Thiers wasn't a programmer herself, she had to hire contractors to create the site, which meant taking a full-time job to pay them. Her nonstop evangelizing was on top of the day job, and she was doing it by the seat of her pants, one user at a time. The man Thiers was dating—whom she'd met on Match.com and who is now her husband—combined business skills with a belief in her idea, and he found her personal approach woefully inefficient. "'How can you be talking to one person at a time?' he would say. 'It's not scalable.'" But she didn't want to spend time on long-term strategy, and countered, "If I talk to this woman right now, she'll do it."

At one point, she sought VC funding, and when she managed to get some meetings, her pitch fell on deaf ears: the VCs just didn't understand the enormity of the problem she was trying to solve. "Find me a 60-year-old guy who *gets* babysitting," she says now. Even VCs with young children weren't attuned to the potential of a market for child care. "My wife handles that," one man told her.

But in truth the need was drastic, and once the business took off it did so in a big way, just as two-sided markets are famous for doing. "It's like you drop water on a map and you watch it blow up," Thiers says of the rapid spread. As her service grew in the Boston area, and the business became profitable, she expanded it to other cities, where the company had to start the process with a new community of moms and sitters. "I found out there's a tipping point for every market, but the tipping point was kind of low because moms are insanely viral."[42] The words "insanely viral" are a marketer's dream—who wouldn't want their product or service to spread like an epidemic through sheer word of mouth? Moms do talk a lot, in part because they are clustered in the kinds of tight-knit groups that breed communication and trust. They have many opportunities to share information—while watching their babies in playgroups, standing outside the preschool classroom, or participating in an online support group—so word of a valued service can spread fast, especially when there are plenty of sitters to go around. Because of the returns to scale in a two-sided market—a large network is more valuable to its users than a smaller one—it's actually easier to get your thousandth user than it is to get your tenth.[43]

Unfortunately, no sooner had SitterCity became nationally known—Thiers appeared on the *Today* show five times as a child-care expert—than me-too businesses started cropping up. "When you've done all this work, and you finally see it take off, it's copied almost instantly," she says, comparing what happened to SitterCity to the many clones of Groupon. Whereas in 2000 the online market for child care was nonexistent, today there are no fewer than 84 businesses offering essentially the same service as SitterCity. Care.com, which came along after SitterCity, now boasts more users. When there are so many players, Thiers says, it becomes a game of outspending the competition. Many of these businesses will doubtless lose the war of attrition; others may join forces. Having pioneered the industry won't necessarily give SitterCity an edge in the long term. One thing is certain: despite SitterCity's current success, it is far from the unique bridge Thiers had set out to create.

This is the fundamental problem with trying to capitalize on being a Bridge: once people see someone profiting from filling a structural hole, they try to get in on the action, too. Middlemen in real estate are a good example. Stoxstill-Diggs, the Craigslist middleman, got a real-estate license after seeing how much of a commission his own agent had earned for what didn't seem like a whole lot of work. (The ease with which newcomers are able to obtain a real estate license is a big part of the problem in itself.[44]) But the job hasn't been as lucrative as Stoxstill-Diggs had expected. "Sometimes I make more in washers and dryers than a house commission," he told me. Those of us familiar with the image of a BMW-driving real estate agent might be surprised to learn that fewer than 10 percent of American real estate agents earn more than $100,000 per year; the median annual income is only $39,800, and those in the 25th percentile make only $27,800.[45] One reason for these lackluster numbers is that we have too many agents chasing after the same number of listings, with newcomers rushing in as soon as the market heats up. For example, MIT economists analyzing multiyear data from the real-estate market in the greater Boston area found that when housing prices reached a local peak in 2007, the number of agents nearly doubled from their number in 1998, reducing each agent's market share. This competition didn't benefit consumers either: since commission rates are fixed, consumers paid the same as they would have with fewer agents, yet didn't receive higher-quality service.[46] Another study along the same lines found that when the price of land in a city rises, so does the fraction of real estate agents as agents flock to the potentially more lucrative market—yet the increased competition means that the actual wage of a typical agent doesn't change.[47]

I asked Stoxstill-Diggs whether he was concerned about competition on Craigslist: won't the success of his book create a glut of middlemen going after the same opportunities he's been seizing? He told me he wasn't worried, that there's enough for everybody. I wasn't so sure, and sought the opinion of Jim Angel, the Georgetown finance professor. To some extent he agreed with Stoxstill-Diggs. "He's lucky that he's in a business that's geographically isolated," Angel explained. A bunch of new Craigslist hustlers in Los Angeles or Detroit won't hurt business in Nashville. But every market can get saturated. "If an infinite number of people started bidding on every used appliance, then competition would drive out all but the best and most efficient," he said. "What will happen is that as more people will get in the game, you will see spreads get more narrow, transactions get snapped up more quickly, and the players who remain will be those who have a comparative advantage—those who are good at seeing the ads and acting on them fast." Some of these survivors will be people with no better use for their time than to trawl Craigslist all day long, Angel says. Others will become full-time managers coordinating the efforts of specialists: "people who can put together a little business where they have cousin Vinnie who's the guy who watches Craigslist and makes deals on the phone, and cousin Joey is the guy with the pickup truck who goes to pick up the stuff, and sister Maria is the one who keeps the books and collects the money when people come to pick stuff up."

As a middleman on Craigslist, Stoxstill-Diggs already brings a specialist's advantage to the market, but that doesn't mean that carving the job into even thinner slices won't lower costs even more.

However, competing on cost can only get you so far. A more profitable, harder-to-copy way to create value as a middleman is to be more than a Bridge by providing additional services that buyers and sellers value. Each of the following chapters shows one way successful middlemen are doing just that.

2

THE CERTIFIER

Applying the Seal of Approval

THE ROLE: *Sellers often know more about the quality of what they're offering than buyers do, making buyers wary of the goods on offer. By scouting for what buyers want, screening the options, and staking their own reputations on what they buy and sell, Certifiers provide value for both buyers and sellers. To profit from this role, Certifiers must invest in their ability to tell the wheat from the chaff and in a reputation for quality that pays off in the long run.*

"Indiana Jones Meets *Sanford & Son"*

One day several years ago, Mike Wolfe, in an episode of his hit cable TV show *American Pickers*, pulled his Mercedes-Benz van up to a rural property that looked particularly promising: out front were several beat-up old pickup trucks bearing "For Sale" signs, and scattered farther back stood more than a dozen trailers.[1] Accompanied by his "picking" partner, Frank Fritz, Wolfe was in upstate New York, somewhere between Saratoga Springs and Syracuse, far from Wolfe's home base of Eau Claire, Iowa.

When a friendly-looking woman answers the front door, Fritz gives one of their typical introductions. "We're pickers. We're always out buying and sellin' stuff," Frank tells her, handing her a flyer listing the kind of stuff the pickers are looking to buy.

As always, they're on a quest for what they call "rusty gold"—old motorbikes, signs, and other Americana sitting around in people's attics, barns, and woodsheds. Things that may look like trash but that are worth real money to collectors and antiques dealers. To uncover these hidden gems, Wolfe and Fritz log sixty thousand miles each year, crisscrossing America's heartland and driving up and down the country's coasts. And when they reach a promising spot and are lucky enough to be allowed in, they must rummage around to try to find something of value. The work is both exciting and humble. As if still pitching the show to TV executives, Wolfe often describes his vocation as *"Indiana Jones meets Sanford & Son"*—a cross between treasure hunter and junk dealer.

In looking for properties to pick, Wolfe completely reverses our notions of good and bad. Staying away from freshly painted McMansions with satellite dishes and manicured yards, he gravitates toward houses with tall weeds out front, buildings and cars painted in dated colors like avocado and harvest gold, and rust on just about anything. The more signs of age and disrepair, the better.

"Our secret to making a profit is that we skip the middleman, meaning we don't buy from thrift stores, antique malls, or flea markets," Wolfe and Fritz write in their book, *American Pickers Guide to Picking.*[2] "Instead, we go straight to the source." Of course they do: to find undervalued treasure, you can't go to a store or market, whose treasures will already be marked up. To have any hope of making a profit, you have to go off the beaten path.

And that's exactly what happens on this day in upstate New York. The woman who lets the pickers in explains that her father, who recently died, had been a "collector-hoarder" for as long as she'd known him. Looking for money to pay off her father's debts and keep the farm running, the daughter is ready to sell some of Dad's belongings. "We'd be honored to look through this stuff," Wolfe says, his ever respectful demeanor on display.

We're led into the first building, where the camera pans to reveal a long-abandoned mess: an old ladder, naily lumber boards sticking out every which way, rusty metal, random piping. Heaps of junk to most people. But Wolfe sees potential. He shines a small flashlight under one heap, wondering what's hiding beneath. "There could be like a car under there," he says, only half-jokingly. Tall and limber, his muscles flexing through his jeans and T-shirt, Wolfe quickly climbs up for a better view of the room.

Looking around, he spots the first bit of rusty gold: vintage bicycles. As he hauls a bunch of bike frames and wheels out into daylight, we see that the wheels are warped and brown with rust. Wolfe instantly knows he's found something of value. "1890s," Wolfe says. He's not out to swindle anyone, and takes the time to explain to the daughter what makes the bikes special. "Wooden rims, pneumatic tires, very cool stuff. Cork grips." He dumps all the bike parts on the grass and makes a package offer. "For all this, I can do $200."

"1890s?" she asks.

"1890s," he agrees, "But condition is everything." Then he shows where the frame is broken, separated from the casting. She pauses to think, and he ups his offer. "How about $250?"

"Sounds all right," she says quietly, and they shake on it.

With an enthusiasm more common in little boys than in grown men, Wolfe speaks to the camera, and says he thinks he can piece together one whole bicycle and still have extra parts left.

Wolfe is a bike collector himself, so he may keep his find after fixing it up a bit, but if he decides to part with it, he can resell it for several times more than he paid for it. For example, later on the same pick, he buys a Harley VL tank for $75, figuring he can sell it to the right guy for $200. Later still, he spends $20 on a toy boat. It's covered with caked-on mud and has a large rip in its sail, but Wolfe thinks he can sell it for much more than $20 because it's the kind of toy Benjamin Franklin was writing about back in the 1770s—a true collector's item. ("That's what's great about digging in barns in New

York," he tells us. "You find so much more earlier stuff than you do when we're in Iowa.")

The Middleman Who Skips the Middleman

The show plays up the simple "buy low, sell high" logic of the picking business by displaying, in numbers on the screen, what Wolfe paid for each item and what the item's worth. But these numbers ignore Wolfe's less obvious costs. At the end of the pickers' visit, the hoarder-collector's daughter and son-in-law are happy, and Wolfe and Fritz look happy, too—but after picking through fourteen trailers, haggling over their picks, and packing their haul into the van, the picking partners are exhausted, and it's not at all clear they really made a profit. The two men spent the better half of a day in the hope of making a few hundred bucks.

That's not the whole of it, either. For one thing, not every back road takes a picker to treasure he can buy. "We can be out for weeks at a time and come back with next to nothing in our van, or we can make one unplanned stop on some back road we take out of sheer curiosity and find a huge honey hole," they write, using picker slang for a stop full of rusty gold that its owners are willing to part with.[3] He's making a point about unpredictability, but his comment also says something about search costs. Imagine driving for days, buying gallons of gas, without scoring a single buy. The search costs in the picking business are tremendous, of which travel expenses alone can eat away any profit. Until his TV show brought fame and fortune, Wolfe would sleep in his car to stay within his budget, and you can be sure that car was nothing like the shiny Benz you see on his show.

The high costs of the picking business are a serious problem, and it's one we'll return to later. But for now let's focus on the value Wolfe provides to his clients; it's important to appreciate because it is much the same value so many other middlemen provide in other industries. A large part of what makes him valuable to the dealers and collectors who buy from him is precisely his willingness to go far and wide—to bear those search costs.

Sure, Wolfe skips the middleman, just as he says—but he's a middleman every bit as much as the dealers who buy from him are. Think about it: if an antiques dealer bought directly from a guy with an old barn, instead of from Wolfe, the dealer would say he's skipping the middleman, too. But the antiques dealers *want* the middleman—they value the picker—because any markup they pay to him is worth the price to them. Why? Any one of Wolfe's clients might not buy everything he shows them, but they know that what he's offering is closer to treasure than to junk. Having painstakingly separated the wheat from the chaff, he brings them only the wheat, and stakes his reputation with buyers on his ability to do that. That's why, although he may not be making a killing, he is a Certifier just like the other skilled middlemen we'll meet in this chapter.

Scouting, Screening, and Vouching: "Oysters Proven to Contain Pearls"

The Certifier is probably the most prevalent and useful role a middle-man can play. Through deep expertise and a hard-won reputation, the Certifier saves buyers time while reducing their risk of being duped by a seller. Whether you're going into a grocery store with confidence that the produce really is organic, driving around with a real estate agent who doesn't waste your time showing you houses that are all wrong for you, or reading a magazine that you trust will contain only accurate, timely, and well-written articles on topics relevant to you, you're counting on the store, the agent, and the magazine editor to act as a Certifier. If you're a middleman yourself, no matter the industry, your customers are probably counting on you to act as a Certifier, as well.

So what exactly does a Certifier do? The work boils down to three things: scouting, screening, and vouching.

Scouting means casting a wide net: going far and wide in search of potential picks. If you're Wolfe, it's driving around upstate New York hoping you'll find the 1890s bicycle, and it may mean having a door slammed in your face when you approach a potential seller.

Screening means using your know-how to separate the wheat from the chaff: it's being able to tell, once you gain entry to the old trailer, whether the dirty toy boat is a valuable antique or a worthless piece of junk.

And *vouching* means staking your reputation on the quality of what you ultimately present to your buyers. It means understanding that if the toy boat turns out to be a piece junk, that buyer won't be inclined to do business with you in the future—and certainly not to recommend you to others. As a Certifier, you're always taking the long view: less interested in any one deal than in protecting your good name, which will lead to many more deals down the road.

This all seems like common sense, right? Here's the thing, though: many people we turn to for these services fail to deliver. Middlemen who can do them well will be ahead of the pack.

As consumers, we often have trouble appreciating the effort and the expertise that go into scouting and screening. In fact, when we see the end product, we sometimes forget that scouting and screening has taken place at all. These are things we tend to notice only when they're *not* happening. We may not notice when a loan officer turns away a prospective borrower (unless we are that borrower). But when the loan officer rubber-stamps an application for a mortgage, giving a loan to a person with a high risk of default, we know that the Certifier has failed to do proper screening. The same goes for Certifiers responsible for conducting the process of due diligence: when an investment bank hired to orchestrate the sale of a company neglects to vet the financial health of the acquiring company, nobody might be the wiser—unless the acquiring company goes belly-up and leaves the seller empty-handed.[4] Some marriage matchmakers do such a poor job screening their clients that women have been known to be set up on dates with married men.[5] Similarly, brokers in the international marriage business had done such a horrendous job of screening prospective husbands—allowing men with criminal backgrounds to meet and marry women from overseas—that the United States Congress passed a law specifically to protect mail-order brides from such abuses.[6]

Most successful Certifiers, however, do screen the people and goods they represent: in a competitive market, they wouldn't stay in business for long if they neglected this crucial part of the job. However, though the work of screening is largely invisible to those not doing it, it is not trivial and can be quite onerous: in searching for treasure, a big part of a Certifier's job is to sift through stuff that is *not* treasure.

Effective Certifiers in other industries understand this. Paul Hawkinson, a distinguished corporate recruiter who has long given advice to other recruiters, once compared the pool of potential hires to a sea of oysters. Only some of those smelly oysters contain pearls. "Recruiters only give you oysters proven to contain pearls," Hawkinson explained to the people who might wonder why recruiters are worth their fees.[7] As a result, the recruiter makes the client's job much easier. Rather than having to dredge for oysters (scouting) and to shuck them (screening), the hiring manager can look at a neat row of open oysters and determine which pearl is the best.

Bad recruiters don't bother with shucking the oysters. Instead, they take what people in the industry derisively call a "spray and pray" approach—they gather a bunch of résumés and send them out to hiring managers without much screening at all. They're hoping that one of their aimless shots will hit the target. If they're lucky, one shot *will* hit the target, and the recruiter will get a fee. But most hiring managers don't want to work with such recruiters because they provide hardly any value, doing very little that the manager can't do as easily on her own.

Hawkinson was writing about oysters and pearls in 2005, and a lot has changed since then: LinkedIn, which has since grown to more than 300 million users worldwide,[8] now makes scouting easier, with a central database of résumés easily searchable through LinkedIn's sophisticated "sourcing" software designed with recruiters in mind. But the basic need for scouting, screening, and ultimately vouching hasn't changed nor has the need for professional recruiters to perform these tasks. In fact, professional recruiters make up LinkedIn's highest-revenue customer segment.[9] Someone actively looking for a new job might get a premium (paid) LinkedIn account for the year of the job search, but a full-time recruiter needs a powerful account all the time. And because finding candidates is recruiters' bread and butter, and they must do it every day, it makes more sense for them to invest in scouting and screening tools than it does for hiring managers or, in some cases, even for in-house recruiters.

The Middleman as Expert

Howard Robboy, a partner and co-president of a Seattle-based recruiting firm that fills 150 jobs each year, says that in some ways LinkedIn has made his work harder and no less necessary. "Everyone's on LinkedIn, and they're besieged by people trying to contact them. You have a million pests bothering you."[10] Many of those pests, of course, are recruiters—with sites like LinkedIn, it's become easier than ever to call yourself a recruiter, which means that good recruiters, those who know what they're doing, have to work harder to get a candidate's attention. "But it's also sped up our ability to fill searches because everybody's on LinkedIn; I can quickly make a target list of 50 candidates, so it saves me a lot of time."

Robboy got his start in sales, working for Johnson & Johnson, and when I spoke to him, he had been working as a recruiter for

28 years, specializing in hiring sales managers who work with consumer packaged goods. Robboy's firm, Consumer Connection, only handles searches in the field of consumer packaged goods—products that most people use every day, like food, clothes, and toiletries. Because of his narrow focus in just this area, he was able to develop deep expertise. "I know exactly what [sort of candidate] our clients want to hire." That, he says, is in contrast to many "talent acquisition people," those working on-site in the client's staffing department. "In the staffing world, probably 25 percent of the people who work on-site are really good, but probably 40 percent are really bad. They don't know what they're looking for. It takes them a couple years of training to get to the point of getting good, and their training consists of sending bad candidates." On-site recruiters, Robboy is saying, can't properly scout and screen even if they wanted to. As a result, hiring managers can't count on them.

The hiring managers do know what they are looking for, but they'd rather spend their time running their department than screening candidates. That's certainly true in Robboy's niche, since the hiring managers who enlist him are typically VPs of sales. "A VP of sales doesn't have the time: they're flying across the country, they've got really busy jobs, so the last thing they want to do is run a LinkedIn ad and get 300 résumés." Because then they'd have to screen those résumés. The VPs could turn to their own staffing department, but again, the results of those efforts are hit or miss. Not only do the in-house staffers often lack the expertise to do good scouting and screening, they lack sufficient incentives to do it fast, Robboy suggests. Robboy does have that sense of urgency because he works on a contingency basis: he gets paid only if he actually fills a job opening.

But it's not just about motivation. "The other thing is we're experts," Robboy explains. "If a client has an opening, we figure out that these are the 30 companies we should recruit from." Because of their knowledge of the industry and their connections made over the years, Robboy and his colleagues can find the most promising candidates from those firms. "We'll network through buyers, and through distributors, through brokers. The internal people can't do that. They don't have the time, the knowledge, the contacts, the relationships. They have no idea." Perhaps more surprisingly, this deficiency can be just as true of hiring managers (like the sales VPs): hiring managers may know what they're looking for, but they don't have as good a sense of the talent pool as does the specialist who deals with candidates every day. Hiring managers have less experience in interviewing candidates and in comparing them with a realistic target. As a result, a hiring manager is much more prone than a recruiter to settle either too quickly or too late, either seeing too few candidates to make a great hire or wasting time on too many candidates because of a mistaken belief that someone more qualified is still out there. A full-time recruiter like Robboy, in contrast, has the experience to know when to keep searching and when to stop.[11]

Robboy's expertise comes from specializing narrowly, which makes him a go-to person when a client needs a very particular candidate. A client might come to Robboy and say that the company wants "someone who's sold natural skin-care products, not mainstream skin care or L'Oreal or Revlon. They don't want someone who's sold personal care or cough-and-cold." That's a very narrow search, but because Robboy knows the client's industry, that narrowness can help him home in on the right candidates more quickly. "It takes hundreds of companies out of the equation. You have to be able to cut to the chase to know: here's my pool, here's where these guys work."

That's just the scouting stage, but his expertise obviously helps with screening, too. "I may call a candidate, and it may be the first time I've talked with him, or it can be a candidate I've known for 28 years. But what I do know is what they do for a living. I can find out [when talking to a sales manager]: are they dealing with the head buyer, the general manager, the person who's doing pricing, schematics, special events? How proficient are they with this software? I can learn all that stuff in 10 minutes. Are they relocatable? Are they content to leave for a $5,000 raise? If you're a specialist, you know all the kinds of questions to ask. If you're a generalist you don't know what these résumés mean."

That kind of expertise translates not only into a higher success rate in filling jobs, which means a higher rate of getting paid and getting hired again, but also in lower search costs, since Robboy can scout and screen candidates much more quickly than if he were recruiting outside his niche. That's why he turns down jobs outside that niche, even if he could fill the job eventually: "It would take me ten times as long to fill the job—it's a waste of time." Time is money for everyone, of course, but the savvy and busy Certifier understands opportunity costs especially well. Why take a project that will take 100 hours to complete if you can fill ten other jobs during that time?

It is sometimes tempting, when you are starting out, to be a generalist so you can stay busy; after all, it can take years to ramp up your business to the point where all your work is in a specific niche. But successful Certifiers learn to resist the temptation to be jacks of all trades. That's because they understand that breadth comes at the cost of depth, so they choose one area in which they can provide the kind of deep expertise that it is hard to compete against. For Robboy, it is consumer-packaged goods; for Mike Wolfe, it is Americana and, more specifically, motorcycles, transportation, and advertising collectibles. And for a Certifier we'll meet shortly, it's gently used designer fashion.

Why does it pay for a Certifier to invest in becoming an expert? The economist Gary Biglaiser, writing in 1993, offered a simple explanation. He observed that "a middleman buys many more goods than an ordinary buyer."[12] It would be a waste of time for an ordinary buyer to invest in knowledge and skills that the buyer would only need to use once in a while: for the same reason you wouldn't train to be an auto mechanic just so you can work on your own car, most ordinary buyers don't want to spend a lot of time and money developing deep expertise in buying a particular good.[13] A middleman is different because he or she will be buying a particular type of good all the time. As a result, a middleman has "an incentive to make a large investment in skills that enable him to detect a good's true quality," as Biglaiser put it.

That simple observation has several implications for the would-be Certifier. For starters, it reinforces the value of specializing: a tight focus helps you develop expertise sooner than if you are a generalist. The sooner you develop expertise, the sooner you can start reaping the benefits. For the same reason, it's a good idea to invest in yourself early in your career, so you have more time to enjoy the payoff. Finally, if you already have expertise in some area—because of a hobby you've long cultivated or a skill you learned at home—you already have a head start.

The Middlemen of eBay: The Four Percent Who Make Half of All Sales

Ann Whitley Wood, who runs a luxury consignment shop on eBay, got a head start from her early love of fashion. Having grown up in Dallas, home of Neiman Marcus and a culture of dressing to the nines, Wood had been keenly interested in fashion since she was a young girl. "I was always a clothes horse, with an interest in fashion since I was ten or twelve."

Talking to Wood can make you want to open your own store on eBay, as she did years ago: compared to Mike Wolfe's often dirty and thankless work, her job looks easy and highly profitable. Wood, who still lives in Dallas, nets a quarter of a million dollars per year (on sales of a million dollars) working part-time and rarely venturing farther than the post office. She gets most of her merchandise from well-heeled women right in her fashionable town, most of them repeat clients and referrals, and usually insists that they bring their Prada purses, Chanel sweaters, and Hermes scarves to her.[14] "Anybody with the competency of a 12-year old can sell on eBay," Wood says.

At its most basic, selling on eBay means you post pictures of the item you're trying to sell, write an accurate description, set a price, and sit back for the buyers to come to you. Because sales are conducted online, you don't need traditional sales skills like building rapport with customers or coaxing them out of indecision. And because people from all over the world are shopping on the site, a properly priced item will almost always find a buyer, sometimes within minutes. "It's like shooting fish in barrel," Wood says.

But although anybody can make a sale on eBay, not everyone can turn a profit, let alone the kind of profit Wood makes. The site started out as a consumer-to-consumer marketplace: like a global garage sale where anybody could sell just about anything to anyone directly. In eBay's early days, when most sales were through auctions, the prototypical eBay item was a Pez dispenser that one collector might sell to another. Very quickly, though, the site evolved into a place where more and more sales would go through professional middlemen. Some were owners of brick-and-mortar stores wishing to expand their market or people like Mike Wolfe who found eBay so helpful (and time-consuming) that he hired a full-time person to run sales through the site.[15] Some were "trading assistants"—companies like AuctionDrop and iSoldIt, that made it easy for occasional sellers to off-load their castoffs without the hassle of going on eBay themselves. And some were people like Wood, who wouldn't be in sales at all were it not for eBay.

Before there was eBay, Ann Whitley Wood was an appellate lawyer. It was a job she loved—and would still be doing if she didn't have to give over so much of her life to it. She still misses aspects of her legal career—the writing, the company of colleagues—but as a mother of three, Wood doesn't wish to spend these years working sixty-hour weeks. So when the opportunity to become a middleman on eBay fell into her lap, she welcomed it. Since her childhood, she appreciated the kind of items she now sells—from crystal and china to shoes and handbags.

When eBay came along, she began selling things from around her own house. "I was able to sell them because I had them and I understood them." Then, one day, a makeup artist she knew told Wood about someone who needed a bunch of stuff sold on eBay. "I talked to her assistant," she recalls, "and the next day my garage was full of Gucci and Prada." That's how Wood got her first consignment client. (Even though the people consigning the goods to Wood are selling, not buying, Wood calls them clients because she is providing them a service, the kind described in the Concierge chapter.) Other consignment clients came from word of mouth. As word spread among people in Dallas over the years, her sales volume grew. Wood's feedback score on the site blossomed, too, so she earned "PowerSeller" status on eBay, the company's label for its most active and reputable sellers.

People want to do business with PowerSellers because the designation provides a level of assurance you don't get with ordinary eBay sellers. To become a PowerSeller, you have to provide quality service and meet a monthly sales quota, with different quotas for each tier, from Bronze to Titanium.[16] Wood is a Platinum PowerSeller, a level that's just right for its balance of income and part-time schedule.

But whatever tier you want to be in, it's almost impossible to become a PowerSeller just from selling your own stuff—you have to have a steady supply of new stuff to sell, which you must get from other people.[17] That's why just about all PowerSellers are resellers and retailers. Only four percent of all eBay sellers sell enough to become PowerSellers, yet more than half of all eBay sales come through these four percent. Middlemen are where it's at now. "In the same way that eBay is a juggernaut because it's so advanced in terms of providing a marketplace, certain sellers are juggernauts as well," is how Wood puts it.[18] What's happened on eBay is very similar, in other words, to what's happened on LinkedIn. The recruiting site's original premise was that you could find new people through people you know, but it's become much more about professional middlemen using it to find candidates for their clients. Jobs on LinkedIn aren't found through personal networks as much as through the headhunters who make it their business to scout and screen and vouch for the people they hire on behalf of others.[19]

Wood's eBay store, Willow-Wear, has a stellar reputation on eBay: with nearly 8,000 reviews, it currently has an average feedback score of 100.0 percent, meaning that it got absolutely no negative ratings whatsoever in the past 12 months. "I protect that feedback rating very carefully," Wood says. The day Wood and I spoke, for example, someone who had bought a pair of men's shoes from her wanted to cancel the transaction because it was a mistake. "I could refuse to cancel the transaction and basically hit him with an 'unpaid item strike,' but I'm not going to do that because there's just no need. I know I can sell his shoes to someone else, and I engender goodwill. I'm not a pushover by any means, but I'm going to allow him to cancel the transaction." Wood understands that she has much more to gain long-term from her customers' satisfaction than from whatever she'd make on any one sale. The men's shoes example is a no-brainer: of course, she'll allow the cancellation, since she hadn't spent the time and money to ship the order. But even with more costly cases, she considers it worthwhile to keep the customer happy by standing behind what she sells. What Wood is doing when she accepts returns is vouching. She has already screened the items she accepts for consignment, and she stakes her reputation on them being every bit as good as her pictures and descriptions and prices make them out to be. She knows that if they weren't, she wouldn't just lose that customer, she'd lose many more customers because her all-important feedback score would suffer. "I care about my reputation more than about any individual transaction," she says.

Do some buyers abuse this system? Of course: some ask for their money back even when the item they bought arrived exactly as advertised. Although Wood finds these situations annoying, she sees them as just part of the cost of doing business—an ongoing investment in her good name.

The Value of a Good Reputation

Wood knows from personal experience that higher feedback scores translate into higher prices, and economists studying eBay and other marketplaces have reached the same conclusion. In one of the best-known experiments on the value of reputation on eBay, researchers recruited an actual eBay seller, a man with a strong, positive reputation in selling vintage postcards, and had him sell the same cards under an alias with no track record. Buyers had no way of knowing that the cards were identical, so they had only the sellers' feedback scores to go by, making for a clean test. How much more would the reputable seller be able to charge for the same cards than the new, unknown seller? The answer in that experiment turned out to be about 8 percent.[20] There is nothing magic about that number: the difference could be higher or lower depending on a host of factors, such as the price of the goods, the magnitude of the reputable seller's positive track record, and the fraud protection available to the buyer; all things being equal, though, positive reputations pay off. That's true on other websites that track reputations. A study of hotels rated on Booking.com found that hotels with the highest guest ratings charged the highest nightly rates.[21] Similarly, studies using data from Yelp.com found that higher restaurant scores increase the chance that a restaurant will sell out all its available seats during peak hours[22] and that restaurants with a higher reputation earn higher revenues.[23]

All these studies suggest that better reputations translate into higher revenues, but you probably want to know about profits. How do we know that reputable sellers' higher prices improve the bottom line instead of merely offsetting the higher costs that reputable sellers incur? That's a much more difficult question to answer with data (since it's harder to gather information about sellers' costs and profits), but economic reasoning predicts that the profit margins of more reputable sellers *must* be higher, or there would be no incentive to build up and maintain a reputation for quality. The economist Carl Shapiro laid out this argument clearly in a classic paper in 1983. Shapiro pointed out that when a seller's reputation is the only way for buyers to tell the quality of a product, a seller who wants to become known for selling high-quality goods must, for a time, sell these goods at a loss. Why? Because until the seller has built up a reputation for quality, buyers won't pay enough to cover the full cost of providing quality; those initial sales below cost are the seller's investment in reputation. However, the seller is only willing to accept losses, Shapiro argued, if the investment will pay off—if, in other words, that seller can eventually command higher prices as a result of a well-earned reputation. What's more, once the good reputation starts to pay off, the return to reputation must be high enough for the seller to continue to provide high-quality products, and that means that the reputable seller's profit margin has to be higher than a low-end seller's; if it weren't, a reputable seller would be tempted to lower quality. "After all," Shapiro pointed out, "quality reductions will yield immediate cost savings, while the adverse effect on reputation will arise only in the longer run."[24] A reputable seller who takes the long view, as Ann Whitley Wood does, will see that it pays to maintain a reputation for quality products and quality service even if it were possible to earn a higher margin in the short term by cutting corners.

For Wood, it is also well worth her while to maintain a sterling reputation with her consignment clients, the other side of the business. They must see her as a trustworthy service provider: someone who can be counted on to sell their valuables at a good price, to pay them after the sale, and to do so without delay or hassle.

"The consignment client can't be sought out—they only trust you through word of mouth," Woods says. "I get the repeat business over and over again because they know they can trust me."

The upside of that, of course, is that as long as she continues to act in a trustworthy manner, clients come to her. Notice how different that is from Wolfe's business: no matter how decent he is with the people he buys from, he cannot go back to them for more collectibles to buy: once a honey pot has been tapped, it has no more to give. And because his sellers are scattered around the country, and each transaction is so small, they don't talk him up to each other. So he's stuck with making cold calls. Every time he wants to buy, he must knock on a new door and introduce himself all over again. He has no way to develop a reputation with sellers, so he cannot capitalize on his honesty and decency.

This is an important lesson for middlemen: your profits will be higher if you can build up a reputation, ideally with both sides of the market. And if you are already doing good work, it behooves you to find ways to let that be widely known. That is something that LaJuan Stoxstill-Diggs, the Craigslist hustler from the Bridge chapter, hasn't done yet. He told me that when he buys a used appliance, he always turns it on to make sure it works: he does at least minimal screening, in other words. He also seems exceedingly courteous and helpful, and he probably has other fine qualities that customers value. He knows it, and his past customers know it, but new customers don't know it because he has not made a name for himself. He gets a tidy markup each time he flips an appliance—but if he had a reputation, he could probably do better. The tried-and-true way to do that is to maintain a storefront.[25] Stoxstill-Diggs doesn't want to open an actual store, he says, for lifestyle reasons; for example, he likes the flexibility of buying and selling appliances on his own schedule. If he plans to stay in this business for a while, he might do well to invest in an online presence, even if it's just a website with client testimonials. Stoxstill-Diggs actually has a considerable web presence already—but only in relation to his book about Craigslist, not about himself as a reputable seller even though he earns most of his income from selling appliances rather than books.

Why Buying Direct Is Overrated: Lemons at the Farmer's Market

You might have noticed a pattern among several of the middlemen in this chapter: Wood, Wolfe, and Stoxstill-Diggs are all resellers of used goods. There's a good reason for that. Whether it's a dryer, a designer handbag, or a piece of Americana, the quality of a used product is hard for a nonexpert to assess, and as a result, most sellers know more about the quality of what they're selling than most buyers do. This imbalance between what the seller knows and what the buyer knows (what economists call an "asymmetry of information") leads to a series of problems.

For starters, sellers might try cheating prospective buyers, charging more than the item is actually worth given its actual quality. As an extreme example, someone with a Gucci knockoff might try to pass it off as the genuine article, pricing it higher than a fake is worth. Buyers, aware of this possibility, might therefore be wary of buying a used anything from someone they don't know, or they might be unwilling to pay the price asked for. As a result, honest sellers (unable to show that they are honest) would have trouble getting a good price for their goods, driving some of them out of the market—a decision that leaves the market overpopulated with dishonest sellers, which further erodes buyers' trust and prices and so on in a vicious cycle called "adverse selection."[26] The original paper about adverse selection, "The Market for Lemons," dealt with the case of used cars, but the phenomenon is so pervasive, rearing its head in important markets like those for insurance, that the economist behind the lemons model, George Akerlof, eventually earned a Nobel Prize for this insight.[27]

The lemons problem explains why middlemen so often appear in markets for used goods: they not only have the expertise to judge quality, but they can vouch for it with their reputation. But it is not only with used goods that we need middlemen to protect us against lemons. It is with any case of hidden information. Part of the reason we need headhunters like Howard Robboy is that workers keep important information about themselves hidden. And as a series of scandals in California revealed, hidden information also plays a key role in the market for fresh produce.

Many people enjoy the idea of buying local and buying direct from farmers, but if they aren't close enough to a farm, buying direct usually means going to a farmer's market. Unfortunately for these consumers, this situation creates the ideal setup for fraud. As a Los Angeles TV investigation uncovered, several stands claiming to be selling locally grown produce had actually been importing their avocados and other produce from Mexico, where a warm climate and low wages made produce prices far lower.[28] In fact, the fraudulent resellers would sometimes buy Mexican produce from a wholesale market before bringing it to farmers' markets in affluent towns like Santa Monica and Century City: they knew that through this efficient supply chain they could make a higher profit than by growing the produce themselves in California.

The problem isn't limited to Los Angeles—cases of fraud at farmers' markets have been reported elsewhere in the United States and overseas.[29] As with many other products and services—from a used car to an anti-aging cream—a casual buyer of "local" produce can't know until after the sale whether the product is everything that the seller claims it is, and sometimes not even then. This is one of the big problems of buying direct. Unless you're buying from the same people over and over again, it's hard to be sure you're getting the level of quality you want.

Fraud at farmers' markets in California led the state government to enable funding for an army of inspectors to police the markets.[30]

Unlike most shoppers, a well-trained inspector can tell, for example, that white specks on a mango are probably scale, a pest from South America—not local.[31] Government oversight is one solution. Middlemen are another: if a reputable store labels an apple "local," you can be pretty confident that it is, because you trust the brand. Each brand has a hard-earned reputation to protect, and if these stores were to be caught cheating, they'd have much more than legal troubles to contend with. Just like the PowerSellers on eBay, middlemen are in a better position than producers to establish a reputation with end consumers.

One of the key lessons to building a reputation is the need to make costly investments up-front, to the point of not earning a profit initially. One middleman I spoke with, a modeling agent named Carol Shamon who started the Shamon Freitas Talent Agency in San Diego 25 years ago, told me that it took years for her reputation to set in. In her first year in business she made about $2,000, and the year after that it was $5,000: poverty wages. She might have made more money in the short run by sacrificing quality for quantity—by signing aspiring talent without much screening and making promises she couldn't keep—but such myopia would surely have come back to bite her by damaging her reputation with buyers. Likewise, when models have a choice of agents, it pays in the long run to maintain a reputation for good work and honest dealings among them, too. "When you take a business that's not traditionally honest, and you are the honest person," Shamon says, "it might take a long time but you rise to the top."[32]

The Myth of the Gatekeeper

A prevalent view of middlemen is that they're gatekeepers, keeping talent and quality out of the reach of buyers. Especially in the culture industries, where taste is largely subjective, it's common to vilify gatekeepers. But by now you should see that being selective is actually how the gatekeeper provides value: part of the value of a middleman to the buyer is precisely to keep out the people and products that buyers are not likely to want, like the rusty bike that's from 1990 rather than from 1890. But keep in mind that that's just half the story because the Certifier wants very much to scout out the talent to sell, to open the gate to the right person. Many people believe that the culture industries—books, movies, music—are wildly different from other fields, and that what succeeds in these highly unpredictable markets isn't a matter of quality so much as of luck. There is a good deal of truth to that view, as we'll explore in the Risk Bearer chapter; in fact, to some extent a mix of skill and luck is at play in any human endeavor. Judgments of skill and quality may be more subjective in the arts than in other fields, but Certifiers in all fields have this in common: they must anticipate what their buyers value. Just like Howard Robboy, the contingent-fee recruiter, the cultural gatekeeper gets paid only if she makes a successful sale.

Consider the role gatekeepers played in the career of Tom Clancy. When Clancy died in 2013, at the age of 66, he was one of the most commercially successful novelists of our time. Seventeen of his novels had made it onto the *New York Times* bestseller list, and he had 100 million copies of his books in print. But when he was starting out, he faced his share of rejection, and was "discovered" not once, but twice.

The first time was by Deborah Grosvenor in 1982 when she was working as an editor at a small publishing house called the Naval Institute Press, an offshoot of the US Naval Institute in Annapolis, Maryland. The press, which specialized in books about naval and maritime affairs, had just decided to branch out into fiction, as long as it had a naval setting or theme, when she received an unsolicited manuscript for a novel called *The Hunt for Red October*. The title's *Red October* was the novel's Soviet submarine, so the book fit the publisher's theme. But its author, who was selling insurance back then, was a complete unknown to readers. Still, when Grosvenor read the manuscript, she could tell she had a diamond in the rough. "I knew immediately that Clancy was a storyteller and had a strong, assured voice, a sense of humor, and a fast-moving, intricate plot. His mastery of technology was amazing," Grosvenor recalled.[33] "But the story was bogged down by too much technological description and explanation, and the multiple, intertwined fast-moving time lines and scenes were occasionally confusing."

She was so interested in acquiring Clancy's book that she worked with the author to revise it even though she knew her boss and the editorial board might ultimately pass on it. Clancy was willing to make the changes she suggested, turning in a better, leaner manuscript than the original, but unfortunately for Grosvenor, her boss hadn't even bothered to read it. Grosvenor pushed harder. "I wrote him a memo saying that we had a potential bestseller on our hands that we could lose any day to a big house in New York unless we acted quickly."

Thanks to Grosvenor's advocacy—essentially selling the book to her boss—the Naval Institute Press did agree to publish Clancy's book. And though initial sales were modest, the book's audience grew and grew: paperback rights, foreign sales, and of course the 1990 movie, which became a blockbuster starring Sean Connery and Alec Baldwin.

Yet another middleman has a claim on discovering Clancy: the literary agent Robert Gottlieb, who is now the chairman of Trident Media Group, one of the largest literary agencies in the United States. "Tom had published his first novel, HUNT FOR RED OCTOBER, with a small press," Gottlieb says, referring to the Naval Institute Press.[34] "I was at a stage in my career where I was constantly reading magazines, small press books, looking for authors and ideas," he explains. "I read that novel and was blown away—I knew I was onto something big. I contacted Tom, and we worked together for twenty years."

By discovering Clancy—pulling him into the gates, vouching for him, and helping him reach an ever-growing market—both gatekeepers saw their stars rise along with Clancy's.

As Robert Gottlieb and Deborah Grosvenor show us, Certifiers in the arts don't just act as a filter for whatever happens to come their way. They actively seek out treasures their buyers might want. Put another way, they're not only screening, they're also scouting—just like Mike Wolfe and Howard Robboy are. Scouting isn't for everyone, to be sure—as Gottlieb implies, he is no longer at the stage of his career where he has to be reading obscure books and magazines to find an author: authors now usually find him. But for a hungry middleman starting out, active scouting is essential because it's the only way to find something to sell.

The other flaw of the gatekeeper-as-villain view is that it presumes a kind of conspiracy among the middlemen, in which they're somehow colluding against talented newcomers. In reality, of course, middlemen compete against one another, just as Deborah Grosvenor suggests when she urged her boss to act fast. If one gatekeeper is too picky, rejecting what buyers actually want, then other middlemen have every incentive to swoop in so they can make a sale.

The Villain of Cost and the True Reason Pearls Are Expensive

If you diligently keep doing what a Certifier does, sooner or later, you become a valued Certifier, with your labors appreciated by buyers and sellers alike. Unfortunately, that alone doesn't make you a business success. That's because most business people's goal isn't just to create value: it's to make a profit. And if that's your goal, then becoming a valued middleman is not enough—you also have to watch the costs you incur in doing the very things that make you valuable. Those costs threaten your profits at every turn. You might spend a good deal of time and effort scouting for the goods and services your buyers want. The more time you spend and the farther you go out of your way to find those valued gems, the more likely you are to find what your buyers want—but is the payoff worth the cost? That's the question you must ask yourself. Unfortunately, the more effort you put into scouting, the more you end up spending on things like travel expenses, quality assurance, and simply time (opportunity cost). It doesn't seem fair: in a more just world, the harder you work, the higher would be your profit. But in the real world, costs mean that that's not always the case. In fact, the labor you put in isn't what creates value at all.

Something being hard to find isn't enough to make it valuable— it has to be valuable first to be worth the chase. Remember Paul Hawkinson's comment about recruiters giving you only the oysters proven to contain pearls? He's right, of course, and the hassle of shucking those oysters explains why hiring managers prefer to delegate the task—but it doesn't explain why the task is valuable. The nineteenth-century economist Richard Whately was probably the first to articulate that insight, and he used the oyster-pearl analogy, too. He pointed out that "if a man, eating an oyster, should chance to meet with a fine pearl, it would not sell for less than if he had been diving for it all day."[35] The value doesn't come from the amount of effort expended, but rather the other way around. As Whately famously put it elsewhere, "It is not that pearls fetch a high price because men have dived for them; but on the contrary, men dive for them because they fetch a high price."[36] Before then, most people believed just the opposite—that the value of a good comes from the human cost of producing or finding it. This false belief is the "labor theory of value," and you shouldn't fall for it: just because something is hard to find doesn't mean it has value to anyone, as any piece of junk hiding in your grandparents' attic will show. Plenty of things take a tremendous amount of work—picking grapes in stifling heat, mastering a Beethoven sonata, reporting an investigative story—but that doesn't mean you'll get paid for doing these things, let alone enough to cover your time and effort.

The same is true for Certifiers: the items Ann Whitley Wood resells fetch more than Mike Wolfe's do, even though her work is easier than his. Howard Robboy could spend 100 hours finding a candidate outside his specialty, but he rejects those assignments because the 100-hour job wouldn't pay him any more than a 10-hour job in his area of deep expertise. Being a profitable Certifier is a matter of working smart. Other things being equal, it's more profitable to focus on certifying goods and services that customers especially value. Also, if you take the long view and invest in building your reputation, you are more likely to reach the point when sellers come to you so you don't have to do as much scouting. In fact, a successful Certifier might find herself so inundated with sellers that to stay efficient she must hire gatekeepers to do initial screening.

Finally, a word about vouching, or staking your reputation on goods and services: it's not just for professional Certifiers. Reputations are famously harder to build than to destroy, so when you vouch for someone in your personal life, you are taking a real risk, too. Let's say you try to fix two people up. Or you recommend someone for a job. Whether you know it or not, you're not just connecting people—you are vouching for them and thus putting your reputation on the line. If all goes well, your reputation rises, but if something goes wrong, your reputation takes a hit. Think about whether you want to take that risk next time someone asks you for a referral.

In the next chapter, we will look at a role that often goes hand in hand with that of the Certifier, especially when the middleman is vouching for people.

3

THE ENFORCER

Keeping Everyone Honest

THE ROLE: *The Enforcer makes sure buyers and sellers put forth full effort, cooperate, and stay honest. When they run two-sided networks, where the behavior of one side can have positive or negative effects on the other side, Enforcers understand the importance of designing and upholding rules that will create a more valuable network. Therefore, they watch over their partners' dealings, parlay their relationships, and establish shared standards for good behavior.*

Why Services Require Enforcers

When you're selling *goods*, being a Certifier is enough—you can vouch for the quality of the Prada handbag or the Ben Franklin–era sailboat because these products' quality is not going to change before it reaches your buyer. Not so with *services*: regardless of service providers' underlying ability, they can decide how much effort to put in and how honestly to conduct business. Sussing out hidden information about sellers, as Certifiers do, won't protect buyers from shirking and cheating, problems that can come up after buyers sign on the dotted line. These problems of shirking and cheating, variously called moral hazard, postcontractual opportunism, or hidden action[1]—are especially acute when a player's actions are hidden and when buyers and sellers don't have an ongoing relationship. An ongoing relationship can protect against such problems, as long as the future value of the relationship is higher than the gains from cheating or shirking today. The lack of such a relationship, on the other hand, gives players an incentive to act opportunistically. This isn't to say that everybody or even most people will cheat or shirk—but even if there are only a few bad apples, would-be trading partners don't necessarily know who they are. For buyers and sellers to trust each other under those conditions, they need to know that someone—a third party—will reliably and fairly enforce the contract. That's the job of the middleman I call the Enforcer. Whereas Certifiers protect against the precontractual problems of *hidden information*, Enforcers protect against the postcontractual pitfalls of *hidden action*.

The word "enforcer" can evoke images of violent criminals who are only looking out for their own good, the sorts of characters we see in *Breaking Bad* and *The Sopranos*. It's no accident that Enforcers, as we usually think of them, are prevalent in the illicit economy: because buyers and sellers in the underworld can't turn to the courts to enforce contracts, they need a system of private enforcement. In these settings, middlemen who play the Enforcer role become indispensable.[2] But although they often resort to violence or the threat of violence, violence isn't the point. The sociologist Diego Gambetta, in his study of the Sicilian mafia, argued that the mafia's stock-in-trade is genuine protection—not a protection racket in which the mafia extorts money from business owners, but an actual service offered in the absence of an effective system of public justice.[3]

I argue in this chapter that any situations that provide reasons for buyers and sellers to be unsure of one another creates a need for Enforcers—in noncriminal environments and among people who mean well and even when both sides do have legal recourse.

Nonetheless, to best understand the way Enforcers serve both sides, and to see how this role works in concert with that of the Certifier, it helps to look first at middlemen in an illegal industry.

The Pimp at the Truck Stop

Several years ago, a group of health researchers set out to study the sex trade in a roadside town in southwest Uganda.[4] Uganda is one of the poorest nations on earth, and even in places that are thriving by Ugandan standards, as this town was, many women turn to prostitution to make ends meet. Among their biggest customers are commercial truck drivers, who are away from home for long periods and have the money to spend on sex. In Uganda and elsewhere, truck drivers have long been known to be among the biggest spreaders of sexually transmitted diseases, so they tend to be a target of attention from those who study public health. For this study, the researchers interviewed dozens of truckers traveling through this town as well as a dozen prostitutes. The academics were most interested in a third group—the middlemen who connect truckers with prostitutes. These middlemen, who mixed pimping with other forms of wheeling-and-dealing with the truckers, were reluctant to participate in the study, but truckers and prostitutes spoke more or less freely, explaining quite clearly why they did business through a middleman.

For the truckers, the answer boiled down to a single often-voiced comment about the middlemen: "They know the women." Many of the prostitutes work in bars that cater to visitors, sometimes as waitresses; to a visitor passing through it's not apparent which of the women are there to sell sex. And the truckers, who must get back on the road early the next morning, don't want to spend the time figuring this out on their own. The truckers also care a great deal about another piece of information the women want to keep hidden from view: their HIV status. Many women are infected with the AIDS virus, but truckers obviously prefer prostitutes who are known to be "safe." When truckers say that middlemen "know the women," they're talking about all these things. Because knowing the women is the middlemen's stock in trade, they are able to provide the screening and vouching that their customers value, just as the Certifiers we met in the preceding chapter.

But the middlemen at the truck stop served as more than Certifiers. If a trucker meets a woman through a middleman, then if he does get cheated or robbed, he can go back to the middleman to demand compensation. In fact, the prostitute is less likely to cheat a customer she met through a middleman because she knows that whereas the trucker will leave town the next day, the middleman will stay to settle the score.

The middlemen at the rural truck stop, in other words, aren't only there to select appropriate women before the deal is struck: they also stick around to make sure the prostitute keeps her end of the bargain. What's more, the middlemen are able to act as Enforcers for the prostitutes, too, making sure the customer pays and doesn't abuse the woman. Notice how these activities go beyond the Certifier role. By playing the Enforcer role, the middleman keeps both sides honest.

What does this have to do with legitimate business—isn't that what police and the court system do? Even in those conditions, though, private enforcement becomes useful whenever resorting to the legal system is impractical for one reason or another. Think about international business deals, where it's not clear who has jurisdiction or which rules should apply. In domestic dealings, a different set of problems calls for private ordering: going through courts is expensive and time-consuming—so people look to other ways to keep each other in line, from working with individuals and companies they already know and trust to using third-party services, such as credit bureaus, Yelp, Angie's List, mediators and arbitrators, and, naturally, middlemen.

Unlike mob enforcers, who aren't afraid to use brute force, the middlemen we'll look at in this chapter take a diplomatic approach: although firm in setting standards for good behavior, they elicit more admiration than fear from buyers and sellers. They show fairness in their dealings, and they work hard to preserve ongoing relationships with both buyers and sellers. They're often able to leverage these relationships to help one side or the other, thus making good behavior pay off for everyone. But being an Enforcer is perhaps the toughest role middlemen play, sometimes requiring them to be lawmaker, police, and judge in one. It means figuring out what it means to be fair when you have to balance the often competing interests of the two sides. And it means risking one or the other side's loyalty when mediating disputes that can arise.

Playing the Watchdog

The most basic way Enforcers keep people honest is by watching over buyers or sellers in ways that it would be too costly or even impossible for them to do on their own. It is a fundamental truth of human nature that people act differently when they're being watched. They're nicer, work harder, and behave more honestly. Just think of how motorists slow down when they see a police car. (Conversely, think of TV's hidden-camera undercover investigations, which reveal terrible things some people do when they assume that no one is looking.) Whether it is fear of punishment or concern about how others see them, people respond to the presence of watchful eyes. In a clever experiment at MIT, researchers used a sociable robot named Kismet—a hodgepodge of metal parts with a pair of eyes capable of tracking movement—to watch over participants as they chose to contribute money to an honesty box; when Kismet was "watching," contributions rose by 29 percent.[5]

In an even more dramatic demonstration of the same effect, a different group of researchers found that the mere picture of a pair of eyes made participants more honest: college students who could leave money in an honesty box when getting drinks from a coffee room left three times more money when in the presence of eyes, even though those eyes couldn't actually see.[6] Sensitivity to the feeling of being watched seems built into our DNA. In fact, patterns of behavior along these lines have led some social scientists to theorize that the concept of an all-seeing, all-powerful God evolved as a cultural solution to the problem of cooperation in large societies: when you can't count on fellow tribe members to watch everyone's every move, what better way to keep people in line than to have them believe that an almighty being knows when they've been naughty or nice?[7]

Middlemen are neither omniscient nor omnipotent, of course, but when it comes to watching over dealings between buyers and sellers, they have a far better vantage point than either side has of each other. In this way, they are like a stand-in for the small-town gossip networks that keep neighbors civil: able to observe the actions of the buyers and sellers they work with, especially over a long period of time, Enforcers can deter bad behavior, reward honest dealings, and thereby make buyers and sellers less wary of dealing with each other. As this chapter will show, that's an important role in a wide range of middleman businesses, from online marketplaces to agencies that match workers with temporary jobs.

How OpenTable Secured Restaurants' Trust in Diners

One middleman business that has done an admirable job of deterring bad behavior is OpenTable, the company that revolutionized the way diners make restaurant reservations and was recently acquired by Priceline for $2.6 billion. Instead of having to call up one restaurant at a time until they find an open table at the desired time, diners can go online, put in the size of their party and their preferred seating time, and see a list of restaurants that have openings during that window. Not every restaurant has come on board—whereas diners can use the service for free, restaurants have to pay a monthly fee and a smaller fee for each seat booked through OpenTable—but, despite some competition, the service has a vast reach, especially across cities in the United States. Through the service, restaurants can attract more diners, and by taking online reservations up until the last minute, they can reduce idle capacity. Diners win, restaurants win, and OpenTable wins.

When Chuck Templeton founded OpenTable in 1998, though, the concept was so novel that restaurants resisted, he says. "Nobody understood the Internet back then," he recalls.[8] To make it easy for diners to try out the service, reservations required nothing more than a first and last name and an e-mail address, and a diner could sign up as something like johndoe@yahoo.com. "So everyone had this concern that there were these anonymous reservations, and the no-show rate would be really high." No-shows are a perennial bane for restaurants: if someone makes a reservation and doesn't show up, those seats, which could have gone to a real customer, are lost forever. With rare exceptions, it's against informal industry norms for restaurants to require a deposit, so diners can no-show with impunity and the restaurant gets nothing.[9] No-shows can happen no matter how the reservations are made. But restaurateurs feared that by taking reservations through OpenTable, they'd be exposing themselves to more no-shows—that a kid bored on a Saturday night, for example, would make online reservations just for kicks, with no intention of showing up.

OpenTable didn't want that, either: if someone doesn't show up, not only does OpenTable not make any money on that reservation, but the restaurant blames OpenTable, fraying the partnership. In fact, without a good system in place to keep diners accountable, OpenTable would have a hard time getting restaurants to become customers in the first place. So Templeton and his team had a strong incentive to create rules to minimize no-shows.

Rules for proper behavior are a crucial element of any middle-man business that hopes to attract enough partners on both sides. In writing about SitterCity in the Bridge chapter, I pointed out that two-sided markets benefit from network effects, whereby buyers want to be where sellers are and sellers want to be where buyers are. But network effects aren't just about *quantity* (the more the merrier)—usually, buyers care about the *quality* of sellers, too, and sellers care something about the quality of buyers.[10] If you go on a dating site or a singles event, for example, you don't just care about how many potential partners there will be, but also whether they're the sort of people you want to meet. When preferences for quality combine with the snowballing effects of two-sided markets, quality can ultimately lead to quantity. One reason Facebook over-took MySpace in popularity, for example, was the way Facebook enforced a certain degree of quality control over its users: whereas MySpace allowed people to join anonymously (or to sign up under multiple fake identities), Facebook forced its users to sign up under their real names and addresses, creating the kind of accountability and trust that ultimately made it a more attractive gathering place. Advocates of privacy and Internet freedom have at times balked at Facebook's real-names policy, but most people were "willing to trade their privacy for the privileges of joining a network based on trust," as the journalist Julia Angwin has written.[11] Other middle-man businesses—think of Airbnb—have learned that it's in their best interest to set and enforce policies for good behavior because these ultimately attract better participants on both sides.

The designers of OpenTable's rules decided to allow pseud-onyms, but through a clever set of rules they managed to create a system that enabled restaurants to trust diners. Today the system works smoothly, and no-shows are no more a problem through OpenTable than they are with restaurants taking reservations over the phone. But figuring out the right set of rules was tricky, a ver-sion of the classic middleman's conundrum of how to balance the needs of both sides—or, in Templeton's words, "How do we not to piss off the diner, but at the same time protect our interest in the restaurant?"

The first rule they put in place was simple: the booking system prevented diners from making reservations the diners couldn't possibly keep. Diners sometimes like to keep their options open by making a reservation at six and seven and eight at three different restaurants, Templeton explains, so inevitably they'd have to bail on two of those, sometimes not bothering to cancel. But with one simple rule, OpenTable wouldn't allow them to do that: there had to be at least a two-hour window between a diner's reservations. Of course, diners could circumvent this rule by making a reservation by phone, but OpenTable wouldn't be a party to such ploys. Users could also, in theory, make additional reservations under a different pseudonym, but for reasons that will be clear in a minute, that didn't happen much, either.

Another straightforward OpenTable policy was sending e-mail reminders the day before the reservation. "They might have made the reservation two weeks ago, decided a week ago that they weren't going to make it, and forgot to cancel it," Templeton says. The e-mail, he says, was a way to remind diners that they could cancel very quickly and open that table up to someone else. Restaurants might not like a cancellation the night before, but even an eleventh-hour cancellation is better than a no-show. It's the same reason many doctors' offices (and some restaurants that take phone reservations) routinely make reminder calls or send e-mail reminders.

The most clever thing OpenTable did, though, happened after the meal. Being an effective Enforcer requires watching the actions of your trading partners, but playing the watchdog can be costly. (Just imagine if OpenTable had to install a representative at every participating restaurant.) OpenTable kept monitoring costs low by letting diners and restaurants keep tabs on each other, with OpenTable stepping in only in case of a dispute. This system runs so effortlessly that most OpenTable customers aren't even aware of it. When a diner who's made a reservation through OpenTable shows up, the restaurant's maitre d' checks the party into the OpenTable reservations system. That means the restaurant pays OpenTable a small fee for a successful transaction—currently $1/seat at most restaurants—and the diner gets credit for having dined at an OpenTable restaurant. These credits, usually 100 points per meal, eventually pay out as a cash bonus, so they're a loyalty program to encourage diners to use OpenTable. The loyalty program also alleviates the pseudonymity problem, since it rewards sticking with the same username for all your reservations.[12] If a diner for some reason fails to show up, the restaurant marks the reservation as a no-show; restaurants don't want to pay for no-shows, so they have an incentive to mark someone as a no-show. Here's where things get interesting: although a restaurant might be tempted to cheat, to save a few dollars on reservation fees by falsely reporting a no-show, they rarely do that because they know OpenTable will be on to them.

How do restaurants know that? Because OpenTable has, in effect, developed a reputation as a good Enforcer: whenever a restaurant reported a diner as a no-show, OpenTable would send diners a tactfully worded e-mail explaining why no-shows are a problem for restaurants and asking diners to let the restaurant know ahead of time the next time if their dining plans change. Think about what the e-mail accomplishes. If a diner really was a no-show, the e-mail would make the person think twice about ditching a reservation next time. In fact, OpenTable kicks out diners for life if they have four no-shows within a year. Depending on your perspective, the policy may seem too harsh—for life!—or too forgiving, since you can incur three no-shows with impunity, and the clock restarts after a year. But the policy does what it's meant to do—it keeps the bad apples out without losing valuable customers. OpenTable doesn't want anyone to incur four no-shows: the company would rather use each no-show as a warning, a teachable moment on how to be a good citizen in the OpenTable ecosystem. What's remarkable is that the e-mail made restaurants accountable, too—"a good way to keep both buyer and seller honest," Templeton says. That's because diners have an incentive to make sure restaurants don't mark them as a no-show, just as restaurants have an incentive to report no-shows. If a restaurant reports someone as a no-show who was actually there, and that diner complains to OpenTable, the discrepancy actually gives OpenTable a bit of useful information. OpenTable doesn't even need to investigate. "If that happens once, then that doesn't matter," Templeton explains. "But if you start to see a pattern on either the restaurant side or the diner side, we could then quickly tell who's the one doing the shenanigans."[13]

In other words, through OpenTable, each diner and each restaurant developed a reputation within the system. And, as always, reputation is a powerful motivator for good behavior. Just as the threat of getting kicked off OpenTable keeps diners from incurring too many no-shows, so does a track record of contested no-shows keep a restaurant from cheating OpenTable. As Templeton says, "A restaurant can't do it more than five or six times before we're calling them saying, 'Hey, we've got all these customers saying they were there and you're no-showing them. Is everything OK?'" The wording of this question is deliberately vague and diplomatic. OpenTable doesn't want to catch its restaurant partners in a lie: it wants them to save face, to stick with the relationship, and to do the right thing in the future.

This is a stunning feat: even though OpenTable is never on the scene, it has better information about no-shows than anyone else. Most restaurants don't even have a record of who has dined and who turned out to be a no-show at their own restaurant; no one but a middleman can see that kind of information across restaurants. OpenTable can and does, creating the kind of virtuous cycle all two-sided markets aspire to. In securing the restaurants' trust, OpenTable attracted more restaurants, and the more restaurants there are to choose from, the more attractive OpenTable becomes to diners; the more reservations are made through OpenTable, the more worthwhile the site becomes to restaurants, and so on.

Other successful online businesses do the same thing, using both sides' feedback about each other to keep both sides honest.[14] These systems seem obvious in hindsight—but they're actually a challenge to create in a way that works well. It took eBay years of effort—and experimentation by economists—to develop a feedback system in which the fear of seller retaliation for poor reviews by buyers didn't create a chilling effect on honest feedback.[15] A simple solution used by the latest reputation systems is making feedback blind—in effect, simultaneous—so that neither side can see how the other side rated them before giving their own rating. Another improvement: limiting who can post a review to those who've used the service, thus making it costlier to post fake reviews.[16] Finding ways to elicit honest, reliable information is one of the big jobs of Enforcers by which they benefit both sides and from which they can profit themselves.

This sort of policing isn't just for Internet marketplaces (like OpenTable and Airbnb), and it does not rely heavily on cheap, crowd-sourced reviews. This chapter looks at middlemen operating off the Internet, too—a modeling agency, a temporary placement service, a wedding planning business—all of which enjoy the profits of a well-designed two-sided network. Because middlemen's profits depend on the economic value of their network, they have a strong incentive to govern what happens in those networks.[17] All the middlemen in this chapter collect information about participants on both sides of a deal, strategically parlay that information into the kind of accountability that increases the value of the network, and end up with a larger profit from the extra value created. Even though middlemen incur costs in playing the Enforcer role, middlemen can play the role more efficiently by spreading the costs among their trading partners.

How Watchdogs Amplify Reputations

When watchdogs broadly share information about past behavior, research shows, buyers and sellers enjoy higher returns for doing good work: watchdogs amplify good reputations. Ginger Jin, an economics professor at the University of Maryland, worked on one such study.[18] She and her colleagues examined an online marketplace she describes as an "eBay copycat"—the Chinese trading platform called Eachnet—as it moved to eBay-style centralized feedback from the catch-as-catch-can word-of-mouth feedback we're all familiar with.[19] Just as PowerSellers on eBay act as Certifiers for the goods they sell, so eBay acts as an Enforcer for the sellers; the better eBay's feedback system is, the more effective an Enforcer eBay is. Jin, whose past studies of the effects of information on markets have looked at restaurant hygiene report cards and baseball card sales, points out that word of mouth is inherently "random, idiosyncratic, and may not be easy to find," whereas the centralized feedback system broadcasts information to a lot of people and reaches them much faster after a transaction. Her study confirmed this intuition. Before centralized feedback, the most reputable sellers on Eachnet (users similar to the PowerSellers on eBay) had to rely on repeat business to make the best use of their track records. After Eachnet introduced centralized feedback, reputable sellers no longer relied only on their past buyers and on those who happened to hear something from those past buyers. The "good news" about past sellers' good behavior spread far more broadly—to new customers, into new regions, and into new product categories, Jin explains.

Researchers studying the market for small-business loans found a similar effect. Traditionally, a small business could get a loan only from a local bank, because local banks could best monitor a would-be borrower's financial health and judge the business's credit risk. For a long time, small-business lending therefore was driven by relationships. But credit scoring began to change that.[20] Once a business owner's credit score became widely available through credit-reporting agencies, a local bank had no informational advantage over a large distant bank: both types of banks could cheaply learn about the credit risk by buying the borrower's credit report. That change benefited creditworthy borrowers, who no longer needed to rely on their local bank. Broad knowledge of their credit history opened up more choices of lenders, much as a PowerSeller's reputation on a centralized feedback system opened up sales opportunities with more buyers. In general, the more broadly middlemen broadcast information about past behavior, the more open trade can become. By enlarging the size of the pie—the volume of the market—the watchdog middlemen can charge to take a piece of it.

How the Mere Threat of Consequences Can Improve Behavior

The examples we've looked at so far show how middlemen can reward and punish participants by amplifying their reputations, good or bad. But middlemen have a simpler, more immediate way to punish players—and that in itself can elicit better, more trustworthy behavior.

To see how middlemen can do that, let's look at a lab game economists use to study trust: the Investment Game.[21] The standard version of the game is simple, and it involves just two players: the Investor and the Trustee, each of whom must make exactly one decision.[22] The Investor gets $10 at the start of the game and has an opportunity to earn more by entrusting some or all of that money to the Trustee. How much to send over is the Investor's only decision in this game. As soon as the Trustee receives the investment, the money triples—if the Investor sent $2, that becomes $6; $10 becomes $30. At this point, the Trustee needs to make a decision: how much to send back. If the Trustee is trustworthy, the Trustee will send back a good part of the total back to the Investor. For example, if the Investor sends over the full $10, and the Trustee sends back half of the tripled funds, both players end up with $15, which is considerably more than either one started out with. If the Trustee is greedier or less worthy of the Investor's trust, he or she might send back considerably less, even nothing, keeping the tripled endowment. The problem deliberately created by this rule is that the Investor might get cheated—and, knowing this possibility, the Investor will send less to avoid being cheated. That is exactly what tends to happen when people who don't know each other play the Investment Game.

The payoffs in the Investment Game capture the relationship between trust and mutual gain in all sorts of business and personal interactions, including, of course, all forms of buying and selling: when trust between two people is high, both players tend to be better off, and both can enjoy the full gains from trade. For example, if a buyer is willing to pay a premium for high-quality service and the buyer trusts that the seller will indeed provide high-quality service, the buyer will pay the seller more than for mediocre quality. Conversely, the lower the trust between the players, the more both lose out: if a buyer is willing to pay a premium for high-quality service but thinks the seller might shirk, the buyer won't be willing to pay a premium price, and the seller will have no incentive to provide the higher quality she is capable of delivering. Even if you ignore the level of quality, for exchange to occur at all some degree of trust is absolutely essential.

That's the basic two-player game, but what happens when a third player—a watchdog Enforcer—can intervene? That's a question once tested in the lab of Gary Charness, an experimental economist at the University of California–Santa Barbara.[23] The idea behind this particular series of experiments, Charness explains, was to see if having a third party who can punish the Trustee will cause Investors to be more trusting.[24] (Since the Investor makes the first move, Charness calls the Investor the first party.) "If the first party believes that the second party is going to respond more favorably [to the possibility

of being punished], then the first party should actually trust more."
And that's exactly what happened in the experiment: investments
and returns were higher when a third party watched over the other
players' actions and could punish Trustees for acting selfishly.[25]

What's most interesting about the experiment's results is that
regardless of the Watchdog's willingness to punish, the Investors
evidently believed in it, and this belief was enough to increase the
Investors' trust. When third-party punishment of the Trustees was
possible, the amount sent over by the Investors was more than 60 percent higher than in the standard Investment Game. The basic take-
away from this experiment is that even without the threat to your
reputation, just being watched (with threat of punishment) increases
cooperation. Middlemen are in a great position to watch, as we have
seen, and they can make immediate, one-time punishments—for
example, by docking a seller's pay if the service wasn't all that was
promised. What Charness's experiment suggests, though, is that the
actual punishment sometimes won't be necessary to keep players in
line as long as they believe in the threat of punishment.

Charness didn't have middlemen in mind when he conducted
this study. He originally thought of the third-party punishers more
as community enforcement—something like Neighborhood Watch.
But the same principle can apply to professional watchdogs, too—
the watchful eyes that third parties, such as rating agencies, auditors,
and consumers on feedback forums, can provide. The principle can
also apply to Enforcer middlemen, people who act as watchdog as
only part of their job.

Weak Enforcer, Strong Enforcer

These third parties work, however, only if they are credible themselves, points out David McAdams, an economist at the Fuqua
School of Business at Duke University who consults on applying
game theory to business situations. One example McAdams uses is

the American Bar Association, which can slap a sanction on a lawyer who violates the rules of the trade: the organization is credible, he says, because if you're a lawyer who gets one of those sanctions, "you can't go to those guys and have them take it off." The ABA and others like it won't be bought because their own reputation is based on conveying honest information—and their reputation is worth a great deal. In fact, many economists and political scientists believe that the best way to thwart corruption among police, politicians, and other government agents is to pay these third parties well: if your continued employment is worth a lot of money, the thinking goes, you won't be tempted to do anything (such as taking bribes) that jeopardizes your job.[26]

The polar opposite to an incorruptible watchdog is a third party that deliberately posts negative information to extort money for having it removed, as some online "reputation management" companies have been accused of doing.[27] This kind of third party is a parasitic middleman because it generates absolutely no benefit, only costs. The vast majority of middlemen are neither perfect watchdogs nor parasitic ones: they're on a continuum from strong to weak enforcement, and many could do better. Consider, for example, the difference between eBay and Craigslist—neither of which is a parasite. With its feedback system and fraud department, eBay serves as a pretty powerful watchdog in protecting buyers from unscrupulous and incompetent sellers—and in eliciting the very best behavior from good sellers such as Ann Whitley Wood.[28] Craigslist provides a lot of value as a Bridge, but it does very little in the way of policing the trading activity it facilitates, a shortcoming that's opened up entrepreneurial opportunities for the hundreds of specialized startups that do a better job of ensuring honest buyer and seller behavior in a particular niche (on top of better user interfaces with more specialized search tools).

Perhaps the best-known of these "spawn of Craigslist"[29] is Airbnb: you can rent (or rent out) a room through Craigslist, but how comfortable would you be dealing with a stranger directly?[30] In his book *Game-Changer*, David McAdams contrasts Airbnb, an effective Enforcer, with a rival company, HomeAway (which runs the site VRBO.com, Vacation Rental By Owner). Unlike Airbnb, HomeAway allows property owners to get away with deceptive descriptions of their rentals[31]—in part because, unlike Airbnb, it allows individual owners to opt out of reviews.[32]

Now, you might be saying that VRBO is not trying to be an Enforcer. In fact, VRBO might that say it's right there in the name: "By Owner," not by agency. And VRBO's fine print—the terms and conditions on the site—disclaims that the site is "not a party to any rental transaction" and that "the truth and accuracy of the listings are the responsibility of each user." But these disclaimers, which say that VRBO is neither a Certifier nor an Enforcer, are lost on many customers, who apparently pay more attention to the bold promise on the site's front page: "Book the vacation of your dreams." That's my conclusion from the numbers of renters who complain online and to the press about unpleasant surprises, such as no heat, peeling wallpaper, even rat infestations[33]—and about VRBO's unwillingness to step in to resolve complaints.[34] Although VRBO doesn't intend to be an Enforcer, it appears that many of its customers signed up with the implicit expectation that the site would play this role. Business scholars have long known that people bring unstated expectations to a contract, and violations of this "psychological contract" tend to damage relationships between the contracting parties even if there's no legal breach.[35] If VRBO doesn't want to be in the business of enforcing honesty, it would do well to say so loud and clear. Better yet, though, VRBO and similarly weak Enforcers might find it necessary to become stronger Enforcers just to keep up with the competition.

How so? A little legal backstory will help. In the United States, a website cannot generally be held liable for the actions of its users, whether or not there are consequences beyond the site; the reason is Section 230, an influential provision of the Communications Decency Act of 1996. Most laws impose greater legal obligations on businesses, says Eric Goldman, a law professor at Santa Clara University who has published widely on Internet governance—but Section 230 says that Internet businesses can maintain their immunity from liability even if they do nothing to police users. That's because lawmakers didn't want to stifle technical innovation, and they also didn't want to create a perverse incentive for websites to do *too little* screening and policing. Without legal immunity, Goldman explains, "Congress was concerned that websites would feel like if they tried to help and failed, they would face more liability than if they didn't try to help." The goal of Section 230, therefore, was to get websites to do more policing. That way, if you're a website and you fail in your efforts, "you're not on the hook for failure, and the idea is that websites would do more."[36]

Section 230 appears to have worked as intended: we have indeed seen impressive leaps of innovation among Internet businesses in recent years. Strong reputation systems that keep users accountable have become standard among the most successful middleman businesses—think Airbnb, eBay, TaskRabbit, even Uber; these systems have raised the bar for other middlemen. As a result, any site that becomes known as a poor Enforcer can fall behind.

But let's return to the specific case of VRBO, which currently appears as a weak Enforcer. It's easy to see how a weak Enforcer harms its reputation with renters, but you might think a weak Enforcer could continue to enjoy strong profits from property owners. So far, that seems to be working for HomeAway, VRBO's parent company. But something different seems more likely to happen in the long run, especially in the presence of a rival who acts as a strong Enforcer: a weak Enforcer will disproportionately attract dishonest owners. People trying to pass off shoddy properties as good ones won't want a strong Enforcer meddling in their business, but owners of lemons will gravitate toward a less-discriminating platform. Owners of good properties, meanwhile, will prefer a site that rewards them for good behavior through higher prices for a good reputation. Not only that, but owners of all types of properties will have a greater incentive to invest in improving the quality of their rentals (refurnishing them, repainting, calling the exterminator, and so on) if they believe they will receive a return on their investment, which they're more likely to see on Airbnb than on VRBO. Renters, in turn, will pull even farther away from the weaker Enforcer, making that platform less attractive to all kinds of owners. To prevent this downward spiral, the middleman running the marketplace should become a stronger Enforcer.

"You Are a One-time Customer and Wedding Planners are Repeat Customers."

The punishers in the version of the Investment Game that Charness tested had one-time interactions with all the Trustees. The threat of immediate, one-time punishments can deter the most opportunistic behavior, as that experiment showed, but a more powerful way to motivate good behavior is to link current behavior to an ongoing stream of future rewards. For example, if a seller believes that doing a good job today will lead to more business tomorrow and the day after and the day after that, the seller has a stronger incentive to do a good job today than if the reward (or punishment) stops today. That's why ongoing relationships tend to create a climate of trust. We see this again and again in lab studies of repeated games, which create much better behavior than one-shot versions of the same game. In the Investment Game, for example, when researchers tell participants that they'll be playing the game with the same people over and over, experiments show a sharp rise in both trust (as measured by how much people invest) and trustworthiness (how much people send back).[37] Trustees know that if they keep too much of the Investor's money in the first period of the game, they'll earn less in subsequent periods because Investors won't trust them again. This reputation effect mirrors what happens in real life, where repeat dealings between buyers and sellers enable what's essentially a self-enforcing contract: these arrangements work not because of the shadow of the law (the threat of being sued) but because of the shadow of the future[38] (the threat of loss of future business).

Many business dealings in the real world are repeated games, enabling lots of trust and cooperation. This is often true, for example, when people work within the same organization or live in the same household. The logic of repeated games can also work between firms, when companies go back to the same suppliers again and again. In fact, ties between coworkers and between buyers and suppliers can become so strong that they're more than just repeated games: they're relationships, guided as much by feelings of commitment as by the cost-benefit calculations of economic games.

But some situations are more like one-shot games or nearly so: how often do you need to hire someone to paint your house or replace your roof? How often do you sell your company? How many times in your life do you need to hire a band to play at a wedding? The one-time buyer can't use the threat of withholding future business to induce trustworthy behavior from the seller. Yes, a bride can refer business to the vendors she's hired—she can tell friends if her photographer was a doll or disaster to work with, for example—but most brides can tell at most a few people. A wedding planner, on the other hand, advises brides on such matters every day and refers them not only to the photographer but also to the florist, the baker, and the wedding-dress maker. As a middleman between many brides and many vendors, a wedding planner can use her ongoing relationships with vendors to transform a one-shot game (between the bride and a wedding photographer, for example) into a repeated game between each vendor and the wedding planner.

McAdams, the Duke University economist, calls this approach leveraging relationships. "What we're really talking about is changing incentives," he explains. "In the context of game theory, we're talk-ing about changing payoffs because that's where incentives come from." You can change the payoffs in the current game, which is what the Watchdogs in Gary Charness's Investment Game did. "Or you can change future payoffs—or linking what's happening now to a future consequence."

To see how a successful wedding planner leverages relation-ships on behalf of brides, I spoke with Julie McKenney, whose com-pany, Bliss Elevated, serves brides in the Denver, Colorado, area. McKenney, who's won several "Best of" awards from local media, has been in the wedding business for seven years, and during this time she's seen an abrupt change in who buys planning services. "It's not just people who have a ton of money to spend and want really crazy designs," she says.[39] "All of a sudden there was this shift that you can have a wedding planner on the 'day of' and maybe they just recommend vendors, and it can be more affordable." Yet, as planning services have become more affordable on the whole, McKenney's rates have tripled in the past five years: she now charges an average of $4,000 per wedding—and up to $8,500 for her full-service pack-age. Most of her clients have wedding budgets of between $30,000 and $70,000—significantly higher than the recent national median in the United States of $18,086.[40]

When we spoke, she told me about a June wedding she was planning for one of her brides. "I've spent probably four or five hours on various phone calls, and I have over 200 e-mails in her folder—just e-mails with the vendor that she's not even looped in on. Right now, I'm finishing up picking a florist for her. First, it's getting to know exactly what she wanted. Then I take that and I shop it around to different florists, pretty much florists I have worked with before who are highly recommended. Then I pres-ent it to the bride and groom: 'Here are three options, here is their pricing, they are available.' And if they want to have meetings with those vendors, I'll coordinate a conference call." The same goes for all the other vendors a bride might need to hire, from caterers and bakers to DJs and photographers.

That in itself is a valuable middleman service (the role described in the Concierge chapter), but McKenney also understands that the value she provides goes beyond saving a bride's time. At a minimum, her presence ensures that, as she puts it, "everything goes smoothly and vendors show up and you get what you paid for." If a vendor's quality ever slips—as it did with a DJ who seemed to not be as on top of his game as he used to be—she quietly pulls the company off her vendor list.[41] But there's more she can offer. On her website, McKenney puts it this way: "A vendor is likely to perform at an even higher level for you if you are working with a respected wedding planner. Think of it this way. You are a one-time customer and wedding planners are repeat customers." The most visible form of this higher level of performance is little perks many vendors add on to their standard service. Any florist she works with, for example, includes a free toss bouquet (normally priced at $35). Some venues will throw in an extra hour when selling an eight-hour block. A photographer can include an engagement session in addition to the shoot on the wedding day. Some bridal shops will provide McKenney's clients a free garment bag, and one catering company always gives chocolate-covered strawberries and champagne on the house. Many vendors are inflexible on prices, but if McKenney asks for a perk, they're often happy to oblige.

McKenney sometimes refers to her clients as "my brides"—they are, after all, her clients—but her wording also gets at a deeper truth: that a bride working with McKenney isn't really the same player in the bridal market as that same bride hiring vendors on her own would be. Even if a bride knew exactly who was on McKenney's vendor list—knew, for example, to avoid the DJ whose quality had slipped, and knew that all the florists on McKenney's list throw in a toss bouquet—that bride coming to the same vendors off the street won't get quite the same level of service. McKenney sees a few reasons vendors are willing to go the extra mile for her and her brides. Like the bride, most vendors appreciate having her orchestrating the big day because they know the wedding will go more smoothly for everyone. ("If you don't have a planner there, the photographer and the DJ are the ones managing the timeline of the day, and it causes a lot of stress and expense for vendors if things are running behind," she explains.) But more important, she is also, as she implies when she talks of being a repeat customer, in a position to give each vendor more business. In fact, some vendors—and photographers are notorious for this, she says—offer kickbacks for referring clients to them, but McKenney prefers to redirect that money toward the clients themselves. Like a well-paid cop or building inspector, she isn't tempted by bribes and kickbacks because she's happy with what she earns; she'd much rather burnish her reputation with brides by getting these perks for them than to risk tarnishing her good name by accepting money herself. "I think the repeat business is what keeps vendors doing a really good job for my clients—repeat business and visibility." Visibility? "I'm on boards in the community with other planners," McKenney explains, "so vendors may not even just get brides from me, but they may get me talking to other planners. Just yesterday somebody e-mailed out, 'Does anyone know someone local who has sequin linens? I really need sequin linens and I don't know where to find them.' Within a couple of minutes she had five responses from other wedding planners recommending linen vendors. So not only are we providing repeat business through our own pool of brides—we talk with other planners and other vendors." A photographer, for example, might call McKenney trying to help his or her client. "They'll say, 'Julie, I have this bride who's struggling to find a dress,' and they'll tell me what she's looking for. 'Can you give me advice?' And I'll say, 'Yeah, call Kate at Little White Dress. She's the owner, she's amazing, tell her I sent you, and she'll give your bride extra-special treatment.'" Even though McKenney plans only about 15 weddings per year—and only five this past year, when she had a baby—her many relationships in the business give her clout with vendors that brides alone simply can't match.

Make no mistake: although these relationships provide powerful leverage, they don't come for free. McKenney must spend time (and occasionally money) attending bridal fairs, participating in board discussions, answering questions, and generally being helpful. Nobody pays her for that, and any benefit she reaps from these networking activities is indirect. Still, her networking costs are much lower than they would be for someone not committed to the business, and that puts her in an excellent position to invest in these relationships and to profit from them.

Trading in Private Information

How exactly does someone like McKenney profit from these relationships? After all, the barriers to entering the profession don't seem high—you don't have to take classes or pass a licensing exam, for example—so what enables her to charge increasingly higher rates when many eager newcomers could conceivably drive down prices? This is a version of a much more general question that network researchers have been asking about middlemen for years: what keeps these boundary spanners from being jostled aside by others who also want to profit from connecting buyers and sellers?

One compelling answer comes from a fascinating study that analyzed a trove of proprietary data from an international placement agency.[42] This particular agency's job was to find web designers, graphic designers, and similar professionals to staff short-term projects for the agency's clients. The agency received payment that amounted to the difference between the rate negotiated with the client (the buyer) and the rate negotiated with the worker (the seller). For example, if the client paid the agency $150 per hour for a worker the agency had sent, and the agency in turn paid the worker $100 per hour, the agency would earn a margin of $50 for every hour the worker spent on that assignment. While a worker could be at only one job at a time, each middleman was collecting a commission on all the workers currently placed at various clients' sites. As a result, a productive placement agent could earn more than some of the highly skilled workers he or she was placing. It's the sort of disparity (some would say inequity) that can make workers resent an agency—and can make placement work seem attractive to would-be agents. So what do the middlemen do to make themselves hard to compete with and hard to cut out?

The researchers, Matthew Bidwell of the Wharton School and Isabel Fernandez-Mateo of London Business School, found that the first key was the middlemen's ability to gather private information about workers they had placed over time. At the beginning of a relationship with a worker, no middleman knows more about the worker than any other middleman. Each agency knows only what it can glean from a résumé and an interview; because everyone has access only to public information at this point, neither the client nor the worker has good reason to prefer one middleman over another. But as soon as the agency places the worker, additional information begins to emerge, and this private information remains exclusive to the agency. For example, the middleman might learn from the client how quickly the worker completes certain tasks, how well she works with others, how proficient she is with a specific tool, and other important nuances that competing middlemen aren't privy to.

The middleman's newfound knowledge has an effect both on the worker and on clients, including clients who've never hired this worker before. The more the middleman learns about this worker, the better a match he will be able to make on the next assignment—thus enabling a new client to benefit from information gleaned through another client's project. As a result, the middleman can charge a little more for the same worker with every subsequent assignment. For the worker's part, the longer a track record the worker has with the agency, the easier it is for the agency to show clients what the worker is able to accomplish and to persuade clients that the worker is worth a high wage. As Bidwell and Mateo-Fernandez write, "The broker with private information can credibly vouch for the seller"—that is, the worker—"in a way that brokers with short-term relationships cannot." The worker, in turn, is able to earn a higher rate from an agency he or she has a longer history with, which implies that the worker will tend to prefer this agency over another one with whom the relationship is less established. In short, the agency creates value for both sides and creates an increasing amount of value over time.

Many people talk about the importance of building relationships, but it's not always clear how to do that and why it pays off. This study shows these things in a concrete way: long-standing relationships help you gather information that enables more valuable collaborations in the future. That's interesting in itself, but the study goes further than that to reveal something even more interesting, particularly for middlemen and those who work with them. By looking closely at the numbers—the bill rates charged to the client firms, the pay rates given to the workers, and changes in these rates for each worker over time—the researchers discovered that as the value created grows, the middleman captures *a larger share* of that added value than the worker does. Remember that for a middleman to be profitable, it is not enough to be good to your trading partners: yes, middlemen have to create value for buyers and sellers, but they must also be able to capture some of that value. What, then, enables a middleman to capture more of the added value than the worker, the seller in this three-party relationship?

The answer to that question is the second big insight from this remarkable study. It turns out that although the worker and the middleman are partners, each benefiting the other and each dependent on the other, the relationship is not perfectly symmetrical: each worker is more dependent on the agency than the agency is on the worker. That's for the simple reason that the agency is able to maintain relationships with more workers than the number of agencies or employers with which each worker is able to maintain a relationship. As the researchers point out, if a worker could maintain as many relationships as the agency does, it's not clear why the worker needs an agency at all. This asymmetry gives the agency more alternatives than the worker has, which gives the middleman more clout in the negotiation over wages. A worker would prefer to get $120 out of the $150 the agency bills the client, while the middleman would prefer to pay $100, but since the middleman has better alternatives to a negotiated agreement than the worker does, the rate they settle on will tend to be closer to the one the agency wants. If a worker turns down a middleman's offer, the middleman can turn to a number of other workers he also knows would be a good fit for the assignment.

A wedding planner is different from a placement agent, of course: unlike the temporary placement agents Bidwell and Mateo-Fernandez studied, McKenney charges a fixed fee rather than an opaque markup, so bargaining with vendors over price won't give her a higher payoff. In fact, I wondered if the fact that she is recommending vendors allows those vendors to charge brides more for their services. McKenney doesn't think so. Clearly, they want to keep her happy, and presumably they want to do the same for other wedding planners who are active in the Denver area. Most vendors do this by providing the best service they can and staying competitive on price, knowing that McKenney has a choice of vendors—just as a temporary placement agent has a choice of workers to suggest to a client. McKenney has clout and she has information, and the longer she stays in business the more of both she has. As a result, she can make better matches and elicit better work from her vendors. It is this very real improvement in quality that probably explains why she can command significantly higher fees today than she did when she started several years ago.

Setting Shared Standards

In looking at research into how third parties keep others honest, I became intrigued by the work of Riccardo Boero, an economist and sociologist working at Los Alamos National Labs who had run several experiments on the Investment Game.

Boero was motivated, he explained, by important economic changes in his native Italy.[43] Thousands of small firms, usually family-owned, had long sustained a prosperous economy in the country's industrial districts. Boero likens these industrial districts to Silicon Valley without the focus on technological innovation. Each firm cared about its own financial well-being while also acting like a good citizen with others in the district. There were norms about how to treat suppliers, workers, customers, and so on. For a long time, these shared norms created a high level of trust that gave the districts an edge over competitors who operated in a less organized ecosystem. Then, in the 1990s, the system began to fray: economic growth in China and globalization more generally, Boero says, forced Italian firms to focus more on their own self-interest and less on the common good.

He and his colleagues began to wonder if there were other ways through which trust among business people could develop: if you couldn't count on long-term relationships with the same partners to foster shared norms and a high degree of trust, what could you do?

In one experiment to investigate this question, the researchers tweaked the Investment Game to enable strangers (who'd been randomly paired up) to evaluate each other after each round of play.[44] These evaluations would then follow the players as they moved from partner to partner, so that when you met a stranger in a later round of play you'd know something about the player's reputation. This change to the rules of the standard Investment Game increased cooperation quite a bit, just as you'd expect: even though player A knew she might never play with player B again (and would therefore have some incentive to cheat B), she would act trustworthy because she knew that if she didn't, then B would tell C and D and E, and these strangers would cease to trust A; A's cheating would fail to pay off in the long run, and so A would act more trustworthy. This is the classic way reputation works.

When the conditions are right, this kind of gossip-based system works beautifully. But in many real-world settings, the conditions aren't right. One problem occurs in large societies: when there are many players, gossip is hit or miss because even though B might tell C and D about her experience with A, other players (E and F and all the rest) might never find out. In this environment, "players are not sure the information about them is going to reach future partners," Boero says, and under those conditions, cheating is no longer always bad for business. "In general, our idea is that the more the transmission of reputation is uncertain, the more likely the reputation mechanism can fail." In fact, this is what Ginger Jin's research on the Chinese eBay copycat suggests: without the wide dissemination of reputational information, systemwide trust is low, and people then tend to restrict business to those they've successfully done business with in the past or to those they happened to hear good things about.

Spotty diffusion of gossip is one reason people aren't on their best behavior. Boero's research also suggests another reason: simply a lack of a well-established norm for good behavior. Think about the Investment Game: what does it mean to act trustworthy? Does it require sending back half the amount ($15)? The full amount? Or maybe just anything over the $10 the Investor sent over? The norm for good behavior, even in a game as simple as this one, is really not obvious. Similarly, norms can be unclear in actual business dealings, where notions of right and wrong can vary by industry, by culture, and even by company. For example, what does it mean to be on time or to pay on time? Lack of agreement on norms can lead to tensions even between well-intentioned players who both think they are doing the right thing. One person might show up to an appointment five minutes after the appointed time (or pay an invoice a few days after receiving it), thinking she's on time or early, while the other person sits waiting and fuming. We'll look at how actual middlemen help reduce these conflicts in a moment, but first let's see how they did so in the lab.

Like Gary Charness and his colleagues, Boero and his fellow researchers introduced a third player to the basic Investment Game. But whereas Charness's game was a one-shot game, and the third party had the power to materially punish the Trustees, Boero's game involved multiple rounds in which the entire role of Boero's third party was to just report on the behavior of the other players. Since reputational information doesn't always spread well through a large group, a specialized third party might help, the researchers thought. The idea, Boero explains, was to see if the third party's "gossip" worked to sustain trustworthy behavior despite the fact that the third party received no payoff. Indeed, this third-party gossip did work: when the third party reported on the actions of the other players, the other players acted more trustworthy than in the one-shot Investment Game. These Trustees were also just as trustworthy as in the game in which players reported their own, first-hand experiences.

I have read about many reputation experiments over the years and have even participated as a player in one, so when I first read about Boero's experiment, I was struck by a big difference. In most reputation experiments, players see (typically on their computer monitor) a detailed history of other players' actions—for example, a table reporting how much each person returned in each period of the Investment Game. In Boero's experiment, on the other hand, the third party didn't report the exact action of each player; instead, the third party simply rated the player as positive, negative, or neutral.

Boero set up the experiment that way for a couple of reasons. First, just to make life easier on the players: if you're an Investor and you see exact numbers for each Trustee over the course of several periods of play, that's a lot of information to process, and most people will translate whatever they learn into a simple label in their minds anyway: is this person trustworthy or not? The second reason for this way of reporting behavior is more interesting and tells us more about the way an Enforcer functions in the real world: to teach, however subtly, what the norms are.

Before the start of the game, Boero explains, people's judgments of what is good and what is bad behavior in an Investor is quite subjective and varies a lot from one player to the next. For example, some Investors might think that sending back anything between $10 and $15 is neutral, whereas others believe that sending back $15 is positive. There's some disagreement about good behavior and no common standard. But then people start playing the game. Investors interact with Trustees, and they get feedback from the third parties. With the very first evaluation, subsequent behavior begins edging toward the standard in the mind of the evaluator. Players start to adopt the third party's standard even though the third parties are every bit as subjective as the Investors themselves. Boero, speaking as if he were the third party, says that "If I start saying that the player who contributes less than ten is a positive guy, nobody tells me that that is wrong." There's also no incentive for the third parties to uphold a common standard even when they do come to sense what that standard might be. And yet, somehow, the range of opinion about what is good and what is bad starts to narrow: the players converge on a common standard of good Trustee behavior. "It is astonishing that there is a convergence," Boero says, because it happens simply through interaction with the third parties.

Economists tend to assume that given the chance, many people will shirk and cheat. Much of the time, they are right: hidden action is a problem because it creates openings for such opportunism, behavior that economist Oliver Williamson famously described as "self-interest seeking with guile."[45] Opportunism is an important force to be reckoned with, which is why this chapter has focused on it, but a preoccupation with opportunism can obscure a more benign reason people sometimes fail to live up to our expectations: they simply don't know what we expect. Players sometimes make honest mistakes, acting badly not out of guile but out of ignorance.

In the real world, middlemen are much like the third parties in Boero's version of the Investment Game: able to see and establish the norms in the industry, teach them to new players, and keep everyone accountable to those norms. The only difference, really, is that professional middlemen, unlike the third parties in the game, receive a payoff.

A clear illustration comes from the business of fashion modeling, where the buyers and sellers don't always understand each other and where an effective middleman acts as a kind of cultural broker between the two groups. One person who exemplifies this role is Jenna Adams, a director at the Philadelphia-based Reinhard Model and Talent Agency, one of the top agencies in that city.

On one side of the agency is the talent: the models and actors the agency represents. On the other are the agency's clients—mainly photographers, film producers, and advertising agencies who, for specific projects, need to hire some of the talent Reinhard represents. For the clients, the agency's basic service is to find models that fit the client's current need and to do so within the client's budget; for the models, the agency negotiates the fee so the project is worth the model's time and level of exposure. Being seen on too many ads and billboards tends to devalue the model, Adams argues, so more exposure should be more expensive. "We work on behalf of both sides," she says.

The agency therefore does its best to make sure each side does right by the other; this can be difficult when the seller doesn't understand the buyer's expectations. A common source of misunderstanding is in attitudes toward time, specifically punctuality: the buyers, such as photographers, can't abide lateness whereas the models, especially beginners, sometimes think nothing of it. Adams understands where each is coming from. "I think you're dealing with more flakiness because we're not saving lives here," she says of models' notorious unreliability. Modeling work has the image of being fun. "It's glamorous, it's lighthearted, and it doesn't necessarily strike people as serious." It doesn't help, Adams adds, that many models are young—people who've never had adult responsibilities. The buyers, on the other hand, come at a modeling shoot from an entirely different perspective. They're not only more mature, but they have more money on the line. If a model shows up late or even cancels at the last minute, she loses at most the fee she would make on that assignment, or so she thinks. For the buyer, on the other hand, even a seemingly small snag can cost tens of thousands of dollars. Adams recalls a time when a model showed up at a shoot with a new haircut; since her long hair had been a major factor in getting picked for the job, the new cut was a big deal indeed.

In many social situations, arriving 10 to 15 minutes late is no big deal—but a professional photo shoot isn't a cocktail party. Adams understands better than the young models that every time increment is money—not just for the other models but for the crew, Adams says. A delay of 15 minutes, therefore, can amount to several person-hours' worth of losses. That's too costly for photographers to take a chance on, which is one reason they turn to a modeling agency even if they could find a model with suitable looks on their own. A modeling agent like Adams can set a common standard—one that, at least in this case, is closer to what the buyer expects than to what a model might prefer. When both sides work through a reputable agent, "there's an accountability factor," Adams says.

As with wedding planners who manage vendors, that accountability comes from the agent's role as a repeat player, which enables her to tie today's actions to consequences for many tomorrows. It's as simple as that: "The easier [the models] make everyone's job, the more they'll be working." On the flip side, "if they're unreliable, if they've been troublemakers, . . . we will only be patient for so long," Adams says. She would never speak ill of a model with a client: the agency would simply terminate the contract.

The fact that Reinhard has had to "release" models it can't vouch for shows that the agency is acting as a powerful Enforcer: a weaker agency, with less ability to attract top talent, might let the model get away with bad behavior longer because its agents don't want to turn down assignments.[46] By being willing to act as an Enforcer, a powerful and successful agency takes the long view, which ultimately benefits both itself and its clients. Cutting off a business relationship with a flaky model protects the agency's clients and its own reputation with clients, much the way Julie McKenney, the wedding planner, protects her good name among brides by taking a poorly performing DJ off her vendor list. Even though the modeling agent terminates a formal contract while the wedding planner simply stops referring future brides, both middlemen are simultaneously helping their buyers and themselves.

Caught in the Middle?

At the same time, the middleman must not lose sight of the interests of the seller, who is as important to the success of the agency as the clients who pay the bill. Even though models are the ones who need to be taught what clients expect in terms of punctuality and appearance, clients can be just as clueless on other important issues. "It's not unheard of to run into a client who doesn't know how to explain what they need, or what their true intentions are in terms of images," Adams says. "We've had a situation where the model didn't know she was expected to do lingerie," a job that would call for a higher rate than what had been settled on. "Or it's supposed to be print-only, and when the model arrives there are video cameras there." Clients have also been known to use images past the agreed-upon date. All of these situations call for a conversation with the client to protect the interests of both the model and the agency.

To minimize unwelcome surprises from both sides, the agency makes every effort to "dot our i's and cross our t's," Adams says. "It's one reason we use e-mail now: there's a lot less room for human error when you're confirming everything with both the client and the model. We are following up and following up." Notice that this is the tack OpenTable uses to make sure diners show up for their reservation: both middlemen understand that to err is human and that it's a bad idea to chalk up to malice what can be explained through cluelessness.[47] And although a middleman can inadvertently add to the confusion—distorting messages as in a game of telephone—an effective Enforcer does the opposite: clarifying messages, strengthening signals, and improving communication between the people on either side.

Not every conflict is due to a misunderstanding, however, and mediating situations when it seems clear that one side intentionally acted badly is trickier, especially if that side is the client. "I absolutely have had clients try to pull fast ones," says Adams, "and usually we have to push back." Pushing back naturally risks angering the client, which business people are loath to do. For example, Chuck Templeton, the founder of OpenTable, told me that as much as he wanted to protect the interests of both diners and restaurants, that wasn't always possible, so when push came to shove, the company would rather not lose a restaurant partner, because, as he put it, "The restaurant is the one paying the bill." But an agency model, who is probably more valuable to an agency than an individual diner is to OpenTable, does expect the agency to protect her interests against an opportunistic client. Sometimes, despite the agency's attempts to be evenhanded in these disputes, the agency will be caught in the middle, with both sides feeling that the agency didn't treat them fairly. At least once that Adams can recall, a conflict that the agency was unable to resolve to anyone's satisfaction caused Reinhard to lose both the client and the model, which, of course, seems like the worst possible outcome.

Because of her agency's position of strength, though, Adams can keep these rare incidents in perspective. The people involved may not have cared whether the resolution was fair, she points out; perhaps they were just unhappy to get the answer they didn't want to hear. In any case, Adams understands that acting as a firm Enforcer is, in the end, the right course of action. "You do get to a certain point," she says, "where we can feel confident in our professionalism and our level of talent where we can lay down the law—and if that doesn't work for a client, they can look elsewhere." The talent agency, it seems, benefits from the same indirect network effects that help OpenTable and other successful two-sided markets: if the agency can do a good job of protecting the interests of the model, it can attract the best models, and the best models attract good clients, who are willing to abide by the agency's rules of professionalism, rules that in turn benefit both the agency and the models, and so on.

One way to think about both the Certifier and Enforcer roles is that they protect buyers from risk. But that's not all there is to managing risk for your trading partners, and the next chapter explores more broadly how middlemen can play the role of Risk Bearer without exposing themselves to unnecessary risks.

4

THE RISK BEARER

Reducing Uncertainty

THE ROLE: *From banks and insurance companies to wholesalers, some companies earn a premium for bearing risk. By building diversified portfolios, they're better able to weather volatility than their trading partners. The same principle holds true for nonobvious middlemen, from gallerists and venture capitalists to Internet platforms that deliver on-demand services: all are better able than their trading partners to bear risk. One key to being an admirable Risk Bearer: being able to discern internal from external risk, avoiding the former risk while embracing the latter.*

Heads I Win, Tails You Lose?

Every business person deals with risk, but middlemen are in a unique position to profit from it. To play the Risk Bearer role well, they must understand the workings of risk.

When we put middlemen and profiting from risk in the same sentence, you may picture the sort of middleman who enjoys all the gains from taking risks without any of the losses—the sort of "heads I win, tails you lose" risk taker who, of course, isn't taking any risk at all. An egregious example of this parasitic type is AIG, the insurance giant that, deemed "too big to fail," got an $85 billion bailout from US taxpayers after the company's financial products unit, which had sold highly risky credit-default swap contracts, lost billions of dollars when the subprime mortgages crumbled.[1] The company proved unable to pay all the highly speculative securities that it had insured.[2] (You might recall from the Introduction that a study of the warmth and competence of famous brands found AIG to be among the most contemptible, perceived as both incompetent and not having other people's interests at heart.) Unfortunately, AIG is not an isolated example of the risk-shifting middleman. Much more routine are the many financial advisors with no skin in the game: people who happily collect a portfolio management fee even when your portfolio suffers large losses or who play fast and loose with other people's money. Examples outside of finance abound, too, such as the spray-and-pray recruiters who see their work as just a numbers game: if you throw out enough résumés, something will stick. That's not risk-bearing, that's capitalizing on dumb luck.

You might also be thinking of predatory middlemen like the high-frequency traders Michael Lewis excoriates in *Flash Boys*— people who get an unfair edge against the very investors on whose behalf they're supposed to be trading and who increase volatility rather than reducing it.[3] The general phenomenon of powerful middlemen shifting risks to the little guys is more widespread than that. General contractors often shift risk to their subcontractors through pay-if-paid clauses.[4] Insurance companies are notorious for taking policyholders' premiums for years and later weaseling out of paying out claims in a capricious, highly unpredictable way.[5] I call these "predators" because they use their power to push around the people they are supposed to serve, instead of harnessing this power for the little guys' benefit.

I am focusing on the admirable type of Risk Bearer, the partner. Admirable Risk Bearers prosper only when their partners prosper— and suffer losses when their partners do—and while they harness the power of risk, they don't rely on dumb luck but use their skill in discerning the type of risk they should embrace.

"Then the Art World Changed Dramatically"

When you're a middleman in the highly uncertain market for contemporary art, you can't stay in business for long without coming to understand risk, and Jason Horejs, the owner of the Xanadu art gallery in Scottsdale, Arizona, learned an early lesson the hard way: he had the bad luck of opening his gallery on September 11, 2001.

The son of a professional artist who had worked in someone else's gallery when he decided to open his own, he thought he understood the business: seeing his employer's gallery flourish emboldened him to venture out on his own.[6] He opened Xanadu on palm-tree–lined Main Street, right in the heart of the city's downtown arts district, where tourists and owners of Scottsdale vacation homes go to browse and shop (and where the rent for the 2,300-square-foot gallery is suitably high). "Then the art world changed dramatically," Horejs recalls. The economic aftershocks of 9/11 and of the dot-com bust affected everyone, but these shocks hit the art market especially hard: fine art is just about the most discretionary spending category there is, so when people lose jobs or see their investments plummet in value, art becomes one of the first expenses to go. Even the very wealthy tighten their purse strings when conspicuous consumption makes them look bad. Thus, instead of the strong sales Horejs had been projecting from past experience, Horejs saw red ink. "We were living off savings and investments from family members and financing the business on credit cards," he recalls. "It wasn't until 2004–2005 that sales had finally stabilized enough to kind of make the business self-sustaining and start paying off some of the debt."

That stability didn't last long, though. The Great Recession of 2008 hit, forcing Horejs to lay off staff. Several Scottsdale galleries went out of business.[7] A gallery can't buy insurance against recession risk, but Horejs was able to tap into the time-honored informal insurance known as the family. "I was very fortunate to have my mother come in and work in the gallery on a volunteer basis," he says. When business picked up again, he was able to hire her, for pay, as the gallery's director.

These sorts of risks remain invisible to most people, including to artists, who sometimes grumble about high gallery commissions. (Xanadu's commission of 40 to 50 percent of the retail price, which leaves the artist with 50 to 60 percent of the proceeds for every piece sold, is typical.) Horejs says that complaints about commissions typically come from inexperienced artists, because artists who've tried to sell their own work come to see the effort and challenge required. Artists have options, and those who turn to the gallery appreciate what the gallery does on their behalf. But even when the marketing efforts are apparent, tough times for a gallery are hard to see, in large part because galleries deliberately make it so. "Even when times are tough, it's to the gallery's benefit to try to project an image of success," Horejs explains, "because you don't want your customers to think you're facing difficulties, to wonder whether you'll survive. So you can't afford to project the downturns—the artist is likely not going to see that."

The phenomenon Horejs describes applies to other middlemen, too. All of us whose livelihood depends on attracting clients have an incentive to play up our successes while downplaying our failures, even if those failures aren't our fault: would-be partners tend to judge us by our results, regardless of how big a role luck rather than skill played in those results. Thus, a talent agent touts her most famous and successful clients, not the clients you've never heard of. A real estate agent reports the many houses she successfully sold but doesn't tell you about the ones that sat on the market for many months without a sale. A venture capitalist's website is more likely to name the highflyers his firm has funded than the also-rans. The resulting image is skewed by design, distorted through the middleman's deliberate attempt to create a positive impression. In addition to these intentional efforts at impression management, there are innocuous sources of risk distortion: entrepreneurs who are successful will often mention a history of setbacks and even failures, but those whose ventures ultimately failed (who might impart the lesson that persistence doesn't always pay off) don't get as wide an audience.[8] We often see ticket scalpers peddling tickets well above their face value; if we rarely see scalpers scrambling to sell tickets that proved less popular than expected, it could be because the resellers would rather stay home than pour more resources into a bad investment.[9] Even if audiences are aware of this "success bias," they may not appreciate its magnitude enough to properly correct for it.[10] The result: risk takers' jobs appear less risky than they actually are.

"I Don't Want to Become Dependent Suddenly on One Artist"

Still, though middlemen's work is risky, middlemen are usually in a better position to bear risk than their trading partners are. That's because they deal with many more buyers and sellers than the buyers and sellers do, which gives them more ways to diversify away some of the risk. Take the difference between galleries and artists. As Horejs puts it, "It's hard to imagine any business with more risk than the art market is for an artist." He not only sympathizes, he also realizes that he wouldn't be in business without the artists, and he encourages them to diversify as much as possible. Although most galleries require geographic exclusivity—for example, the artists Horejs represents can't sell their work through another gallery in Scottsdale—artists can spread their work across the country and around the world, and Horejs urges his artists to do just that. That way, if one city suffers a downturn, there's at least some chance that another's relative fortune will counterbalance that. Since taste in art is largely subjective, it's also possible that what sells slowly in Scottsdale will be hot in Portland. And yet volatility is almost inevitable, such that sales of even a reasonably successful artist's work can be quite unpredictable. "One month they may do very well," Horejs observes, "and then it may be months and months before they see another sale."

There's only so much a gallerist can do to avoid this feast or famine, which isn't even regular enough to be called a cycle. The gallerist faces risks, too, as Horejs saw immediately upon opening, but by being able to represent a large number of artists, he is in a much better position to deal with the uncertainty of a fickle art market. First, no matter how successful any of his artists becomes, he doesn't put all his eggs in that one basket. "I don't want to become dependent suddenly on one artist," he says. "That would put me in a very vulnerable position."

The same principle also motivates him to represent a mix of artists. In the vast spectrum between the blue-chip galleries in places like SoHo that work with the world's most famous artists and the vanity galleries where artists actually pay the gallery to show their work, Horejs sees Xanadu as "squarely in the middle,"[11] a swath that still leaves plenty of room for diversification. The gallery's many artists, from emerging to regionally and nationally known, work in a variety of styles and media, not only painting, sculpture, and photography but also glass, jewelry, and more. The prices of the artwork vary quite a bit, too, to cater to the broad range of potential buyers walking through the door, with some sculptures priced at tens of thousands of dollars and most pieces selling for $1,500 to $7,500. Horejs also hedges his bets by selling online, a channel that enables him to carry more inventory and charge lower commissions.

Horejs can't get rid of the kind of systemic risk that nearly wiped him out in 2001 and 2008, but he seems to have done a great job of managing diversifiable risk. In his business, diversification doesn't just help him: to some extent, it also reduces the risk of his trading partners: without the gallerist, an artist would have to pay rent and other marketing costs without knowing if or when those expenses would pay off. That's a bigger gamble than most artists could bear. For example, if the artist had her own gallery, displaying only her own work, then a few months without a sale could wipe out her marketing budget. Horejs's diversification, on the other hand, enables him to keep carrying that artist's work until a sale comes through because other artists, whose sales are largely uncorrelated with the first one's sales, could continue to cover the rent and more. In other industries, the middleman's ability to diversify becomes a major benefit to the trading partners. This idea comes to life in a place with a chain of middlemen: the world's largest hub for buying and selling seafood.

Middlemen at the Fish Market

If you've ever had *maguro* in a restaurant in Tokyo, it's almost certain that the tuna came from Tsukiji, the city's famous fish market. The size of about 40 football fields and selling everything from seaweed to caviar, Tsukiji distributes about $5.5 billion of marine products each year, making it the largest seafood hub in the world. And it's where all restaurant tuna comes from. It doesn't matter whether you dined atop an office tower in Shinjuku, had a quick bento box at a lunch counter in a subway station, or noshed in a cozy neighborhood sushi bar miles from the center of town: all restaurateurs in Tokyo buy their *maguro* at Tsukiji, arriving around sunrise and selecting whatever quality of fish their customers expect in the quantities they'll consume that day.

Fish, of course, is notoriously perishable, and since chefs come in person to make their purchases, it might surprise you that *maguro* passes through at least two sets of middlemen before it reaches the chef. The first are Tsukiji's auction houses; well before dawn, they receive the fish on consignment from the dozens of fisheries they regularly do business with. The auction houses make money from commissions on winning bids made by the second set of middlemen. This second set are the wholesalers who buy whole tuna and, one or two hours later and in their own stalls in Tsukiji, sell chunks of it to *their* customers, the thousands of restaurants and mom-and-pop grocery stores that dot the city's food map. The whole process unfolds within a few hours, and not just for tuna but for every other seafood at Tsukiji, from farm-raised *hamachi* to lobster shipped in from Maine, with different auction houses and different wholesalers and different restaurateurs selecting their own assortment.

On the surface, these supply chains appear to be a classic case of "bulking and breaking," of one player buying from many sources and then distributing, in smaller quantities and greater variety, to others down the chain. And it is that, but it's also something else. That "something else" begins and ends with tuna's spectacular size and price, which dwarf those of other fish. A typical trout, for example, weighs 4 to 8 pounds and can be bought wholesale for two or three dollars. A bluefin tuna, on the other hand, easily weighs over 600 pounds, far more than do any of the burly buyers who peer above it to settle on their bids. Thanks to tuna's popularity and increasing scarcity, it now fetches a hefty wholesale price—a whole tuna typically costs between $10,000 and $20,000.[12]

The upshot of all this is that the wholesalers who bid on the tuna at Tsukiji are taking a big risk. As the anthropologist Theodore Bestor explains in his thorough study of Tsukiji, even if the buyers had hours to inspect the day's catch, they'd have little to go on to determine the fish's quality: things like the shape of the body, the condition of the skin, and whatever they can discern from the palm-sized cross-section visible from where the tail's been cut off. What if a tuna that looks fine on the surface is infested with internal parasites?[13] What if it's suffered from freezer burn? Both have happened, and either situation, as well as others like them, are a huge loss for the buyer; unfortunately, there's just no way to tell for sure until the wholesaler buys the fish, brings it to his stall, and cuts it open.

It's a risk the restaurateurs don't have to worry about. By the time they arrive at the wholesalers' stalls, the *maguro* on offer has been cut into halves, quarters, or more, its distinctive ruddy flesh laid bare for all to see. If the tuna was diseased or damaged in some way, the wholesalers and auctioneers have already worked things out among themselves, with the help of Tsukiji's tuna court.[14] Whether the court determined that the wholesaler could have seen the problem through more careful inspection, or the judge ordered the auction house to refund the wholesaler all or part of the price paid, the sushi chef need not even know. The middlemen bear all the risk.

Across many industries, that's usually as it should be—especially if the risk is not preventable. It's one thing if problems are a result of the poor judgment or low effort of one party or another; it's quite another when the source of uncertainty is Mother Nature, or what lawyers call "acts of God."[15] The Risk Bearer helps buyers and sellers weather the random vagaries of business, from insurable catastrophes to currency fluctuations to the day-to-day swings in product demand.

Why should middlemen bear the risks? For one thing, they're usually better able than their trading partners to pool and thus diversify risk, spreading their bets so that gains can cover losses. A gallery owner representing dozens of artists can diversify away much, though not all, of the risk, as the Xanadu gallery shows. Similarly, a book publisher putting out a dozen or more titles a year can more easily have a "win some, lose some" attitude than an author, who typically writes just one book every couple of years. Accordingly, publishers typically reduce an author's risk by providing authors with a certain guaranteed portion of future sales, the advance. Although the industry's declining revenues are pushing publishers to shift more of the risk to the author, such that the "advance" has become something of a retreat,[16] publishers continue to bear much of the risk by paying for editing, cover design, printing, and other costs. Authors who choose to self-publish have to pay for those things themselves and hope to defray the costs through a larger share of their sales, but they have a small chance of doing so in a market where most self-published books sell fewer than 150 copies.[17] A publisher that puts out dozens of books each year can bear the risk much more easily than an author.

The Promise and the Perils of Sharing Risk

It is a general principle that when the party that's best able to bear the risk does so, both parties are better off. The middleman who is able to bear risk can profit from doing so by charging a risk premium, while the more risk-averse party doesn't mind paying the risk premium to reduce risk. So why don't we see middlemen bearing most of the risk?

The answer to this risk-sharing question goes back to the old problems of adverse selection and moral hazard. Most economic outcomes in the world are some combination of effort and chance (or skill and luck). How many widgets a sales rep sells, for example, depends on how hard the rep works, how good the rep is at sales to begin with, and factors completely outside the rep's control, from the quality of the widget to the state of the economy. The rep shouldn't be held responsible for those external risks, and the company she works for (which has many reps) is in a better position to bear the risk. So should the company pay all sales reps a fixed wage, no matter how many widgets they sell? It's a difficult question, and based on a host of factors we see either hourly workers or commissioned salespeople[18] in successful firms, but often a fixed-pay scheme can disproportionately attract lousy salespeople (adverse selection causing better salespeople to prefer pay-for-performance employers) and may induce even the skilled ones to slack off (moral hazard). In general, the more risk one party assumes, the less incentive the other party will have to work hard. So there's a tension: on the one hand, both parties stand to benefit from sharing risk; on the other hand, sharing risk changes incentives and increases risk. Economists are very familiar with this trade-off between risk sharing and incentives, which occurs in many contexts and not just in sales.[19] Successful middlemen, whose livelihood depends on sharing risk and providing proper incentives to buyers and sellers, also understand the problem. But judging by how ordinary people evaluate the decisions middlemen make, it seems that many of us don't quite get it. Consider the following cases:

- A single mother struggling to keep up with mortgage payments on her condo tries to refinance, but the lender rejects her application because she had recently lost her job, which is the very reason she is struggling.[20] On the other hand, Mark Zuckerberg refinances the loan on his $5.95 million mansion and gets an interest rate of 1.05 percent, less than half the national average.[21]

- A 50-year-old man gets advanced-stage prostate cancer, begins aggressive treatment, and applies for life insurance to protect his family if the worst case should happen. The insurance company turns him down, telling him he can apply again in 12 months.[22] Meanwhile, the same insurance company advertises to young families, eager to sell them policies with low monthly premiums.

- An aspiring children's book author who's never been published before wants to reach a wide audience, so she sends her manuscript to a literary agent specializing in this market, but he ignores the submission completely. Meanwhile, a movie star with a first manuscript has agents vying to get her a book deal.

Do you see the pattern? Many people find these situations ironic, even morally wrong—why wouldn't you do business with the people who need you most? But those whose business depends on managing risk don't see it that way.

An interesting example of this disconnect between public perceptions and risk bearers' views comes from a study commissioned by the

Society of Actuaries seeking to understand public views of life insurance companies.[23] The report points out that risk classification—or grouping risks based on their costs—is such a fundamental part of the insurance business that, if it's not done right, it can lead to dire consequences. One actuary quoted in the report tells the story of one company that got it wrong, a casualty insurer that decided to get into the auto insurance business. "The new management believed that people who lived in Chicago's blue-collar neighborhoods were being unfairly discriminated against, because they were being charged auto insurance premiums that were too high," an actuary recalls. "On the basis of this belief, management ignored the actuarial evidence and wrote auto insurance for drivers in these Chicago neighborhoods at rates that would have been right for a population with far fewer auto accidents," the report says. The company was named Prudence Mutual, the actuary notes dryly, since the decision proved extremely imprudent. "Prudence Mutual went belly up."

Through focus groups, the researchers found that the public didn't appreciate that insurers try to avoid this type of calamity, which harms both the insurer and its policyholders. In fact, the public's views of risk classification were diametrically opposed to those of the industry. The industry view was that risk classification is an equitable practice, since it means that low-risk individuals don't have to subsidize those known to pose a higher risk, but the public saw risk classification as unfair. The industry saw writing policies as its goal, whereas the public saw insurers as people who deny policies. Insurers understood that risk classification is designed to avoid the problem of adverse selection, which will hurt the entire pool and raise costs for everyone, but the public believed its purpose is to squeeze profits.

Insurance is the classic industry that profits from bearing risk, but other middlemen in the business of risk face the same confusion. The view of insurers as people who deny policies is similar to the view of middlemen as "gatekeepers," both cases ignoring the fact that middlemen can never make money if all they say is no. To prosper in a climate of uncertainty, it's essential to take on risk with an upside. And yet, as the chapters on Certifiers and Enforcers showed, middlemen must be discriminating to avoid adverse selection and moral hazard. Therefore, to profit from risk, middlemen, like successful insurers, must be astute at teasing apart these two types of risk:

- **Internal risk.** This is my term for what finance scholars call counterparty risk, or risk due to the characteristics or actions of a trading partner. In other words, internal risks are risks caused by asymmetric information (adverse selection and moral hazard). Risk-bearing middlemen should avoid internal risk because it can only harm them and their partners on the other side. That's why, for example, a lender should be wary of lending money to someone with no job and no assets.

- **External risk.** This is what economists call exogenous risk and what lawyers call acts of God or force majeure: risks that trading partners cannot control. This is the type of risk that risk-bearing middlemen should embrace if they are able to diversify away some of the uncertainty. Avoiding external risk seems like a safe way to go, but it fails to take advantage of the upside of risk, which follows the age-old principle of "nothing ventured, nothing gained." When middlemen who are able to diversify away a lot of external risk nonetheless shy away from it, they provide less value to their trading partners. When, on the other hand, they embrace external risk (while avoiding internal risk), they stand to profit from bearing risk; if they are especially bold, they can elicit admiration for the kind of heroic risk-taking that benefits others.

To see how this separation of internal from external risk works in practice, let's look at how a highly successful venture capitalist decides where to invest.

The VC: Opening the Floodgates

Mike Maples, Jr. is the founding partner Floodgate, a small venture-capital firm (a "micro-VC") that quickly built its reputation through its founder's early bets on Twitter and DemandForce, among other highly risky ideas that paid off.

After leaving his job as a founding executive of an enterprise-software firm in Austin, Texas, Maples began investing his own money in start-ups. Having established himself as an angel investor, he started Floodgate in 2006. As of this writing, Floodgate has invested in 129 companies, 31 of which have already experienced "exits"—30 have been acquired by larger firms, and one (the textbook-rental company Chegg) has gone public.[24] Several of his other holdings, particularly Lyft and TaskRabbit, seem poised for successful exits as well. Maples projects a confidence in his ideas that is leavened by humility about his achievements; his lingering Texas accent seems to amplify the aw-shucks tenor of his words, as when he chalks up his early success to beginner's luck or when he credits others for his first lessons in investing.

Like other VCs, Maples aims to find and fund companies that will become massive winners. Unlike so many other ambitious investors, though, he and his partner in the firm, Ann Miura-Ko, never invest in a company that has already become everyone's darling. Instead, they aim to discover what they call thunderlizards, Godzillas in the making.[25] And because Floodgate places bets that are relatively small—typically less than a million dollars, and once as little as $50,000—it is able to back ventures that would seem far too risky to VC firms whose typical investment is $10 million. "As an investor, you handicap yourself a lot by investing large amounts of money in very disruptive ideas," Maples told me.[26] "The more disruptive the idea, the crazier it'll sound early on, and the less comfortable you'll feel putting a lot of money in—whereas if you're putting a lesser amount of money in, you can afford to take a basket of risks. So I guess my view is if you want to fund something truly disruptive, you'd be better off making ten $500,000 whacky bets than one $5 million less-risky bet." He is not implying that large funds typically put all their eggs in one basket—all VCs hold a portfolio of companies—only that large investments tend to make you more cautious, which means that your portfolio will be less likely to yield exceptional returns. "Larger firms with more partners that invest more money per deal are always going to be more risk-averse," Maples says.

Paul Graham, founder of Y Combinator and likewise a believer in investing at the seed stage, put it more bluntly in his essay "A Theory of VC Suckage." Each deal is for several million dollars, Graham argues, because management fees give firms an incentive to build up large funds. That, Graham writes, "explains why VCs take so agonizingly long to make up their minds, and why their due diligence feels like a body cavity search. With so much at stake, they have to be paranoid."[27]

Some large firms do quite well—Sequoia, Accel, Andreessen Horowitz, and Greylock are a few such exceptions—but size can definitely be a handicap in the pursuit of high returns. Large firms don't just invest large sums, they also have many partners and typically use a voting system to make decisions. So even if one or more partners in a large firm wants to invest in a crazy new start-up, odds are they will get voted down by the other partners, and this makes it harder for these funds to back the most controversial companies, according to Maples. Floodgate, in contrast, not only has few partners, but it doesn't use voting at all. The partners don't second-guess each other, and their internal motto, Maples says, is "Just win, baby."

Embracing External Risk: Nonconsensus and Right

What Maples is saying when he talks about investing in crazy ideas is that he embraces external risk, because this is where the opportunity for a huge upside lies. This is not to say that Maples believes in rolling the dice and seeing where they land. He is clear that, as he puts it, "We don't believe a company is a lottery ticket." He owes it to his limited partners looking for huge returns to be highly selective, and to that end every idea he backs has to fit two criteria: "nonconsensus and right," a popular idea in elite VC circles.

The nonconsensus part is the one that refers to crazy ideas. "One of my favorite things to hear from an entrepreneur in a pitch is, 'I'm not sure this is legal,'" he says. This is exactly what he heard from the founders of Lyft, Logan Green and John Zimmer, who were pretty sure their ride-sharing business was running afoul of current taxi regulations. Maples isn't one to advocate shady, unethical start-ups, but rather those that challenge laws that, while originally designed to protect consumers, may no longer be in consumers' best interest. This is similar to the discussion in the chapter on Enforcers of state-of-the-art reputation systems that can sometimes do a better and more efficient job of eliciting good behavior than government institutions. You might say Maples prefers to back what is righteous rather than what is legal. Why does he love pitches in that legal gray area? "Those could be good businesses to fund because a lot of times there are not a lot of competitors," he explains. (Even though Uber has a competing ride-sharing service, UberX, Maples points out that Lyft started before Uber launched UberX.) Whether the laws eventually side with the entrepreneur's venture or against it is a huge risk—the kind that many people are afraid to take—but that is precisely what makes the bet attractive; if it turns out to be right, the gain will be enormous and, because it is a nonconsensus venture, it won't be shared by many others. Notice that it is also an external risk, and not an internal one: the entrepreneur has no incentive to undermine the VC's goals by shirking, for example, because doing so would sabotage the entrepreneur. Maples knows how to embrace external risk while avoiding internal risk.

Mike Maples didn't come up with the idea of investing in ventures that are nonconsensus and right, and he is certainly not the only venture capitalist to think this way. Marc Andreessen, perhaps the best-known VC working today, plots start-ups on a two-by-two matrix in which VCs should aim for the quadrant corresponding to nonconsensus and successful.[28] It should go without saying that you cannot know for sure which ones will be successful, and even the best VCs are often wrong, but you *do* know which are nonconsensus. Andreessen and partner Ben Horowitz picked up much of their investment philosophy, probably including this idea, from investment advisor Andy Rachleff, a former partner at Benchmark Capital and founder of Wealthfront, a firm that uses technology to transform the investment advisory business.[29] Rachleff, in turn, credits his "investment idol," Howard Marks, with this framework.[30] When the entrepreneur-turned-VC Peter Thiel asks, "What important truth do very few people agree with you on?" he is getting at the same sort of exceptionalism: the contrarian truth, something that is nonconsensus and right.

Understanding that the biggest returns will come from nonconsensus ideas is only a first step, though, because it is very hard to figure out the "right" part. Consider Twitter, which Maples invested in before founding Floodgate. It's easy to look at a triumphant company and conclude, with the clarity of 20/20 hindsight, that the choice to invest in it was a no-brainer, but things are rarely that obvious at an early stage. For several years, Maples recalls, others made fun of his Twitter investment. "In the early days, people said, 'How can you possibly have a company where the product only lets you say things in 140 characters? That's the stupidest thing I've ever heard.'"

This is the problem with the advice to invest in ideas that everyone thinks are nuts: as Andreessen has pointed out, people thought that Einstein was crazy, and they also thought Charles Manson was crazy;[31] only in retrospect do we know for certain which one was fit to be locked up. Crazy ideas are inherently more risky, leading as they do to more extreme outcomes: either spectacular successes or total failures. But who knows before the fact?

Benefiting from Power Laws

But VCs have something working in their favor to help them make such bold bets: the two extremes don't mirror each other. Even a monumental failure has a limit to its losses, whether it be $500,000 or $5 million, whereas a spectacular success knows no bounds: the top companies come to be valued at $500 million or more at exit. This is why the risk analyst Nassim Nicholas Taleb, best known as the author of *The Black Swan*, considers venture capital to be what he calls "antifragile," something that actually gains from randomness.[32] To achieve antifragility, Taleb writes, the potential cost of errors needs to remain small and the potential gain needs to be large. "It is the asymmetry between upside and downside that allows anti-fragile tinkering to benefit from disorder and uncertainty."[33] When your downside is limited and your upside is potentially infinite, you should embrace risk taking.

That rule fits venture capital perfectly because returns in venture capital follow a power-law distribution, a pattern many of us are familiar with as the 80/20 rule,[34] although many power-law distributions are even more extreme. For example, according to a study released today, the 80 wealthiest individuals in the world collectively own $1.9 trillion—a total about equal to the "wealth" of all the people in the poorer *half of the world*.[35] In *The Black Swan*, Taleb coined a memorable word to refer to such highly skewed distributions: they occur in "Extremistan," where a single event or data point has a disproportionate impact on the total.[36] Venture capital lives in Extremistan in that only about 15 start-ups out of several thousand vying for VC funding each year are responsible for the vast majority of profits: just one of those megahits—the next Google or Facebook or Twitter—will make you a monumental winner even if all your other investments lose money. Peter Thiel calls this "the biggest secret in venture capital," writing in *Zero to One*. "The best investment in a successful fund equals or outperforms the entire rest of the fund combined."[37] Thiel's $500,000 angel investment in Facebook in 2004 (before he became a VC) came to be worth more than $1 billion when Facebook went public in 2012,[38] making it easier for him to take the kind of radical bets that we associate with eccentric billionaires.

The implication of such patterns of returns is that it makes no sense to invest in any company that doesn't have the potential for massive returns; in a "hits" business, particularly when you can make only a limited number of bets, there is no point in betting on something that seems merely good. Even an investment that will double the VC's investment if it succeeds is a bad bet because the expected value of that return will dilute the portfolio returns.

Of course, there is no guarantee that even a single one of the companies a VC bets on will bring in massive returns, but that doesn't mean VCs must rely on luck alone. For one thing, they can gain information to help them make better decisions. For example, Maples had good reason to believe that Twitter wasn't just a nonconsensus venture, but also a right one. That's because Twitter cofounder Evan Williams had an insight from his experiences running the blog-publishing service Blogger. "Evan said, 'When I did Blogger, over a million people did blogs, and my hypothesis is if I make it easier to do microblogs, maybe ten million people will do microblogs,'" Maples recalls. Providing seed funding for the venture enabled Maples and Twitter's founders to test whether that hypothesis was right—and if early results are promising, for the VC to double down through additional funding rounds. (Today, Twitter claims 270 million active users per month.) The idea that microblogging would be popular could have proven to be wrong—but listening to the founder's special insights makes the experiment more than just a shot in the dark.

The Upside of Humility

This willingness to listen to a founder's unique knowledge instead of relying on his own experience distinguishes Maples from many lesser VCs. When economists talk of asymmetric information, they almost always view it as a problem: the risk that the party with more information will take advantage of the less informed party, which in turn causes suspicion, skepticism, and distrust by the other party. But Maples shows us that a middleman who keeps an open mind can benefit from the superior information of the entrepreneurs seeking funding.[39] For example, when he listened to the pitch from Chegg, the textbook rental company, he realized that the founders knew what they were talking about when they predicted that college students will rent textbooks. New college textbooks are notoriously expensive;[40] Chegg's founders believed that if they did for textbooks what Netflix did for movies, students would eagerly sign up—and the company's eventual success showed that they were right. But most VCs didn't get it because they're wealthy enough to pay for their kids' textbooks. "A VC has no visceral understanding of why a debt-strapped college kid is going to rent a textbook—it just didn't compute in a VC's world," Maples says. Maples seems too nice to say this outright, but this story and others like it paint a picture of many VCs as people who are not only out of touch with reality, but also too arrogant to *realize* that they are out of touch; they are too sure of themselves to consider that someone with less business experience might know something they don't. Maples's story about Chegg reminded me of the pushback SitterCity founder Genevieve Thiers faced when pitching her idea to VCs, some of whom said dismissively, "My wife handles that stuff."[41]

The dismissive attitude seems to be an occupational hazard of gatekeeping middlemen, and one that Maples appears to have so far avoided. When a big part of your job involves saying no, and when you have the authority to write a large check, some of this power can go to your head. Psychologists have found that people in power actually see, think, and behave differently, having trouble adjusting their view to encompass alternative perspectives. We are all biased toward our own experience, of course, but research has shown that the powerful are more so. The most vivid illustration of this tendency is the "Letter E" experiment by psychologist Adam Galinsky and colleagues, in which the researchers asked participants to quickly write the letter E on their own foreheads after being made to feel either powerful or powerless. Those who had been made to feel powerful (by recalling a time they had dominated others) were three times more likely to draw the E in a self-oriented direction—as if they themselves were looking at it—than those who'd been told to recall a time they felt low power. The low-power participants tended to write the letter so it faced the audience, a more empathic approach to the task.[42] Maples has gained considerable power, too, but has somehow managed to maintain a healthy humility, which keeps him open to good ideas from founders.

Nowhere is this more apparent than in his openness to ideas from female founders. Recent studies have shown people to be more likely to accept business proposals from men (especially good-looking men)—even when the proposals were identical.[43] It is the sort of coarse decision-making shortcut that may actually have once served investors well—but it is ill-suited to an environment in which anyone can become an entrepreneur. "When I was a kid, the tech industry was really geeks selling to geeks," Maples recalls. "Then it was geeks selling to the rest of the world because the world is connected. But what Ann and I are seeing are new types of entrepreneurs emerging," he says. "In the last decade, to be an entrepreneur you had to raise money, and Sand Hill Road had a preconceived idea of what a tech entrepreneur looked like—they were usually an early-twenties white dude, who was an alpha-geek computer hacker. And that was kind of the canonical person you'd invest in." In B2B ventures, companies that sell products to other companies, the prototypical entrepreneur looked a little different, but it was still typically a he. "We believe that the low cost of starting a company is democratizing entrepreneurship itself," Maples says, "and now entrepreneurs can emerge from any location and they can be any gender and any ethnicity, and so rather than a high priest on Sand Hill Road deciding what a start-up entrepreneur is, people can just *do* entrepreneurship, and whoever gets traction is an entrepreneur. That's going to fundamentally change the nature of entrepreneurship and who starts companies and succeeds." As entrepreneurship becomes accessible to more people and more different types of people, Maples says, he and Miura-Ko want to be accelerants of that trend; even in this climate, entrepreneurs need VCs for access to capital markets. "If you're Leah Busque and you're starting TaskRabbit, it doesn't matter how good the idea is if you can't raise a dime."

How Contrarianism Attracts Opportunity

In pitch fests and media interviews, the Floodgate partners have expressed these ideas many times; the more they do, and the more times they put their money where their mouths are through their funding decisions, the better known these VCs will become as entrepreneur-friendly, especially among entrepreneurs who don't fit the traditional mold. That gives the Floodgate partners an edge in the competition among VCs for good deal flow. A quarter of Floodgate's portfolio companies are women-led, as are a quarter of the companies pitching Floodgate.[44] If the next Leah Busque is seeking seed-stage financing, it's a good bet Floodgate will be high on her list of VC firms to pitch. "We fundamentally believe that some woman will start a company worth more than $50 billion in the next five to ten years," Maples says, "and we have a better chance of winning her preference if we're not a firm full of 6-foot-tall white dudes." Research supports this idea. For example, a 2004 study of venture funding found that offers made by VCs with a high reputation are *three times* more likely to be accepted and that such VCs get a stake in the start-up at a 10–14 percent discount.[45] These days reputational information about VCs is spreading more quickly, enabling newer, entrepreneur-friendly VCs to prosper. Traditionally, says Josh Lerner, a Harvard Business School professor who studies venture capital, "this has been a backwater cottage industry without a huge degree of visibility."[46] But that is gradually changing, Lerner says, with more transparency about the venture funding process than ever. Now entrepreneurs are talking more among themselves through start-up communities and review sites like TheFunded.com, and VCs themselves are blogging and seeking publicity—so entrepreneurs can find more information about VCs than they could even ten years ago. Though in the past VC firms could attract plenty of venture deals despite their partners' arrogance and sexism, these days such behavior can damage a firm's reputation among entrepreneurs; VCs who keep up with the times will have an edge over those who don't.

Maples invests in women because he is after high returns for his investors, not because he wants to right a social wrong, but he comes across as a hero nonetheless. A commonsense definition of a hero is someone who takes risks for the benefit of others. You need both the risk taking and the altruism components, which is why an ordinary firefighter is more likely to be thought heroic than even a world-famous daredevil like Evel Knievel. By risking ridicule for some of his investment choices, showing the courage of his convictions, and benefiting founders and investors, Maples becomes an admired partner to both groups. And when the businesses he funds create jobs and new services that wouldn't exist without him, he becomes a hero for many more people, though an unsung one for most.

Learning from Micro-VCs

Maples seems like a wonderful role model for aspiring VCs, but does his story have anything to teach other middlemen? I think so because middlemen often live in Extremistan: lots of other uncertain outcomes besides the success of start-ups follow a power-law distribution rather than the normal (bell-shaped) distribution that most of us learned about in grade school. Several years ago, a pair of psychologists who analyzed the performance of more than half a million people in a variety of jobs—academic researchers, athletes, entertainers, and politicians—found that across the board (in more than 93 percent of the cases), individual performance outcomes fit the power-law pattern, distributions in which the majority of the people performed below average. That is not so much an indictment of ordinary performers as it is a direct result of the fact that the most extraordinary people in each field performed so spectacularly well: the superstars pushed the average up significantly despite a large total number of contenders.[47] Put another way, the big winners are outliers, just like they would be in a normal distribution—but the losers in the long tail of the distribution are more or less the norm. This is the same pattern we see in start-ups, where the top 15 each year outperform thousands of others.

Such stark inequalities are even more prevalent on the Internet, in part because the rapid spread of information creates even greater rich-get-richer effects. We saw in the Certifier chapter that eBay's PowerSellers, whose strong feedback scores attract buyers, are responsible for a disproportionate share of all eBay sales. A similar pattern holds for the popularity of online content. In a 2003 study of blogs (back when they were still often called "weblogs"), the social media scholar Clay Shirky counted the number of inbound links to each of 433 blogs, finding that the top dozen (or fewer than 3 percent of the total) had 20 percent of the links from other blogs; it's not quite the 80/20 rule, but it points in the same direction.[48] Popularity on Twitter follows power-law patterns,[49] as well, as do videos on YouTube.[50] There's every reason to believe that similar winner-take-all effects also occur in other online networks.

What does that mean for middlemen deciding which risky prospects to back? The answer undoubtedly depends on the costs of those bets. In *The Long Tail*, Chris Anderson explored the implications of power-law dynamics on the Internet, where the costs of storing and distributing products are low (as they are for digital middlemen like Amazon and Netflix); for such middlemen, Anderson argued, it makes economic sense to carry a wide selection: though each niche product brings in a miniscule amount of revenue, "all those niches add up," he wrote,[51] suggesting that collectively the long tail can rival the hits in the short head, especially if offering a wide variety makes the long tail not only longer but fatter. Even if the niches don't add up to much, the digital middleman bears little risk if the marginal cost of each additional item is close to zero.

As more data came in after the *The Long Tail* came out, some scholars have come to disagree with Anderson's conclusions, most prominently Anita Elberse of Harvard Business School, whose book *Blockbusters* is a long retort to *The Long Tail*.[52] But there's no arguing with one of Anderson's main premises: that the Internet has lowered the costs of distribution. That is why, for example, Jason Horejs can offer so many more pieces for sale on his website than in the Xanadu Gallery in Scottsdale and can charge his artists a lower commission for these online sales.

Even online, though, where middlemen's costs and risks are lower, admirable middlemen can offer more value as a Risk Bearer to sellers by investing more in those they believe in. That is because sellers—the producers middlemen partner with—incur production costs, a source of risk for the seller. A writer of blog posts or a performer posting videos, for example, spends time creating this content, sometimes considerable time, but the harsh reality of power-law distributions is that this content will most likely get lost in a sea of other material vying for viewers' attention, and only a few hits will emerge. Unfortunately, whether a blog post or a video succeeds is only loosely determined by its quality or even the creator's efforts to promote the piece on social media. If the middlemen distributing this content pay entirely on a revenue-sharing method (the pay-per-click or per-page-view or per-unique-visitor model), they run into the same problem sales managers do when they pay on a commission-only basis: by shifting so much of the risk to the worker, they have to pay a lot more (on average) to get risk-averse workers to take on that risk—perhaps $1 per page view rather than a few pennies. If the middlemen ask contributors to take on the risk without offering a high-enough risk premium, it stands to reason they will repel many of the contributors they most want to attract. A risk-averse blogger, for example, would prefer to work for a platform (such as a reputable magazine) that pays a guaranteed fee for quality content, with perhaps a bonus for additional traffic.

An online middleman who wants to attract quality contributors, therefore, would do better to follow the Certifier model of selecting likely winners and investing in them through higher pay and a bigger marketing push. Online, some of those investments will pay off stupendously (perhaps the blog post will go viral, for example), while others will go nowhere—but, to borrow a metaphor from Mike Maples, a piece of content is not a lottery ticket. If the middleman can pick content that has a better than random chance of succeeding, everyone will be better off: the middleman, the contributor, and the audience.

Despite all this talk about power-law distributions, I don't want to give the impression that all risk-bearing middlemen live in Extremistan, able to enjoy the kinds of returns a successful VC can. But even in the ordinary world of workaday risks, among phenomena that follow normal distributions (the land of what Taleb calls "Mediocristan"), middlemen have long been able to profit from bearing risk that their trading partners cannot. In fact, this is one of the oldest roles for middlemen there is.

The Truckless Trucking Company

Long before there was Lyft and before there was Uber, and well before mobile devices or even the Internet, there was C. H. Robinson.

The company, founded back in 1905, in 2014 ranked #220 on the Fortune 500, the annual list of the highest-grossing companies in the United States. Its annual revenues of $12.7 billion put C. H. Robinson just ahead of household brands Toys 'R' Us and Nordstrom and well above Facebook and Harley-Davidson. If you haven't heard of this behemoth from Eden Prairie, Minnesota, it's only because its customers are other businesses: rather than arranging rides for busy urbanites, as Lyft and Uber do, C. H. Robinson acts as freight broker for companies that need to quickly find truckload capacity to carry freight from one factory, warehouse, or retailer to another. At its core, C. H. Robinson does much the same thing for buyers and sellers as the ridesharing companies do. Like those companies, C. H. Robinson doesn't actually own a fleet, and instead acts as a middleman between its customers (the shippers) and its suppliers (the carriers). And because of its large network of carriers—43,000 transportation providers in 2013—it's able to meet customer demand much more quickly than shippers could by tapping a smaller network, let alone trying to contract with carriers directly. Carriers, for their part, are happy to sell off extra capacity that would otherwise go idle: if you're going from point A to point B anyway, why not earn some money by picking up a load?

I heard about C. H. Robinson from Sunil Chopra, a professor at the Kellogg School at Northwestern University and one of the world's leading experts on supply-chain efficiency.[53] Providing on-demand services à la Uber is trendy stuff, and the Internet and mobile technologies make it easier than ever to aggregate information about available supply and demand. However, as C.H. Robinson's long history shows, the concept behind all these middleman businesses is not new. Middlemen existed before the Internet, Chopra points out, and the Internet only makes them more efficient at doing what they've been doing all along: smoothing out ups and downs by pooling variations in available supply on one side (supply-side risk) and uncertainty about demand on the other (demand-side risk). "The middleman is going to come into play when the supplier has idle capacity but the timing of the idle capacity is unpredictable," Chopra explains.

Most of us don't think about risk this way; we typically associate the word with danger or loss, what people in finance call "downside risk," and perhaps also with gains, or upside risk. But more broadly, risk can be thought of as variability, volatility, spread, unpredictability—any deviation (positive or negative) from steady, predictable outcomes. This is how supply-chain managers typically view risk. Most systems benefit from predictability, so in most situations, variation is a bad thing: having too little inventory to fill orders (a shortage) is as much of a problem as having too much inventory (an overstock). Similarly, given the same average most people prefer a narrower spread. That, in fact, is what it means to say that most of us are risk-averse. If a game show let you earn $1 million and then offered to double the money if a coin toss came up heads, you would probably reject the offer. The prospect of doubling your money is just not worth the risk of losing it all.

This preference for predictability combined with an environment of unpredictability creates an opportunity for middlemen to smooth out risk for both sides of a transaction. Why are middlemen in a good position to reduce risk? For the same reason a VC is able to reduce investors' risk: diversification. The middleman—like C.H. Robinson—can aggregate uncertainty across many players, pooling the timing of demand risk in much the way insurance companies are able to pool disaster risk. As Chopra puts it, "None of us know when we are going to die, but the actuarial tables can say, 'In this age group, this week about this many people are going to die.'" Each individual outcome is hard to predict, but the aggregate outcome is quite predictable; the profitability of an insurance company depends on it. That same principle allows middlemen to predict roughly how many orders to expect without knowing *which* customers will be placing those orders. What's more, the middleman is able to perform the same feat on the supply side: to predict how much capacity will be available without knowing *who* will have capacity available. This is one of the ways staffing agencies help client firms: providing the short-term labor to meet seasonal or uncertain demand for workers.[54] The beauty of this arrangement is that risk-pooling middlemen really don't care *which* and *who:* to provide value, they only need to know *how many* and *how much.*

For pooling to work, two things have to be present, Chopra explains: scale and unpredictability. Scale enables you to take advantage of the law of large numbers, the finding that as the number of random trials increases, the overall outcome converges around the theoretical probability. For example, the probability of getting heads on a toss of a fair coin is .5 (50 percent chance of getting heads), but with only one coin flip it's absolutely impossible to actually get this value: no matter which way the coin lands, the overall outcome will be either 0 or 1. This all-or-nothing outcome makes a single trial as risky as things get. With a few more coin flips—say, six or ten— it's still quite possible you would get all tails (even though if you're a gambler, you might start to suspect you're playing with an unfair coin). However, as you toss the coin many more times—500, 900, 10,000—the ratio of heads to total outcomes gets closer and closer to one in two. The law of large numbers turns something unpredictable into something that, on average, is quite predictable—so having great scale lets you make better forecasts. That's why insurance companies are big. "You don't want to go to an insurance company that has only 100 subscribers—you want 10 million subscribers," Chopra explains, because pooling across 10 million subscribers produces outcomes that are more predictable. For many types of middlemen, the minimum scale is obviously lower, but a certain scale is always important. A ridesharing service consisting of just ten drivers is less able to cope with unpredictable demand than a service of 100 drivers. A placement agency with just ten contractors can't fill the sporadic needs of a client firm. "In being a middleman, scale matters," Chopra says.

The other thing that matters is unpredictability, of course, because it's how a middleman can provide value to people who prefer predictability: there is no risk pool without risks. This is what Chopra means when he says the middleman comes into play when the timing of idle capacity is unpredictable. If you're a supplier working at full capacity on your own, you don't need a middleman to bring extra demand your way. For example, if you're a limo driver who always has a paying customer (because maybe you work as someone's full-time chauffeur), you don't need Uber to bring fares your way. And if you have idle capacity, you don't need a middleman if that capacity is idle at predictable times: if you're running a restaurant, for example, and you expect no customers between 2:30 and 5 every day, it makes sense to simply close up shop during those hours.[55] But when demand is sporadic, Chopra says, "that's the classic setting of where the middleman is doing uncertainty pooling on both the demand and the supply side."

If you look around, you will see more examples of this kind of middleman. One of the world's largest is Li & Fung; based in Hong Kong, this sourcing firm specializes in high-volume, time-sensitive goods for global brands like Walmart, Sears, Disney, and many others. "Li & Fung won't do your regular orders," Chopra explains, "but when your regular supplier is short and you need someone quickly, that's when you go to them." Or, as a *New York Times* story about the company puts it, "Retailers turn to Li & Fung because its resources make it uniquely equipped to find the Mexican port that can accept a shipment sooner, to persuade a Chinese fabric maker to cut an extra thousand square feet of silk faster, and to coax a factory in Bangladesh to fill an order more cheaply."[56]

The same logic works downstream when manufacturers choose suppliers. A car manufacturing plant that consistently needs three truckloads of steel each day can order those directly from the steel plant; the predictability of this demand makes for a perfect partnership between the car plant and the steel plant. "Here the intermediary is going to add absolutely no value," Chopra says. In contrast, factories can't predict when a piece of equipment will break down, and when it does, which part will need to be replaced; it would be too costly for factories to keep spare parts on hand and too slow for them to wait for the right part to arrive directly from the manufacturer. As a result, they turn to middlemen—companies like McMaster-Carr and W. W. Grainger. McMaster-Carr, for example, specializes in next-day delivery of mechanical, electrical, and other hardware from its catalog of more than half a million products. So if your centrifugal pump fails or a trapezoidal-tooth timing belt snaps, you can get a new one quickly without having to keep it in stock yourself and without having to maintain relationships with thousands of parts manufacturers. Chopra says the "MRO" industry (Maintenance, Repair, and Operations) is full of middlemen for this very reason. "You really do need unpredictability for the intermediary to provide value," Chopra says.

It so happened that the night before I spoke to Chopra, the water heater in my house had broken down, and therefore the repair business was already on my mind. The plumber who had installed our water heater didn't work evenings, so I had to wait until the next morning to schedule a repair. Then I had to wait several more hours for the technician to arrive. Having to carry a kettle of boiling water to the bath, as if living in the nineteenth century, left me wishing for an "Uber for plumbers." If no individual plumber gets enough calls in the evening to justify a regular late shift, couldn't a middleman pool this sporadic demand and match it with the available supply? Indeed, Chopra agreed, this is a business opportunity for a middleman because the high unpredictability of demand enables the intermediary to provide real value.

Researchers who study waiting times have a name for this class of problems: they call it "the repairman problem," whose challenge is to minimize waiting for a repair while minimizing the number of idle repairmen. A basic result is that more repairmen and more machines create economies of scale. In his classic textbook on probability, the mathematician William Feller wrote that "three repairmen per twenty machines are much more economical than one repairman per six machines."[57] For a small plumbing company it'll be wasteful to pay even one extra on-call plumber on the off-chance that someone will call and need that plumber right away, because much of the time that plumber would be twiddling his thumbs instead. To cover the cost of that idle capacity, the company would have to charge a huge markup for the occasional emergency job. But that's not at all the case for a middleman specializing in the emergency plumbing business. Why? Because a remarkable thing would happen in the presence of a risk-pooling middleman: "It would almost be like emergency jobs would begin to behave like regular jobs," Chopra says. The middleman could predict how many calls would come in on the whole and direct those calls to whichever plumber happened to be available at that time. The amount of idle capacity in the whole network would come down, and that reduction in waste would make on-demand services much cheaper. But the middleman is an enabler of such efficiencies only when there's unpredictable idle capacity. "If all plumbers are busy all the time, the middleman has nothing to do," says Chopra.

It turns out some cities have middleman companies you can call to get an available plumber from within the company's network. But all of them must face the challenge of separating internal from external risk: is the plumber idle because of the random vagaries of demand or because the plumber isn't very good? To protect its own reputation for quality, a middleman business must sort these things out by also playing the Certifier and Enforcer roles.

For an example in another industry, consider middlemen who promise to shorten the wait time to get a doctor's appointment. ZocDoc is the pioneer in this important area, matching patients who need a same-day or same-week appointment with doctors in various specialties who have last-minute appointment slots to fill. ZocDoc collects monthly fees from participating doctors, and patients going to the site are right to wonder if the doctors on ZocDoc are worse than other doctors, who presumably can stay busy enough on their own. To alleviate this lemons problem, ZocDoc tracks doctors' reputations by gathering users' (patients') feedback: such reviews not only keep participating doctors on their toes, but may even screen out doctors who aren't good enough to want to be rated by users. A similar service for house calls—Medicast—appears to do even more up-front quality control, promising to match patients with doctors who are "screened and certified." These middlemen businesses understand that to be a successful Risk Bearer, you must also solve the information problems that Certifiers and Enforcers do.

Even without risk and asymmetric information, people face informational problems that middlemen can solve. The next chapter explores these problems.

5

THE CONCIERGE

Making Life Easier

THE ROLE: *These days consumers can perform many traditional mid-dleman tasks themselves: we can book our own travel, find a house in our budget, buy or sell a used car, and manage our own investments. Yet savvy consumers understand that just because we can do something our-selves doesn't mean we should. Middlemen who play the Concierge role can provide value for such consumers, but only if they understand what customers really need from them and price their services with consumers' ever-changing alternatives in mind.*

Survival of the Travel Agent

In 1999, a class-action lawsuit supported by the Association of Retail Travel Agents alleged that more than a dozen airlines had illegally conspired to cut travel agents' commissions.[1] In 2003, at the end of a long legal battle between the agents and the airlines, the federal judge sided with the airlines, saying that the commission cuts could have come not from collusion but from simple oligopolistic competition and natural changes in the travel market: with the proliferation of sites like Expedia and Travelocity, the airlines no longer needed traditional travel agencies to bring in customers, and as soon as one airline stopped paying commissions, others had every incentive to quickly follow suit.

Without the airlines' commissions—typically of $50 per fare—thousands of travel agencies eventually went out of business. But surprisingly many remained, and the best of those have prospered. One of them is Poe Travel, which, from its unlikely home in Little Rock, Arkansas, has earned its president, Ellison Poe, recognition as one of the country's top agents by both *Travel + Leisure* and *Condé Nast Traveler*. In more ways than one, the Internet has been a boon to her business, enabling her to work easily with clients from all over the United States and even overseas. Poe's parents had cofounded the agency in the 1950s, and for several decades after that, most of the agency's clients came from Little Rock; today, only about ten percent do.

How did Poe Travel manage to survive the tectonic shifts in the travel business? Years before the Sarah Hall case, the agency had already stopped relying on the airlines for most of its revenue. It's not that the Poes had seen the writing on the wall. They made the change to their business model well before the commission cuts and for reasons having nothing to do with the airlines. "It started with large families and intricate trips," explains Poe, a vivacious and outgoing 51-year-old who, thanks to her parents' line of work, had circled the globe by the time she was 6.[2] "It was 'faxland' back then," she recalls of the era when they began rethinking their business model. "Sometimes we would plan a three-week trip to France for a client, sending all these faxes back and forth, and then the family would change their minds and would decide they wanted to go to Spain instead."

Under the old model, the agency would get no extra pay for all the extra effort of planning a new trip. And since the travelers weren't the ones paying anyway, they might not think twice about wasting an agent's time. So the agency redesigned its pricing. "We said, 'We're in the service business—we can do anything,'" Poe says with an exuberance so infectious that it makes me start rethinking my approach to my own work. "We'll charge for our time just like the guy who does our taxes does." Today Poe's agency typically charges $150 per hour, although the rate can rise to up to $250 per hour for particularly challenging requests. She sometimes has to work a fourteen-hour day on rush jobs, and the higher rate allows her to avoid resenting particularly demanding clients.

As a result of this pricing system, what her clients pay for trip planning varies widely, but in a way that makes perfect sense to her and to them. "Let's say you're doing a trip to Vienna, Prague, and Budapest, and it is with six months in-advance planning, and it's sightseeing in each city with some trains between cities and some opera tickets—your fees [to our agency] might be $400. If you're a last-minute person doing a two-week trip to, let's say, the French Riviera in high season and want lunch reservations, dinner reservations, a hair appointment, a private chopper, a helicopter transfer, VIP [access] to the nightclub—it could be $6,100. It really is a matter of time." The logic of this pricing system seems so clear and natural that it's a wonder travel agents ever operated any other way.

When I book my annual trip from San Francisco to New York City to attend an April conference, the whole process takes less than an hour: I've learned from experience that the red-eye works best for me, I know the airfares that time of year, and I typically stay in the same hotel, so the decisions are easy. For such routine bookings, doing it myself is usually cheaper, faster, and easier than getting a professional involved. Most of us feel the same way about basic travel planning. As a result, the notion that travel agents have disappeared is pervasive: we smiled in recognition when Tina Fey's character on *30 Rock*, fearing a possible job loss, pictured herself living under a bridge alongside travel agents and other displaced workers. But for the kinds of trips Ellison Poe plans, there's still very much a market for an expert agent's help. "What Poe Travel has done is we are a travel concierge: we listen to what our clients want, and ninety percent of what we do is customized. We will sell a brochure trip from a tour company, but really what we excel in is creating the experience," she says and begins reeling off a list of tailor-made trips her agency has designed—an East Africa safari, voyages to Tahiti and Patagonia, and journeys to Sri Lanka, India, and Kashmir, among many other adventures that would be hard to plan on your own. Her agency's membership in a luxury-travel network called Virtuoso gives her access to trusted contacts around the globe.

When she speaks of listening to what the client wants, she means listening deeply enough to uncover the client's latent needs. "Even though they might say, 'I want to go on a cruise in the Mediterranean,' [if you listen carefully you sometimes realize that] what they really want to do is go to a dude ranch," she explains. To understand such preferences, she asks questions beyond the current trip. "'When in New York, what is your favorite hotel? Did you see this movie? Do you like movies?' You get to know these people and you can guide them correctly."

It's natural that Poe calls herself a travel concierge because we already associate concierges with travel and hospitality; in fact, what Poe does at her agency is, simply on a larger scale, exactly what a hotel concierge does for the hotel's guests. Interestingly, though, middlemen from other industries often use the word "concierge" to describe their work, too, and often rightly so. That is because the Concierge model works well anywhere consumers must navigate a bewilderingly complex field of options to make what feels like a high-stakes decision—whether it is buying a house, planning a wedding, investing money for retirement, or remodeling a kitchen. To begin to understand how the Concierge does that, it helps to see what an effective hotel concierge does in a world full of available information.

"Let's Look at Your iPad Together"

Nina Eberlijn is no ordinary hotel concierge. She works at The Setai, one of the most exclusive hotels in Miami Beach. Before that she worked at Miami's Mandarin Oriental, another five-star resort. She has served as a concierge in the Miami area since 2005. With a master's degree in Southeast Asian Studies, which she earned in the Netherlands, she actually began her career as a foreign correspondent in Jakarta, covering Indonesian elections and the growth of Islamic extremism. Besides knowing Dutch and Indonesian, she is fluent in English and can get by in French and German, too. Eberlijn has an ideal background to give expert travel advice to the many sophisticates from around the globe who stay at The Setai. And yet, a few years ago, an article by a hotel industry consultant made her wonder about the obsolescence of her career.[3] The article asked: "Why, in our advanced technological times, does the modern day traveler still need a concierge?"[4] It was one of several troubling questions Eberlijn was forced to ask herself. "What makes the concierge service so valuable when our guests can look up everything they need on their online mobile devices? For how much longer will we find the concierge in the hotel lobby? How does the concierge justify his or her role and existence?"

These are excellent questions, of course. Substitute "middleman" for "concierge," and you have very much the same questions that are at the heart of this book. Many consumers are asking these questions, too. One avid traveler, a young woman from San Jose interviewed for a CNN piece about the obsolescence of concierges, captured the feeling of many a hotel guest when she said, "Considering how rarely I use the concierge service, I'd rather swap it for free Wi-Fi."[5] Indeed, if you turn to the Internet for everything from restaurant ratings and bookings to theater tickets and reviews, why do you need a concierge?

This question didn't bother Eberlijn for long, though—a quick trip down memory lane assured this particular concierge that even in the age of the Internet she still had what it takes to provide exceptional value. Specifically, she recalled a time when a guest called her from his room, and the conversation went something like this:

> GUEST: I am looking at my iPad and it says that I should visit Ocean Drive.
>
> EBERLIJN: Indeed, Ocean Drive is very famous for its beach and pastel colored Art Deco buildings, often featured in TV series and movies.
>
> GUEST: Oh, there are also beaches in Key Biscayne. I see that on my iPad too.
>
> EBERLIJN: Certainly. There are two parks, Crandon and Bill Baggs.
>
> GUEST: Clubbing, I also want to experience Miami's nightlife. Let me see what I can find on my iPad.
>
> EBERLIJN: Why don't you visit me at the concierge desk instead, so we can look at your iPad together?

In that brief exchange, Eberlijn saw that the guest, although well informed in many ways and not having asked her a single question, still needed something from her. Like many people who do their own research online, he wanted reassurance that what he'd read online was right, or he needed someone to put all the pieces together—neither of which his iPad could do. For example, he knew there were a couple of stretches of scenic beach, but in his limited time, should he go to Ocean Beach or Key Biscayne? He knew he wanted to experience Miami's nightlife and could learn more about his options online, but which option would make the most sense given his choice of beach? Such questions are especially acute for travelers who have little time to do their research once they're on the ground and even more so for those who are coming to a city just once and are therefore fretful that they'll miss something essential. No matter the guest's particular reason for calling her, Eberlijn knew she could help him plan a better visit than he could on his own and that she could do so faster, too.

Indeed, that's exactly what Eberlijn did once the guest came down to the concierge desk. She quickly learned he was Russian, that this was his first trip to Miami, and that he wanted to rent a car—"preferably an Aston Martin," he told her. She filled him in on some local history, chatted with him about other trips he'd taken, and learned more about his interests and preferences. For example, by the time she found out he wanted to bring back gifts for his wife and sons in Moscow, she had a good sense of what kind of stores to steer him toward. Before long, she was pointing out one-of-a-kind Miami boutiques he would like, arranging for a car rental, and helping him get his name on several clubs' VIP guest lists. "While the guest was at the concierge desk, he never looked at his iPad," Eberlijn recalls. "There was simply no need to."

Eberlijn isn't resisting any changes technology might bring. In fact, she embraces the Internet, seeing the iPad and similar tools as a complement to her work, not a threat to her profession. (For example, she runs a blog, where I read this story.) "Doing your own research is fun," she writes. "Your research will start the conversation." The concierge will take it from there.

It would be wrong to conclude from Eberlijn's story, however, that everyone wants a personal consultation with a concierge, let alone that most travelers are willing to pay a premium for a hotel that has one. For every person who, like the multimillionaire from Moscow, seeks out the personalized services of a hotel concierge, there are probably several travelers who, like the young woman from San Jose, would rather just have free Wi-Fi. At least when it comes to travel, these self-sufficient types know their own likes and dislikes better than anyone else does, they find computers to be more efficient than people, and they're more confident in the information they find on their go-to websites than in the advice from a concierge they'd never met before. So the Concierge is not for everyone—not even at the finest hotels, where guests' time is worth a lot of money and where the concierge can usually be trusted to make good recommendations.

If you're looking for a reason why there are fewer concierges today than there were in past decades, you need look no further. But here's the interesting part: the ones who survived, those who provide specialized expertise beyond what computers can do, are actually more valuable as a result of information technology. David Autor, an economist at MIT who has studied the effects of technology on the labor market, argues that for a certain class of worker, automation is a boon, and it is not just software engineers.[6] Technology always has two faces, Autor points out, simultaneously substituting for human work and complementing it. "Most technology is built to substitute for some activity," he explains. A car is supposed to substitute for a horse and carriage, a word processor is a substitute for someone to spell-check your documents, and the Amazon website is meant to substitute for stores. "But at the same time, there's usually a complementarity that comes into play because many things we do involve a mixture of skills and tasks that go together," only some of which can be automated. Autor gives the example of a modern construction worker with his panoply of power tools and heavy equipment, from nail guns and arc welders to cranes and excavators. Construction workers these days are so mechanized, they're practically cyborgs, Autor says. A predictable consequence is that construction workers no longer do the same hard physical labor they did before such technology came along; another is that it takes less time to finish the same job, so you need fewer construction workers for the same number of projects. So hasn't technology reduced construction workers' value? "But of course the answer is no," Autor concludes. "Technology has increased their value because the construction doesn't happen by itself: you still need a skilled person to operate all that equipment and apply their brain to make the decision of what gets used where." By complementing the worker's own skills, the equipment enables the worker to accomplish more.

The same principle applies to jobs in customer service, including middleman jobs. "If I'm a travel agent," Autor says, "there's a mixture of being able to quickly access information, but also having 'meta-expertise' about what's a good place to go, and what do people like to do together, and what do I know about the local environment, and what do I know about the customer and what they enjoy. So in general, making information lookup cheaper can make the sort of 'value added' of the travel agent greater." This is why Ellison Poe feels that the Internet has been an unalloyed good for her business. Far from substituting for her services, it's enabled her to leverage her expertise more powerfully: looking up facts in an instant, drawing customers from far and wide, and communicating with them faster than ever. Computers can automate many human tasks—but, Autor argues, what's hard to automate are tasks that demand flexibility, judgment, and common sense. People who have those skills will always remain in demand.

The bad news, though, is that certain jobs will either disappear or become low-paid jobs. As a middleman, you simply cannot charge the same prices if you are doing for customers what they can easily and cheaply do for themselves—or what any number of other middlemen can do just as well. For example, the biggest mistake travel agents make, Ellison Poe of Poe Travel says, is acting as just an order-taker. "You have to listen to what the client wants. If we're just an order-taker, you might as well call an American Express agent, who *is* an order-taker." Other Concierges would do well to heed her advice, and that's not just because of automation. Even if computers never become the kind of order-takers customers want, any able-bodied person can be a decent order-taker. As a result, the supply of such workers is nearly endless, which is why retail workers typically earn minimum wage and why travel agents who are merely order-takers will never earn the rates Poe charges. To be in great demand, it's not enough to have skills that are uniquely human; you also have to have specialized skills that are scarce among humans. Or, as David Autor puts it, "There's You versus Them, and You versus the Machine."

From the Problem of Scarcity to the Problem of Abundance

Successful middlemen realize that despite customers' ability to find answers online, many people crave someone to play the Concierge role. In fact, the vast volume of information available to consumers is actually making the Concierge role more important than ever. As one writer put it, "With so much information now online, it is exceptionally easy to simply dive in and drown."[7] If you've read about the Certifier and the Enforcer, you already know that middlemen can reduce informational imbalances between buyers and sellers: when sellers know more about the quality of their goods or services than buyers do, middlemen can put buyers and sellers on more even footing, quickly establishing the kind of trust necessary to make a sale. But what if there aren't informational imbalances—what if plenty of information about quality and prices is readily available online, as it is in the travel business? In that case, the problem for buyers isn't too little information to make a good decision, but too much. As the journalist Lisa Miller observed in a *Newsweek* essay, "A simple family vacation requires innumerable visits to destination websites; a suspicious scouring of rankings and reviews; and, at the heart-stopping final moment, a purchase on a site where prices and availability seem to change by the second." In short, for the ordinary consumer, "trip planning has become a time-consuming hell."[8]

This problem extends well beyond the many decisions involved in trip planning. It occurs wherever there's more information than the human mind can easily process and not just on the Internet. The economist and psychologist Herbert Simon, who received the 1978 Nobel Prize in economics for his insights into human decision making, famously summed up the problem when he wrote, back in 1971, that "the wealth of information creates a poverty of attention."[9] That's because information, as intangible and costless as it often seems, actually does consume valuable resources. "A rabbit-rich world is a lettuce-poor world, and vice versa," Simon explained; the abundance of one resource creates a scarcity of another. So it is with information, which consumes attention—a psychological construct that Simon concluded is best measured in a person's time. Think of it this way: to make a decision requires two steps: gathering information and processing that information. The more information you gather, the more time you must spend processing that information. That's why when information gathering is almost costless, as it has become on the Internet, decision making remains costly because of the processing cost of comparing so many options across many dimensions. In fact, for a certain group of people, decision making with an abundance of "free" information is more costly than ever, in large part because it creates a higher processing cost.

Most of us intuitively understand these costs of decision making, and by and large, we behave accordingly. Benjamin Scheibehenne, a professor of economic psychology at the University of Basel who has studied consumer choice, says that experiments show that people do trade off the time and effort to make a decision against the expected benefits they might get from searching further or digging deeper. In other words, they take the cost of choosing into account, settling on a choice once they find one that's good enough for the current situation—they "satisfice," as Simon put it, rather than trying to find the best choice in an absolute sense. "This may not be optimal, but what is the definition of optimal?" Scheibehenne points out.[10] Life is short, so satisficing could actually be the optimal strategy.

But some people refuse to settle for good enough—these so-called maximizers are so anxious about making a poor choice that they don't know when to stop gathering information. Barry Schwartz, the Swarthmore psychologist who has written about the paradoxically negative effects of too much choice, says that the Internet has definitely made maximizers' lives worse. "If you have to get into your car to get to the other store, you may shrug your shoulders and not bother," he told me. "But if all you have to do is go to another website, why wouldn't you? It's so damn easy to check out one more site."[11]

Of course, even without middlemen, we are not entirely left to our own devices when it comes to managing the onslaught of information, with plenty of websites trying to help us—starting with Google. The company's mission, in fact, sounds very Concierge-like: "to organize the world's information and make it universally accessible and useful." It's an ambitious and ongoing challenge for even the brightest minds in computer science, as ever more information in different forms becomes available. As the algorithms used to find and display information improve, they will have to keep pace with the explosive growth in the volume of data. There will only be more websites, more reviews, more tweets, and more maps and photos and videos and countless other pieces of information to look at and weigh as we make decisions.

That presents both a challenge and an opportunity for computer scientists and software engineers—and for middlemen. Duncan Watts, a sociologist at Microsoft Research, points to the middlemen in real estate. Several years ago, soon after he had gone through the process of buying an apartment in New York City, he told me that historically, real estate brokers have thrived on their superior access to information. "They had the listings and you didn't, so you had to go to one to find out what was available. They guarded that very jealously because they understood, I think correctly, that this was their big competitive advantage and that was what allowed them to charge a lot of money."[12] Listings are no longer locked up in the local proprietary databases known as the multiple-listing service; the information is now widely available to anyone with an Internet connection. So where does that leave brokers? "They'll have to do something different," Watts believes, "because once you have all the information in the world, you go from the scarcity problem to the abundance problem," he says, alluding to the twin problems Herbert Simon described many years earlier—a problem computer scientists are still tackling today. "You go from not knowing anything and needing someone to give it to you, to knowing too much and needing someone to make sense of it." In other words, as a buyer you still need someone, but now that person's role has changed. The real estate agent, for example, needs to filter all the listings for you based on what you need, needs to organize the viewings, needs to find you a lender and an appraiser and all the other things a complex transaction requires. In theory, you can do all these things yourself—but, as Watts points out, "it's time-consuming, and you don't know what questions to ask." What you need if you don't have the time and don't know what questions to ask is a Concierge.

The Concierge solves another problem related to the abundance of information: the information is often *deliberately* hard to process. "Firms don't like perfectly transparent markets," says MIT economist Glenn Ellison, who has studied the way producers engage in obfuscation. He likes to use the example of airlines, which have tacked on excess baggage fees, meal fees, charges for changing your ticket, and the like. This nickel-and-diming makes it harder to compare prices across airlines—which is exactly what the airlines want. "If airline prices are too transparent and the Internet makes searching too easy, then the airlines get into this very intense price competition with each other and make no money at all," Ellison explains.[13] "If they can make the world more confusing, customers will do a limited number of searches, and the firms don't need to be five dollars cheaper than the other guy." Middlemen can help the customer by sorting through this mess, and it will be an ongoing job because the producers will continue to fight back with new forms of obfuscation. "Firms selling things would prefer that things be a little more confusing to soften the price competition, and the intermediaries try to make it less confusing to make it easy to buy things."

As computers get smarter and smarter, they will be able to take on more and more of the Concierge role. Think, for example, of the highly personalized movie recommendations that Netflix's recommender software can serve up, a feat of machine learning that just ten years ago most of us couldn't foresee. With software growing more impressive every day, it's not very hard to imagine a time when, with the tap of your finger, your iPad will be able to generate the perfect itinerary for your vacation in Miami: not the kind of generically great itinerary you find in guidebooks and inflight magazines, but one that's customized to your tastes and interests, length of stay, and budget. In a high-tech version of what Ellison Poe does when she asks about her clients' favorite movies and New York hotels, this software of the future might even use your Netflix and TripAdvisor data to build this kind of personalized itinerary and do it for any city you might visit.

To stay one step ahead of technology, to complement it rather than be replaced by it, the Concierge must up her game. Before the Internet and smartphones, a hotel concierge could provide a good deal of value just by giving a list of nearby restaurants or the address of a tourist attraction. A travel agent could provide value by telling you which hotels in your price range have room availability during your travel dates. A real estate agent could provide value by telling you what houses are for sale in your desired neighborhood. Today, when such basic facts are easy to find, there's no point in going to the Concierge unless this person can do significantly more.

Earning Your Fee

Yet many middlemen have failed to adapt as well as many customers would like. The clearest example is the residential real estate business in the United States, in which agents typically earn about 2.5 or 3 percent for helping clients buy or sell a house. One of the most common client complaints about real estate agents (and there are many common complaints to choose from) is not knowing what the agent did to earn this big commission—or being left with the feeling that the agent didn't do enough to justify the high fee. It's not the price itself that clients resent, but the mismatch between price and quality, which amounts to a poor value. Many people don't mind paying Ritz-Carlton prices for Ritz-Carlton service; what nobody can stand is paying Ritz-Carlton prices for the level of service you'd expect from Econolodge.[14]

Hugh Borax, a forward-thinking real estate agent and broker in Santa Monica, is an exception and may just represent the future of real estate middlemen. Borax works hard to make sure customers have no doubt of the value he's providing and the first step is to let customers choose which package of services they want to buy: his prices reflect the extent of the services. For buyers, that range goes from what he calls the Concierge option, which includes everything a full-service agent offers, down to his one-percent option, for clients who find their own house, are willing to do their own comparative market analysis, and therefore need an agent only to shepherd them through the complex process that begins at the point of making an offer on a property.

When Borax was starting to build his brokerage, he was a full-commission agent. As anyone who's bought a house in the United States knows, the standard model is to charge your seller clients a percentage of the sale price (often 6 percent) and split that with the buyer's agent, who typically gets three percent of the sale price. Borax was working mainly with buyers, and the problem he ran into, familiar to most agents who represent buyers, was buyers deciding not to buy a house after all; when that happened, Borax would earn zero commission for all his work, even if it took nine months of showing houses. Sound familiar? This is essentially the same problem Ellison Poe faced when her clients would change their minds about a trip to France—but California real estate regulations, as Borax interpreted them, prevented him from charging an hourly rate for his services as Poe has been able to do.

So what did Borax do? He became a discount broker, focusing on the part of the transaction that comes after someone decides to make an offer. Borax's agency will represent clients who find a property on their own, whether by going to an open house or some other means, for a commission of only one percent. That means that if the deal closes, Borax's agency will refund his buyer client any commission the agency receives above one percent (as long as Borax ends up with at least $7,000). So for a $1 million house, for example, Borax will earn $10,000, instead of the $20,000 to $30,000 he would earn if he were working as a full-service agent. Some clients also want him to do "comps," researching prices paid for comparable houses before they make an offer, and having the agency do comps adds another half a percent to his commission. Many are happy to do that part themselves, too, and he gives them the tools to do so if they wish. "Why should I do work for a client where the client is fully capable of doing it themselves and is interested in doing it themselves?" Borax says. He loves efficiency, and having to duplicate a client's efforts strikes him as the epitome of inefficiency. "So I'd rather do what I know that I do best, let the client do what they're interested in doing, and we both come together, and I can charge them a lower amount."

The key point to notice here is that Borax isn't talking about cutting back on service quality—cutting the price reduces only the *extent* of his service, not its excellence; in fact, specializing can mean offering service of higher quality. That's because most of his clients come to him only after they've already found a house and want to make an offer—so he doesn't have to worry about spending valuable time on clients who never make an offer or who require many months of being shown houses before they find one they like. In other words, clients who know what they want have self-selected into his brokerage. Of course, not every offer he writes up and presents ends in a sale, either, but by working with clients who've already found a house, he's increasing the likelihood of getting his commission. With lower risks and lower costs, Borax is able to profitably provide service in just those parts of the transaction that come after the search. By not spending all his time escorting clients around town to show houses, he can better focus on the tasks that his one-percent and 1.5 percent clients are hiring him for.

The Middle Way for Middlemen

Borax's approach of providing great value through services that customers actually want to pay for might eventually catch on with real estate agents in other communities. But even if it doesn't—the real estate business has been resistant to change for many years, in part from intense lobbying to protect the status quo[15]—his general approach has much to teach middlemen in other industries. To explain his business philosophy, Borax borrows the Buddhist idea of "the middle way," originally taught by the Buddha himself and long espoused by the Dalai Lama: a solution that avoids extremes and leaves both parties satisfied. "That theory can be extrapolated to any problem," Borax says. "There aren't just two ways to solve a problem: there's a middle way that considers the best of both sides." In fact, the Buddha originally used "the middle way" to refer to the happy medium between the extremes of self-indulgence and self-mortification. In the real estate business, the two extremes sellers face are doing everything themselves ("For Sale By Owner") and outsourcing all the work (by hiring an expensive full-service real estate agent). What makes the middle way so widely applicable is the insight that customers don't necessarily want to do everything themselves, even if they can. A middleman's job isn't one service: it is a set of services, some of which can be unbundled.

What is it about real estate that makes agents necessary at all? Why do people need even a one-percent agent? The reason is that buying (or selling) a house is one of the biggest, most stressful transactions many of us will ever experience. The high stakes, the new terrain to navigate, the number of details to get right: all the elements of a tough decision are present. On top of that, it's a one-off transaction, much like planning a wedding. If you planned to get married many times, or to buy and sell many houses, it would probably make sense to invest the time to become an expert yourself; otherwise, hiring a good Concierge is your best bet. In fact, this is one of the reasons economists have put forward for the persistence of high real estate commissions: when so much is on the line, you don't want to take chances by skimping on price. Stanford economist Jon Levin compares the situation to taking a company public, another transaction whose high fees have long puzzled economists. Why would sophisticated business people preparing for an IPO pay an investment bank 5 percent of the value of the offering? That seems like an awfully high fee for this one-time service. "But then you think: it's a huge deal—the cost of something going wrong is just enormous." What's more, you're not going to get a lot of experience going through this process—either buying or selling houses or taking a company public. "So you feel you want to get someone who will absolutely not screw this up."[16] To make sure everything goes smoothly, you'll hire the best Concierge you can, and you won't nickel-and-dime this expert.[17]

At this point, it should become clear that selecting a good Concierge is a decision problem of its own—all the more important given how much trust you place in this person. In fact, it is one reason real estate agents spend so much on advertising and at least a small part of the reason agents' average fees in the United States have remained so high. An experienced consumer will wonder why they should believe that the Concierge's recommendations will be good ones. (Is the Concierge really knowledgeable? How do we know the concierge isn't getting kickbacks from some of the businesses?) When the Concierge is no longer the only way to get things done, a Concierge must work harder to earn a prospective client's trust.

About an hour on the phone with Borax leaves me confident that this is the agent I would hire if I needed to buy or sell a house in Santa Monica. It's not just his Yelp reviews (46 total, all of them five-star reviews). Hearing him talk about what he does, spelling out the process in a patient, step-by-step way, gives me a strong sense that Borax is clear about the value he provides, well-versed in the technical aspects of the business, and organized in his thinking about the process: everything you want in a Concierge. Even though he uses the term "Concierge" to refer to his full-service option—since that word suggests premium service—his discounted options actually fulfill the Concierge role as well. For example, when I asked what he does for the one-percent option, he began by saying simply, "We do everything for the one percent except show properties and perform a comparative market analysis." He then enumerated his services, from setting up clients with an MLS portal so they can do their own searches, to referring them to certain lenders the agency has had good experiences with (stepping in as a Certifier here), to sending a sample offer package to give clients a way to make them familiar with a complicated purchase agreement—and answering questions in laymen's terms. "When the client is prepared to make the offer, we discuss the strategy to get them the property for the lowest amount, as well as the lowest possible terms. We also discuss the likelihood of the offer being accepted, and we always give them the choice of removing those terms."

This is where much of the value comes in because knowing how to prepare a competitive offer comes from experience, especially because an offer isn't all about the price. For example, Borax explains to his clients the pros and cons of including an appraisal contingency—a clause that allows buyers to cancel an offer if the appraisal doesn't come in high enough but whose inclusion can sabotage a deal. Ultimately, the buyer chooses the terms, not the agent, but Borax is there to make sure the buyer understands what's going on. That's what the buyer pays for—not the tasks the buyer has performed on her own.

Offering a middle way, as Borax does, can sound like a no-brainer, yet too often we act is if there are only two options, not three or more. As consumers, we sometimes think we must choose between doing it ourselves and hiring an expert to do it all for us. We think either middlemen will go away or that it will always be business as usual. It's all too easy for service providers, too, to fall into such all-or-nothing thinking. But there are almost always alternatives. Consumers expect middlemen *not* to charge them as if it's still 1980, because consumers do have more options today, and cost-saving technology that's available to consumers is also available to middlemen. These consumers offer an opportunity for middlemen who can find a middle way in whatever industry they want to shake up. Taking business away from traditional full-service middlemen, middlemen who take the middle way provide the services that customers really need at a price that matches the service given.

We've already met a few such middlemen in previous chapters. Think back to Genevieve Thiers, who founded SitterCity upon realizing that parents had no option between a $2,000 nanny agency and posting flyers themselves. Ann Whitley Wood, the eBay PowerSeller, also discovered a middle way; though she exemplifies the Certifier, staking her reputation on the quality of the goods she sells, she also plays the Concierge role for her Dallas-based clients, who neither wish to handle their own eBay sales nor want to limit their market to the local consignment store. Wood offers them the convenience of the local consignment store with the global reach of eBay. That is the middle way, and as the Internet continues to offer itself up to consumers, the middle way is where more and more middlemen will find opportunities to play the Concierge role: not only on eBay, but wherever buyers and sellers need to find each other. As we'll see next, it's already starting to happen in the traditionally suspect business of selling used cars.

"We Want It To Be Simple"

People who have tried to sell their used car, at least in the United States, must have wished for a middle way between a private sale (selling the car yourself) and a trade-in (selling it to a dealer), because neither option is remotely appealing. Selling it yourself is a hassle—it requires taking out ads, fielding inquiries from prospective buyers, meeting these prospects, and negotiating the sale. If you opt for a trade-in, you save yourself the hassle but you lose a huge chunk of what you could sell the car for yourself. According to the car shopping site Edmunds.com, as of this writing, a 2009 Honda Accord 4-door LX sedan with 50,000 miles in "clean" condition sells in my zip code for $10,768 from a private party, but for only $9,648 as a trade-in—a difference of more than $1,000. Unless your time is worth several hundred dollars per hour, you'll probably grit your teeth and go for the private sale. The dealer can retail that same car for $11,865—over a thousand dollars more than you would get on your own. Not that you'd get a share of that difference by selling to a dealer, because you'd get only the trade-in price.

"The folks who are in the market today and who were in the market before we got in"—the used car dealers—"are merchants," explains Mike Bor, the CEO and cofounder of an alternative middleman business called CarLotz, based in Richmond, Virginia.[18] He uses the term "merchants" to refer to people who buy from one person and sell to another, profiting from buying low and selling high. Bor has nothing against the merchant model per se, but from the start his goal for CarLotz was not to be a merchant, with a goal of maximizing the profit of each transaction, but to be a service provider, with the goal of steady profits across a large volume of highly satisfied buyers and sellers. That focus on excellent customer service would set CarLotz apart from the rest of the used car industry. "It's an industry people dislike and distrust," he says, citing (as if evidence were necessary for such an uncontroversial claim) a J. D. Power report that ranked used-car sales in the bottom three by customer satisfaction. "It's really opaque and nobody knows if they're being taken advantage of—it's kind of a dirty industry." To combat this image and offer better value to buyers and sellers, Bor thought CarLotz needed to provide much more transparency and efficiency.

To see how CarLotz does that, it helps to understand the source of inefficiency in the traditional used car market. Until I spoke with Bor, I thought the high dealer markup—the large difference between the dealer's retail price and the trade-in price—could be chalked up to the lemons problem. Since sellers know more about their cars' condition than the dealer does, the dealer must assume the worst and pay accordingly, hence the low trade-in price. Since dealers stake their reputation on the quality of the cars they sell, they can charge buyers more than a private seller does. But although lemon dynamics definitely play a role, the bigger cause for the price gap, Bor explains, is a highly inefficient supply chain.

> The supply chain of a used car from the time it's traded in to the time it's sold can be months and require capital and transportation from a dealer to a wholesaler's lot to an auction to another wholesaler to another dealer; multiple times exchanging paperwork, and signing documents, and exchanging payments, and requiring certain degrees of trust; and over this time period there's the natural decay of the asset that's being transferred, and the potential for it to fall apart.

The middlemen aren't making a killing through the price gap: instead, money leaks out at each step in the long process. To succeed, CarLotz had to shorten the chain and make it much more efficient.

Let's be clear: contrary to popular belief, a long supply chain isn't always inefficient, and often it's the opposite. Trade hubs and multiple specialized players can make a supply chain both faster and cheaper. Think of the way cut flowers move across the world through the Dutch flower market, such that it makes sense for daffodils grown in the United Kingdom to go through a series of middlemen in the Netherlands before returning to retailers and consumers in the United Kingdom. Economies of scale make this roundabout but well-trod trading route more efficient than selling direct. And if each middleman is playing a distinct role, instead of duplicating the effort of other middlemen, then all the links become indispensable. In Euclidean geometry the shortest distance between two points is a straight line, but when it comes to time and money, sometimes the shortest path goes through one or more middlemen.[19] Yet that's only true if the middlemen's value exceeds their cost. In the case of used cars, though, the high transport costs alone make a long supply chain dissipate value. Here's where it pays to cut out some middlemen and become a better middleman yourself.

That is exactly what Mike Bor and his partners did with CarLotz. "You come to us and we look at our data and we say that this is a vehicle that lists for $12,000," Bor says by way of example. "We'll list it for $11,500, and you say, '$11,500 sounds great because my alternative is $7,000 [the trade-in price].'" So you leave your car with CarLotz, which holds on to it on a consignment basis on one of its lots; CarLotz never owns the car. Instead of a merchant model, the company uses a broker/matching model. As Bor puts it, "We are basically a real estate agent for your car." Then, if a customer comes in to CarLotz, notices a lot of wear on the tires, and asks for a price break, CarLotz calls you to ask if it's okay to lower the price. Even that step is less efficient than Bor would like—the transaction would go more smoothly if you had told CarLotz your reserve price in advance, which is what his friends have done when they've used his service. But most sellers don't trust car dealers enough to reveal how low they'd be willing to go. If you accept the buyer's offer, CarLotz closes the deal and pays you the proceeds minus its fee.

The total fee for this service amounts to a little under $900, regardless of the final sale price—$199 when you drop off the car and another $699 when it sells. CarLotz also charges buyers a fee of $299, regardless of the price of the car, so the company earns $1,197 for every car sold. The aim of this flat fee, Bor explains, is to price the company's service at about a third of the value added. This is where CarLotz differs from a real estate agent, who typically charges a commission based on the sale price. "The percentage model assumes that the value that you add as a service provider is proportional to the value of the product you're selling," Bor explains. That may be true of real estate (although many consumers wonder if the value added for selling a $20 million house really amounts to 100 times the value added for selling a $200,000 house). "But in our case, the value we add is the same whether we're selling a Ferrari or a Ford Focus." And because CarLotz is completely transparent about its fees, customers don't have to wonder whether they're being taken advantage of, especially knowing that sales staff have no apparent incentive to push the more expensive cars. "We don't really care which car we sell—we care about making a transaction happen that delights the buyer and the seller," Bor says.

There's a downside to charging a flat fee: it's less attractive to the Ford Focus owner than to the Ferrari owner. Owners of expensive cars enjoy a higher delta between the CarLotz price and the price they'd get from a traditional dealer—sometimes to the tune of more than $10,000—but they still pay CarLotz only $898, which comes out to much less than a third of the value created. Because CarLotz could have charged more for selling expensive cars, the company is knowingly leaving money on the table. Why? There are several reasons, starting with Bor's point about aligning salespeople's incentives with the company's goal of providing equally good service for everyone. Bor doesn't say so, but it's reasonable to expect that this pricing system disproportionately attracts high-end cars to the lot, which in turn should attract wealthier buyers. What Bor *does* say is that he and his partners didn't want to confuse customers with a more complicated pricing system. As he puts it, "One of the keys to our business is we want it to be simple."

Simplicity, it turns out, is a key to any Concierge business. After all, if people are coming to you because they want to avoid the hassles of doing everything themselves, you must make dealing with you as easy as possible. There's also research to this effect. A study by the Corporate Executive Board of thousands of consumers in the United States, the United Kingdom, and Australia tried to get at what makes customers go through with an intended purchase, to buy the product repeatedly, and to recommend it to others. One factor stood out as the biggest predictor: decision simplicity.[20]

Concierges understand that the reason clients are coming to them rather than doing the sale themselves is that they're overwhelmed by the choices and short on time. Therefore, after you establish yourself as the trusted source, you need to truly make life easier for the clients. That may sound obvious, yet many middlemen miss opportunities to play this role. One reason is they may not recognize that they're in a Concierge position in the first place. Retailers, for example, typically pride themselves on a wide assortment but rarely offer the customer service needed to wade through those choices. Another problem is failing to appreciate that what seems like an important distinction (a choice between X and Y, for example) means nothing to the customer or is inconsequential. In situations like that, a wide assortment is actually worse than a narrow one. Customers want the Concierge to narrow choices down for them—or if offering a wide assortment, Concierges must help customers narrow things down quickly. The wedding planner doesn't drag you to every florist in town, doesn't show you every photographer's portfolio, doesn't have you taste every wedding cake. Ellison Poe doesn't show you a list of all the New England packages—if she did, you'd wonder why you're paying her at all. No, these Concierges engage in a process of winnowing—not just screening on the basis of quality as a Certifier would, because a certain level of quality is a given, established at the first cut.

The same thing happens when you provide the Concierge service to sellers. Think back to eBay PowerSeller Ann Whitley Wood: the only thing she asks her clients to do is drop off their clothes; she doesn't make them take pictures, write descriptions, or figure out what price to charge.

This simplicity has to permeate all aspects of your business. Show customers through your website and all your communications that working with you will be easier than doing it on their own, as CarLotz does. If you make things confusing or complicated, prospective clients assume that working with you is no easier than doing it yourself. But remember that the simplicity has to be worth the price: a real estate agent who charges a simple 3 percent commission for all clients keeps things simple, too, as does the dealer who just takes your car off your hands for a ridiculously low price. But customers aren't always willing to pay such a premium for simplicity. So there's a balance that a good Concierge has to achieve.

Simplicity itself isn't simple to achieve: it requires deep expertise to hone a process to its essence. You need, for example, to understand which steps customers find confusing or stressful (even if you as the expert find the same things obvious and inconsequential) and which details are important and which are merely distracting. If you take the time and effort to make things easy for your customers, customizing their purchase or sale to match their goals, you'll be doing them a huge favor in the amount of time you save them.

It's easy to see that CarLotz charges less to sellers than a traditional dealer, but I'm interested in how it plays the Concierge role, so I asked Bor what advantage CarLotz provides to sellers compared to everyone's alternative of selling the car themselves. He had an immediate answer. "We do everything you can do on your own, but we do it perfectly," he told me. No matter who is selling the car—the owner or CarLotz—the basic steps are the same: taking pictures, writing a description, posting ads online, fielding calls, meeting buyers, and at the end, getting the check and signing over the title. The "perfect" part comes from how CarLotz executes each of those steps. Taking pictures of the car is a good example: whereas you might take five or ten pictures before posting them to Craigslist, CarLotz typically takes about 85. Prices to buyers are ten to fifteen percent lower at CarLotz than at traditional dealerships, so buyers come from all over the country; therefore, buyers want to make sure it's worth their time to fly in. "So we are neurotic about taking a tremendous number of pictures," showing the car from lots of angles and plenty of detailed close-ups. To you, that number of photos might seem like a big hassle, but to someone at CarLotz who does it every day, it takes only five minutes longer to take 85 pictures than it would to take only a handful of pictures. The same thing happens with posting the ad: if you were selling the car yourself, you'd probably post your ad on Craigslist, but CarLotz routinely posts ads not only on Craigslist, but also on Autotrader, Cars.com, and several other sites. Then, when buyers start calling or coming by for a test drive, CarLotz is available from 8 a.m. to 7 p.m. six days a week. Few car owners can offer buyers that kind of flexibility. On top of that, CarLotz does things you cannot do on your own at all, like arranging for buyer financing. "In the most simple case, we do everything better, and in the most complicated case, we do a bunch of stuff you can't do."

Many business people talk about providing customer service, but it's not clear what most of them mean. In the case of CarLotz, the message to buyers and sellers is clear, and the model seems to be taking off. Having refined their process and achieved profitability, CarLotz is ready to expand beyond its Virginia locations. As I was writing this chapter, the company announced a $5 million round of funding to finance new stores in North Carolina, Maryland, and Georgia as well as additional locations throughout Virginia.

At about the same time, a start-up in Silicon Valley called Carlypso received a round of seed funding for an even more radical car-selling business model, which relies heavily on technology to minimize human labor. For example, Carlypso uses GPS tracking and a secure lockbox to enable would-be buyers to test-drive the car

on their own. Carlypso also does away with sales lots, since owners can leave their cars in their driveways or on the street. Unlike
CarLotz, Carlypso provides an inspection mechanic, and the company uses commission-based pricing, collecting 5 percent of the sale
price (at least $400 and at most $1,500). Despite these important
differences, the value proposition to sellers is essentially the same as
with CarLotz: save time, do away with the need to meet with strangers, and deliver cash when your car is sold. In other words, sellers
get the money of a private sale and the convenience of a trade-in.
The middle way. The company's name for this hassle-free service:
Carlypso Concierge.

This chapter has focused on houses, cars, and travel, but we
can all think of other fields where a middleman can offer simplicity and convenience at the right price. There are insurance
brokers, for example, who specialize in helping customers pick
the best Medicare plan out of the program's bewildering selection, financial advisors who charge a one-time fee to create an
investment portfolio tailored to the customer (and online advisors who charge less than the standard 1 percent per year to keep
managing the money), personal shoppers who take the pain out
of going to the mall, and interior designers who help homeowners settle on the right combination of colors to spiff up a room.
There are many other such services that don't exist but should:
in every inadequate and overpriced industry norm that continues
to disappoint and frustrate customers lies an opportunity for a
Concierge to do a better job.

There is only one more middleman role left to explore, and it
is in some ways the most different from all the others: the Insulator
deals not so much with connecting buyers and sellers as with figuring out when it might be in their own best interest to keep them
apart.

6

THE INSULATOR

Taking the Heat

THE ROLE: *Usually middlemen bring people together, but sometimes people who already know each other are better off communicating through a middleman who insulates them from blame. This happens when speaking directly and on your own behalf makes you seem too greedy, self-promotional, or confrontational. An effective Insulator can take the heat in such situations—and can also transform what might appear as a client's selfishness into the Insulator's altruism.*

"I Don't Want You to Ruin Your Relationship with the Team."

For the many people who've come to hate Drew Rosenhaus over the years, his 2011 appearance on *60 Minutes* did nothing to improve his image. Representing players on just about every team in the NFL (National Football League), including some of the biggest names in the game, Rosenhaus is unquestionably football's most powerful agent; when he was still only 29, he became the first agent ever to appear on the cover of *Sports Illustrated*. But he's known as much for his larger-than-life personality and bare-knuckle tactics as for the record-breaking deals he's been able to get for his star clients.

In fact, he was the model for Jerry Maguire's backstabbing boss in *Jerry Maguire*, and proudly titled his memoir *A Shark Never Sleeps*. So when he said on national television that he really believed that the NFL would fall apart without him, he was playing true to type, and many football fans immediately wrote off his comment as just the latest ravings of a blowhard. His statement sounded absurd: how can an agent, let alone one as belligerent and divisive as Rosenhaus, be holding together the entire league? But Rosenhaus proceeded to explain why he was simply stating the truth. "When it breaks down between the team and the player, the agent is there to pick up those pieces," he told his interviewer. "When a guy says, 'I want to be traded! I hate this team, I hate this coach,' I say to the player, 'Tell *me*. Don't tell the coach. I don't want you to ruin your relationship with the team.'"[1]

It turns out that Rosenhaus is really on to something. In his own way, he's expressing an idea about conflict resolution that applies far beyond the NFL. He diffuses tensions between teams and players by letting his clients blow off steam with him—and when he does convey his clients' concerns to the team, it is he who takes the heat for being the bad guy. Rosenhaus knows that he's playing a role: the Insulator.

From Black Markets to Regular Business

The idea of taking the heat for someone else's bad behavior might suggest a less than admirable middleman. After all, wherever there are illegal transactions, there are usually middlemen to cover them up. We often read about middlemen in stories about drug smuggling and arms dealing, kidney sales and child trafficking, and tax fraud, bribery, and insider trading. All these middlemen diffuse responsibility,[2] provide plausible deniability,[3] protect their trading partners from the arm of the law, and as lab experiments show, make buyers and sellers feel less guilty about their participation in dirty deals.[4] In fact, with these kinds of middlemen, insulation from blame for unethical behavior is the main purpose of their existence.[5]

But what does that have to do with Drew Rosenhaus and the rest of us? In this chapter, I argue that the same psychological processes that create demand for criminal middlemen also leave opportunities for legitimate middlemen to insulate upstanding citizens.

Many situations call for Insulators. Take employee recruitment. Often, the most attractive candidates are working at a firm in the same industry—either the hiring firm's rival or its customer or supplier. But it looks bad for a hiring manager to poach workers from a competitor. Facebook managers hiring away Google employees transforms what might be friendly rivalry to bitter rancor. So imagine how much worse the fallout is when a company poaches a star employee not from a rival but from a client: the unseemliness of the act could damage the relationship and hurt the hiring firm's bottom line. This problem is one reason companies hire executive search firms: headhunters (as their name implies) can be much more aggressive than hiring managers in going after "passive candidates," those people who aren't looking for a new job but could be persuaded to switch companies if the right opportunity knocks.

A Convenient Fiction

In their study of contingency-fee recruiters in a city in the American South, the sociologists William Finlay and James E. Coverdill explain the politics of the situation this way:

> The headhunter's role is to assume responsibility (and take the blame) when a candidate is recruited from a company that is a client's customer or competitor. Overt raiding of a company for its employees is a provocative action that invites retaliation against the offending organization; using a headhunter is a way for the company that is accused of stealing employees to deflect

the blame by claiming that it was the headhunter's doing. In many instances, though, that is not true: the client identifies the employee it wants to hire and then employs the headhunter as a cover.[6]

The cover works, Finlay and Coverdill suggest, even though all parties know what's really going on. "The pretense that firms do not recruit candidates from their competitors or customers is a convenient fiction for all parties to accept because it reduces the risk that inter-firm tension will erupt into open, tit-for-tat hostility." The headhunters, in other words, absorb the heat and thus help prevent the potentially escalating conflicts that benefit no one. Headhunters, therefore, provide value beyond their expertise and connections. In a pinch, they can become a scapegoat.

Middlemen who play the Insulator role are essential in the many situations that fall within moral gray areas or simply socially awkward domains. By acting as our proxy, the Insulator can enable us to be honest and bold without damaging our image or important business relationships. Instead of connecting two people who don't otherwise know each other, as a Bridge would, the Insulator steps in when it's best to keep the two parties apart.

These ideas about insulation are very familiar to economist Al Roth, who won the 2012 Nobel Prize for his extraordinarily practical work in applying game theory to the design of real-world markets. Roth says that in every market he's ever studied, there are some things that some people consider "repugnant" where middlemen can help. "There are some things you're not allowed to do for yourself but that others can do for you," Roth says.[7] In a negotiation, for example, "It seems impolite for me to say that I have the upper hand, and I should really get 90 percent. But to have my lawyer say, 'My client has the upper hand, and I'm demanding 90 percent for him,' that's sort of easier." That's one reason school boards hire negotiators to negotiate with local teachers' unions, he says. "We're going to have a tough negotiation, but afterward we're going to be friends. And it won't be you and me who made the tough demands."

Interestingly, an agent can be a successful Insulator even when everybody knows who's behind the agent's actions. In one set of studies, a team of psychologists led by Jeffrey Pfeffer tested two versions of a standard situation in the publishing industry.[8] In one version, an experienced author they'd invented (whom they named "Michael Green") is trying to sell a book idea to a publishing company on his own. In the other, Green has a literary agent. Which one ends up better off? As in many other types of deals, "better off" boils down to two separate issues: price and likability (or, put another way, short-term gain and long-term relationship success). It's one thing to impress the publisher enough to command a high advance, but can you come out of the deal well-liked by the buyer?

Both are important if you're hoping for a good working relationship, but sometimes the two goals are in conflict. Flaunting your strengths and accomplishments is a sure way to raise others' sense of your worth, but it can make you seem obnoxious. We don't like people who toot their own horn. Modesty, on the other hand, may endear you to others, but it keeps you from fully displaying your qualifications. Thus, you're damned if you brag and damned if you don't.

The researchers call this quandary "the self-promotion dilemma," and—guess what?—they show that an agent is an effective way out. In their study, an actor playing Green spoke proudly on his own behalf in the first condition, whereas an actor playing Green's agent sang Green's praises in the other condition. Under both conditions, Green ended up with a good deal. But participants who heard Green sing his own praises found him less likable than those who heard an agent do so for Green. Think about what this means: the participants who rated Green as more likable—the students who were dealing with an agent, rather than with Green directly—had been told that the author had retained the agent. They knew that the client had paid the agent to sing his praises, knew that the agent had a financial incentive to extol the client's virtues, understood on some level that the agent was merely doing the client's bidding—and yet they didn't hold all of this against Green. They liked him more when the praise came from the agent rather than from the author directly.

This experiment doesn't prove that hiring an agent is worthwhile, certainly not for insulation alone. An agent charges a commission, and if the total advance is the same with or without the agent, as was the case in this experiment, the author's net earnings from the sale end up lower if he or she hires an agent. If the agent provides no other value, then whether the agent is worth the cost depends entirely on how much the insulation service is worth. To add enough value as an Insulator, you have to make your insulation service worth your fee—something that, as we'll see in a moment, is more likely to happen in situations where likability really pays off.

"I Let My Agent Handle These Things"

Being seen as likable is important in many fields, of course, but nowhere does it pay off quite as obviously as in the world of professional sports and entertainment. Athletes and singers and actors who are both talented and likable not only attract more fans, all other things being equal, but can profit from lucrative endorsement deals as well. In this world, maintaining a likable image is especially good for business.

For an example of how this works, take a look at the phenomenon of the rookie holdout. This is the athlete who plays a game of chicken with the team that drafted him, where the player delays signing until he gets the best contract he can. It's a risky strategy—and not only because the team might be willing to hold off longer than the player. The bigger, more long-term risk to the player who's willing to miss training camp for the sake of a better contract is an image problem. He can easily come across as a prima donna: mercenary and self-important, motivated by money and greed more than by the love of the game or loyalty to his new team. In the 2009 NFL draft, for example, the 49ers' first-round pick (and the #10 pick overall), a wide receiver from Texas Tech named Michael Crabtree, picked up the label "diva" for insisting he was worth more than the considerable sum the Niners wanted to sign him for—approximately five years and $20 million ($16 million of it guaranteed). He held out for 72 days, missing not only training camp but also the first four games of the season. When team and player finally announced in a press conference that they'd reached an agreement, Crabtree made it sound as if all along he'd remained above the fray. "My whole approach was let my agent handle all of my business," he said when a reporter at the event asked what changed in his approach to make the deal happen now.[9]

In saying that, Crabtree was repeating a phrase he must have heard dozens of times from other players on other broadcasts. It would be unseemly for a player to talk in public about money, contracts, and business strategies, which is why "I let my agent handle these things" has become such a cliché in high-stakes, closely watched sports negotiations. Crabtree spent the rest of the conference trying to hammer home the point that all he wanted to do was play ball, do what the coach says, and help his team win. Wearing gray sweats and a Niners practice jersey and saying all the right things, he was the picture of humility, innocence, and good sportsmanship.

You'd think this babe-in-the-woods routine wouldn't fool anyone, and indeed Crabtree's reputation did take a hit from the particularly long holdout, especially one that ultimately didn't give him nearly as much money as he wanted. (In the end, he got approximately $32 million over six years, $17 million of it guaranteed.) But the blow to his image was surely softer than if he had been acting alone, as we can see from the way even professional pundits talked about the situation. During the holdout, Bryan Goldberg, a senior writer for *The Bleacher Report*, wrote a column accusing Crabtree's agent, Eugene Parker, of "brainwashing and ruining the career of a young man who does not know any better."[10] After the deal was done, Pete Prisco, NFL columnist for CBS Sports, proclaimed that "his agent did him a major disservice by keeping him out."[11] The pundits knew that an agent wouldn't do what the client didn't want, but still they blamed the agent.

Having Their Cake and Eating It Too

I first heard Crabtree's story from a young experimental economist named Lucas Coffman, an assistant professor at Ohio State University who had been a doctoral student of Al Roth's. Coffman has more than a passing interest in sports. By his own account, he follows football and baseball and basketball more than he should.[12] He's thought so much about the problems with the NFL draft that he's proposed an alternative. Among the many problems in the current system is that teams pick players one at a time instead of bidding on a group that would play well together. Coffman also has a keen interest in the role of agents, who he's convinced absorb some of the dislike often directed at players.

It so happens that Coffman's father is a middleman: he runs a staffing company. Coffman explains it this way: "Say GE has a big contract at a nuclear power plant. It doesn't seem to make sense to pay my dad to bring in four or five additional workers when GE can hire the same workers themselves." So why call the staffing company? One reason, as we saw from the study of headhunters, might be that GE doesn't want to be seen as poaching workers. But Coffman's father sees a different reason, though very much related to helping the client look good. "One of the values he adds to GE is when they want to downsize a little bit, he gives them flexibility because he goes in and he says the words 'You're fired.' The people he's firing and their coworkers seeing them getting fired—they don't hate GE, they hate my dad." Again, this dynamic isn't strictly rational. "If you ask the other employees, they know it's GE who made the decision, but it's not as salient."

Coffman isn't merely speculating: he and other economists have run controlled experiments that show this exact psychology at work. In one set of experiments, conducted by European economists Björn Bartling and Urs Fischbacher, the researchers had participants play a specially designed version of the famous Dictator Game. In its most basic form, the Dictator Game is a simple, commonly used test of generosity: researchers give one participant (call her Annie) a sum of money (say, $10) and offer her the opportunity to share some part of that sum with another player, typically one that Annie doesn't know. The more Annie the Dictator shares with this stranger (whom we can call Chloë), the more generous Annie appears. The Dictator Game is also often used to measure fairness. If Annie shares half her money, that's considered a fair split. If she shares only $2, keeping $8 for herself, most people consider that an unfair split.

That's the basic Dictator Game, and it's not very interesting in and of itself—it's just a way to gather basic information about an individual or a group, much the way a health researcher might measure a participant's weight before and after a particular treatment. The Dictator Game has been used in so many economic and psychological experiments, with so many variations, that when Bartling and Fischbacher conducted their experiments, they didn't allow economics or psychology students to play since these students' knowledge could taint the results.[13]

But this experiment was different from the basic game in several important ways. It used four players instead of two. Annie was still the dictator, and Chloë was still on the receiving end. But in addition, there was another recipient, whom we can call Charlie. Last, and crucially, there was a middleman (Bobbie) between Annie on the one hand and Chloë and Charlie on the other. In short: A, B, and two Cs.

Here's how the game worked. Annie could either play the Dictator Game herself or she could choose to let Bobbie, the middleman, play it for her. Instead of $10, the researchers gave Annie 20 points, points that could eventually be exchanged for cash. If Annie chose the fair split, each of the four players would get a quarter of that, 5 points each. If she chose an unfair split, she and Bobbie would each get 9 points, with Chloë and Charlie getting only 1 point each.

Finally, the game had an important twist: the opportunity for one of the recipients, Chloë or Charlie (chosen at random), to punish Annie or Bobbie for an unfair split. This opportunity for punishment enabled the researchers to get at what they were really after: who would bear the blame for unfair splits? How much would Chloë or Charlie punish Bobbie as opposed to punishing Annie?

Bobbie turned out to be a major buffer for Annie. For example, when Annie chose to be the Dictator herself, the punishers docked her an average of 4.27 points (out of a possible 7) for every unfair split Annie made. But when Annie delegated the Dictator role to Bobbie, and Bobbie made the unfair split, Annie got an average punishment of only 1.31 points.

But what if Bobbie wasn't making the decision at all, but merely acting as a kind of pawn for Annie? It was this question that Lucas Coffman wanted to answer in his own experiments. It turns out that people punish Annie less when she's acting through a middleman even if the middleman has absolutely no choice but to make the unfair split Annie wants. Thus, using a middleman who's willing to bear the blame lets Annie have her cake and eat it, too.

A Reputation for Toughness

Middlemen who understand the value of being an Insulator can profit from playing this role well. One way is to recognize situations in which concerns about image and long-term relationships mean that clients could really use an Insulator—and then to boldly step into that role. In one exchange broadcast on his *60 Minutes* segment, Drew Rosenhaus is on the phone with a team executive, negotiating for a client who has become a free agent. We don't know the client or the team, but we can gather from the conversation that the player has a strong record in the NFL—he is someone several teams want. Rosenhaus takes full advantage of this situation. At one point, when negotiations seem to be breaking down, he shouts into his handset, "You're taking a huge risk by letting me get off the phone! Because when I get off the phone, I'm calling another team." It's hard to imagine any player being so blunt, no matter how much the team wants him. And that's for good reason: even if the player got his way, he'd leave a trail of ill will behind. Anyone who wants to keep playing would be foolish to do that.

But agents aren't players, and playing hardball in negotiations doesn't hurt agents' careers in the same way. In fact, developing a reputation as a badass middleman can pay off, as suggested by an interesting series of experiments by the economists Chaim Fershtman and Uri Gneezy.[14] The economists had participants play the Ultimatum Game, a game similar to the Dictator Game, except instead of one player simply giving a share to another, the first player makes an offer that the second player can reject. If that player rejects the offer, neither player gets anything. In the middleman version of the game, Fershtman and Gneezy introduced a third player whose role was to make an offer on the first player's behalf. Just as in the Dictator Games with middlemen, using a third party to make offers reduced the rate at which people reject tough offers. For example, in the standard, two-player Ultimatum Game, offers of a 20 percent share or a 30 percent share tend to get rejected; these offers just don't seem as fair as offers of 40 or 50 percent, so recipients would rather get nothing themselves than let the proposer get the lion's share. In a one-shot game this response is irrational—like cutting your nose to spite your face—because there's no chance for the responder to reap any material rewards from teaching the proposer a lesson. Yet, that's how most respondents in dozens of Ultimatum Game experiments behave.

When you bring in a middleman, however, the results change dramatically, Fershtman and Gneezy found. In one experiment, they set up the game such that the middleman got a reward for a proposal that got accepted and no reward for a rejected proposal. When respondents knew that this was the deal, Proposers made tougher offers (through the middleman), and Respondents were more willing to accept these tough offers. In fact, the presence of the middleman actually changes players' perceptions of what is a fair offer, making a tough offer more acceptable than it would be in a two-player game.

But here's where it gets really interesting: when Proposers could choose whether to make offers directly or through a middleman, most of them opted for the middleman. If you notice that people get more acceptances of tough offers made by middlemen, it makes sense to use a middleman.

In all these experiments, the middleman was just the messenger—a pawn for the Proposer—but real-world middlemen can play an active role in their careers by choosing what kind of reputation to cultivate; often it makes sense to establish a reputation for toughness, even becoming known as a badass. It's not just that clients will know they'll get a tough negotiator; the other side (their negotiation counterparts) will know it, too, and clients will know that their counterparts will know it. This common knowledge enables clients to show to their counterparts in a credible way that they mean business, that they won't back down as easily as they might if they were negotiating directly. In this way, the middlemen become what economists call a "commitment device." Gneezy, a professor at the Rady School of Management at the University of California in San Diego who teaches negotiation, explains how this process works in terms of the middleman's high cost of losing his reputation for toughness.[15] "Let's say I am choosing someone [to represent me in a negotiation] who is known to be tough. If a negotiator I choose has a reputation, he has to keep the reputation: if he will be soft in the negotiation, he will lose his reputation. So now when I'm choosing this guy, you know that I've chosen someone who's committed to being tough because otherwise it's going to be very costly for him." The middleman in negotiations is thinking of his long-run reputation (in this case, for toughness) just as the Certifier is thinking of his long-run reputation for quality. "He has to be tough with you, and by choosing this guy I'm committing to being tough."

The real world offers lots of examples of this "badass-agent effect," as we might call it. If you're a sports agent, for example, you have everything to gain by becoming known for your ability to get your players huge deals. Superagents like Rosenhaus are almost as well-known as the star athletes they represent, and sports fans commonly condemn them as money-grubbing sharks or forces of destruction,[16] but the agents let the vitriol roll off their backs—or, in the case of Rosenhaus, embrace the shark label. These agents pull in the kind of clients who want an agent who's not only unafraid of public scorn but who's well-known to team owners and managers for being that way, too.

My favorite example of the badass-agent effect comes from the experience of literary agent Lynn Nesbit, whose clients include Jimmy Carter, Michael Crichton, Joan Didion, and Anne Rice. In an interview looking back on her stellar career, Nesbit once said that when she took Tom Wolfe's first book to auction (rather than letting Wolfe's editor at *New York* magazine offer it exclusively to a favored book editor), she incurred the hatred of this influential magazine editor. But that hatred brought her lots of good clients: other writers at *New York* magazine who, she says, heard the infuriated editor "scream that I was the toughest, bitchiest agent in town."[17] For an Insulator, being bad-mouthed by the right people can pay off.

Can an Insulator Be Nice?

Few people have the stomach for being a Drew Rosenhaus or even a Lynn Nesbit, which is part of what makes them remarkable.

Fortunately, there are other models of successful Insulators, even in the rough world of professional sports. "You don't have to be hated to be an insulator," says Kenneth Shropshire, a Wharton professor and former agent who literally wrote the book on the business of sports agents.[18] (Although Major League Baseball has its own version of Drew Rosenhaus—reviled superagent Scott Boras—Shropshire points out that professional baseball also rewards the approach of agents like Casey Close and Ron Shapiro, nice guys who attract star clients and get good deals for them.) The essence of being a good Insulator—the quality that unites Rosenhaus with excellent representatives of all stripes and from all walks—is championing the client in ways that it would be unseemly for the client to do himself or herself. "The best agents don't have much regard for their personal reputation or their PR platform to the public—but they're actually trying to increase their PR to prospective clients as the agent that looks out for the interest of the client," Shropshire says. Another expert in sports agenting goes even further. "I would actually say that the best agent work is work we never see," says Robert Boland, a sports lawyer who's represented athletes in negotiations and teaches sports management at New York University.[19] But not being in the public eye doesn't mean laboring in obscurity. When an agent does great work, be it by being a badass or a diplomat, word gets around among the people who matter most: prospective clients.

To see how a nice guy can play the Insulator role, I spoke with Dr. Jeff Scott, one of the few professionals in the United States representing only medical doctors. Scott, an unassuming Oklahoma native in his fifties, is just about as different from Rosenhaus as a guy can be. In place of the slicked-back hair and Italian suits, Scott, who continues to practice medicine as a gastroenterologist, favors a simple shirt and slacks under a surgical gown. While Rosenhaus is a bachelor who seems to devote his life to his clients, Scott is a family man with five children. Rosenhaus is a yeller, but Scott projects a calm, quiet confidence. And whereas Rosenhaus jumped into agenting while still in law school, Scott deliberated for 15 years before he decided to start representing doctors—especially rookies just out of their residencies or fellowships—in their contract negotiations with hospitals and medical groups.

In his years of practicing medicine, Scott says, he saw example after example of the problems he's now trying to fix. "Whenever a young physician goes in and talks about their contract, they're talking to someone with a lot of business experience," Scott says.[20] These veteran negotiators, he explains, have seen many contracts and often have corporate muscle behind them—"whereas the resident or fellow doesn't have anyone behind them. So it's not a peer-to-peer negotiation." That's one problem, but young doctors are also hamstrung by role expectations. "One of the things that's pounded into you in residency and fellowship is that medicine is not a money-making endeavor, that it's higher than that. So whenever young doctors come out of their training, they're just very concerned about how [negotiating] will make them look," he says. "They're deathly afraid of asking for more money or more *anything* because they don't want to be seen as money-grubbing. They want to know the numbers, but they're afraid to look like they have that much interest in the numbers. So having me be able to talk about actual money kind of relieves them of their burden, and they can wash their hands of it." By negotiating on a young doctor's behalf, Scott solves both problems: he helps correct the power imbalance while insulating the doctor from senior colleagues' perceptions that the new doctor is in medicine for the wrong reasons.

Scott doesn't have to be a threatening loudmouth to get results because his approach is data-driven, which he finds to be an effective way to keep conversations businesslike. "My style is to say, 'let's look at the objective numbers,'" he says. The numbers he needs are in a volume called the MGMA book. The MGMA is the Medical Group Management Association, a membership organization of hospitals and medical groups that conducts surveys of physician practices.

"They generate all this financial data, so if you're an obstetrician in Florida, then you can look in the MGMA book and see the median salary is this." Because new physicians aren't MGMA members, they don't normally have access to this salary information—but Scott and the people he negotiates with do. "I try to just develop a peer-to-peer type of conversation, and I use objective data," he says simply.

In a system where insurance companies set uniform fees for services without regard to doctor quality (and young doctors come in with no track record anyway), Scott says you should go into negotiations with the assumption that any particular doctor is average and, therefore, should be paid a salary near the midpoint. He tells his negotiation counterparts, "The MGMA says the median salary is this, so that's what we need to go to." He also knows the ins and outs of standard physician contracts, so he can ask that particularly onerous clauses be struck or for missing elements be put in. For example, one chief surgery resident he represented was being courted by a hospital that wanted her to work in its trauma center, but the hospital wasn't offering her any on-call pay. Another client was being hired by a hospital with a paltry retirement plan; to make up for this shortfall, Scott asked that his client get a stipend of $5,000 per month. Coming from Scott, and framed in the logic of numbers, requests for concessions don't seem inappropriate at all; if anything, since a large hospital knows that Scott knows what kinds of salary and benefits are standard, it might seem unseemly for them to deny his requests. It's hard to balk at his numbers and his reasoning without seeming unreasonable yourself.

Since objective data is central to Scott's approach, you wonder whether young doctors could do just as well for themselves if only they had the MGMA book, but Scott thinks that's about as likely as getting a successful appendectomy by giving someone an instruction manual. "Maybe you get the appendix out and the patient survives, and maybe you don't." Negotiation requires people skills—the ability to build rapport, to pick up on subtle cues, to know when to speak up and when to stay silent. Successful negotiation also requires being able to take the perspective of the other person, something that's far easier to do if you've actually been in the other person's shoes before, the way Scott has been during his long career in medicine. But even if you have the skills, there's still the young doctor's concern "that I don't want to come across as greedy and turn them off and get in a fight with a potential employer." As the doctor's representative, Scott is in an entirely different position. "I may bring up that I know you really need a general surgeon for trauma coverage, and I know you're going to make four million dollars a year off the surgeon's fees. I know that it's true, and so I can go ahead and say it. It's almost 180 degrees—if the [young physicians] knew those things, they'd still be reluctant to say it for fear of upsetting the employer." Even if the client is armed with full information, a good Insulator still helps.

Though Scott's world is medicine, he says he learned most of what he knows about being a middleman from his dad, who had owned a small auto-parts store and also often played merchant on the side. "He traded cars, he bought livestock—he was always buying and selling something." So Scott had plenty of opportunity to pick up his dad's ways. "I've seen the over-the-top car salesmen and the Jerry-Maguire-type people, and I'm sure that's fine in a business where everyone is trying to outshout the other person. My style probably comes from my dad being calm, being objective, and treating the other person as a human being. The worst thing is if the physician is excited about this practice and for me to kill [the deal]. If I do that, I've completely failed. So I self-monitor myself to make sure I never overstep those bounds."

Scott learned something else from watching his dad. "He knew that what he had had some value, whether it was a shovel or a cow or a car or whatever it was. And I think he was really good at reading people and kind of gauging how interested they are and what they are willing to do." These skills obviously come in handy when you're negotiating a compensation package or doing any kind of deal.

A Duty-Bound, Heroic Role

After you hear a few skilled Insulators talk about their work, you start to notice a pattern: consciously or not, they cast themselves in a duty-bound, sometimes even heroic, role. Agents and attorneys have a fiduciary duty to their clients—they're trusted representatives with a legal obligation to act in the interest of the client—but in the minds of great agents the duty seems to go beyond that and becomes a higher calling. Drew Rosenhaus has called himself a ruthless warrior, a hit man willing to do anything in his power to help his clients, and even compared himself to Batman. That's Rosenhaus being Rosenhaus, but other Insulators take on pro-client mantles, too. Jeff Scott sees himself more as a protective older brother to his clients, looking out for their financial security and "not letting other people take advantage of them just because they're ignorant of their value." Carol Shamon, the San Diego-based modeling agent introduced in the Certifier chapter, says that though she's a nice person, she sometimes becomes a fierce "mama bear" to protect the talent she represents.

Even a lawyer who's a good Insulator doesn't see himself as merely an expert in the law. That's a point made by Hubert Willman, a seasoned attorney who negotiates deals at the mergers and acquisitions firm Martin Wolf based in Danville, California.[21] When one company buys another or goes up for sale, many millions of dollars and entire careers are at stake; therefore, it makes sense that companies typically turn to professionals to negotiate the deal. Even serial entrepreneurs have limited experience selling a company, but professional mergers and acquisitions firms do it every day. It's more than expertise that these firms offer; they create a protective layer between buyers and sellers. Willman explains it this way: "Sometimes the person who's selling the company wants the opportunity to stay with the company, and in negotiations they don't want a bitterness to arise between them and the buyer. And likewise the buyer who needs the management to stay doesn't want to arouse any bitterness." Willman can present both sides' requests diplomatically and unemotionally; if one side reacts in anger, he can dampen those feelings to prevent the conflict from escalating. And when the deal is done, the buyer and seller can continue a working relationship with no residual ill will. Making that happen is all in a day's work for an Insulator.

Willman stresses that he's not just a lawyer, but an attorney. "The essence of a lawyer is being an expert in the law, and the essence of an attorney is acting on behalf of another," he says. Willman isn't splitting hairs here: the distinction drives his whole approach to his work. "You're representing your client who wants to enter into a transaction or agreement with another party, and the purpose of your negotiation is to reach an agreement—a good agreement," he explains. To him, that means carrying out the negotiation without giving anyone the impression that it's a contest or a game: you're not trying to take advantage of someone else. But representing someone else also means you have no problem asking for things. "If you're negotiating on behalf of a client, you don't look like a bad guy or like you're cheap—you're just looking out for your client." You're not merely a lawyer, the butt of countless jokes; you're an attorney, an advocate and champion of your clients' interests.

Robert Boland, the lawyer who teaches sports management at NYU, makes a point along the same lines. "We're always a better advocate for other people than for ourselves," he says, adding the adage that the lawyer who represents himself has a fool for a client. Boland says that when he took his job at NYU, he not only didn't negotiate, he didn't even ask how much he was going to make. He surely wouldn't neglect asking these questions if he were working on behalf of a client. Why? For the same reason Willman mentioned. When faced with negotiating on our own behalf, we're one person torn between two roles: the individual and the team player. The individual in us wants to look out for our own interest, but another voice inside of us frets that speaking up on our own behalf will jeopardize relationships by making us look cheap or greedy or less than a team player.

To resolve this tension, it's often easiest (and feels less risky) to just drop the role of self-interested individual. Copious research shows that women, who more than men are expected to choose cooperation over competition, are particularly likely to make this sacrifice.[22] But when we negotiate on behalf of another, the role conflict disappears: what's good for our client is also good for us personally. The interests of the individual and of the team (or client) are well aligned, so women end up doing as well or better than men in negotiating on behalf of others, such as friends or protégés.[23] Psychologist Margaret Neale, a negotiations professor at the Stanford Graduate School of Business, says that female CEOs have told her they have no problem negotiating on behalf of their company but find it hard to ask the board of directors for their own raise. "As a woman, it is unacceptable for me to be greedy on my own," Neale explains, "but it's completely acceptable for me to negotiate for someone else, because that is a caretaking thing, a communal thing."[24] A middleman who understands these tensions can provide a lot of value to clients, especially for women, doctors, or other people who have qualms about advocating for themselves. And you can play this role well whether you're a man or a woman. As Willman says, when you're serving as an advocate, you don't come out looking bad—you're just doing your job and doing a good one at that.

In fact, a growing body of psychological research on what's been called the Robin Hood effect shows that when we act on behalf of others, we'll go to great lengths (even moral compromises) to correct inequality. For example, experiments by University of Southern California psychologist Scott Wiltermuth show that people are actually more willing to cheat when the rewards from cheating are split between the cheater and another person.[25] By representing another person, the Insulator can reframe what might be seen as selfishness into a form of altruism.

Since we're willing to fight harder on behalf of other people than we are for ourselves, to be a more powerful Insulator it seems helpful to visualize a specific character or role that matches the kind of professional you want to be known as. Whatever mantle appeals to you—an attorney who champions the client, a big brother who keeps the little guy from being taken advantage of, a mama bear protecting her cubs, or a ferocious warrior who's not afraid to stand up to powerful teams in the face of public scorn—imagining yourself in a heroic role may give you the oomph to do what it takes to play the role well.

Insulation Needs Are All Around

Knowing the value of being an Insulator gives middlemen an underused way to market themselves. An interesting example comes from a woman named Sara Garden, one of the many professionals most of us don't ordinarily think of as a middleman. Garden owns Rocky Mountain Home Staging, a small company in Boulder, Colorado, that helps home sellers make their houses attractive to buyers. Home staging typically entails decluttering, moving furniture, and generally making a space feel bigger and more inviting; Garden, like most professional stagers, understands that people resist making such changes. Even if a house is in bad shape, homeowners don't like to hear it. But Garden has a deeper insight: she gets that the sellers' agents are torn about making staging recommendations themselves. On the one hand, a real-estate agent knows that a well-staged house sells more easily; on the other hand, an agent doesn't want to offend a client. That tension makes sellers' agents a perfect prospect for Garden's services, and on her website she has a section just for them. She says that "75 percent of homeowners think that their home décor is fabulous as is and any mention of changing it can be an emotional minefield," and, immediately after, makes this selling point: "At Rocky Mountain Home Staging our role and relationship with the seller is different. It's ok for us to be the bad guy. We can be the one who tells them straight up that their house smells like pee or that the wallpaper border absolutely must be removed. We will do it kindly, we will do it gently and we will do it honestly."[26] Sara Garden understands role conflict, she gets that even a middleman might need an Insulator, and she pitches herself as the right person to serve that role.

If you keep your eye out, you'll see insulation needs—and opportunities—all around you. Sometimes that creates a niche for a new business, as it did for Dr. Jeff Scott. And sometimes it's just an easy way to do someone a favor. When a colleague of mine accompanied her husband to his class reunion, and a classmate asked him what he'd been up to, he gave a brief answer that she didn't think did justice to his accomplishments, so she piped up to brag on his behalf, mentioning his recent promotion. He came out looking not only more accomplished, but more modest, too. Similarly, the morning Al Roth won the Nobel Prize and Stanford held a press conference, it was not Roth who explained what made his work so impressive, but the department chairman, economist Jon Levin, who mentioned that he was speaking because it would be awkward for Roth to do so. Whether you put in a good word for a deserving colleague or make a request that a friend would feel awkward asking for herself, playing the Insulator is another way to win friends and influence people.

CONCLUSION
THE MIDDLEMAN ECONOMY

MICHAEL DELL, WHO IN THE 1990S TRANSFORMED the PC market by selling personal computers directly to users, begins his book *Direct from Dell* by recounting an early lesson in cutting out the middleman.

His best friend's father had been an avid stamp collector, so young Dell and his friend got into the hobby, too. Soon enough, noticing that prices for stamps were rising, Dell saw an opportunity to make some money. "My friend and I had already bought stamps at an auction," Dell writes, "and since I knew even then that people rarely did something for nothing, I assumed that the auctioneers were making a decent fee. Rather than pay them to buy the stamps, I thought it would be fun to create my own auction. Then I could learn even more about stamps and collect a commission in the process."[1]

Dell goes on to describe how he went about the venture. "First, I got a bunch of people in the neighborhood to consign their stamps to me. Then I advertised 'Dell's Stamps' in *Linn's Stamp Journal*, the trade journal of the day. And then I typed, with one finger, a twelve-page catalog (I didn't yet know how to type, nor did I have a computer) and mailed it out. Much to my surprise, I made $2,000."

If you've been with me throughout this book, at least one of the ironies of this story should leap off the page: in a venture that Michael Dell saw as his first experience of eliminating the middleman, he didn't actually eliminate the middleman. Instead, he went from being a buyer to being a seller—and in the process, he became a stamp dealer himself. After all, he wasn't selling only his own stamps. That wouldn't have made for a lucrative business no matter how quickly stamp prices were rising. Nor would it have made as enticing a catalog for buyers, since he wouldn't be able to offer as wide a selection. No, Dell had gotten his neighbors to consign their stamps to him, earning a profit from connecting people who had stamps to sell with those who wanted to buy them. The boy who would go on to achieve fame and fortune for cutting out the middleman had become a middleman—and even years later, he didn't see himself as one.

There is another irony in Dell's pride in cutting out the middleman, one that wouldn't become apparent until several years after his book's publication in 1999. Although Dell Computers did amazingly well selling without middlemen for a long while, by the mid-2000s the direct-sales approach ceased to take Dell "direct to the top." Hewlett-Packard came to outrank Dell in PC sales, and other competing manufacturers chomped away at Dell's market share, too. In 2007, Dell finally admitted that it was time for a radical change, and began selling its computers through Walmart, Best Buy, and other retailers.[2] Having eliminated the middleman, Michael Dell brought the middleman back.

What happened? Why did direct sales work well before but not a few years later? It was a mix of reasons. Computers got cheaper and more powerful: a standard model became capable of doing everything most PC buyers wanted, so customization, a big draw of buying direct from the warehouse, lost much of its appeal. Lower-cost computers also meant that the shipping costs of a custom order came to represent a higher fraction of the purchase price; buying from the store then became cheaper than ordering from the warehouse.[3] Stores also offered something the warehouses never could: the opportunity for customers to see, feel, and try out a product; that wasn't so important when people were buying desktop models, but it became much more so when they shopped for laptops, which were gaining in popularity at this time.[4] So whereas selling direct in the 1990s enabled Dell to give customers what they wanted at a lower cost to itself, changing market conditions meant that the exact opposite was true in the mid-2000s.

In general, whether it's better to sell direct or through a middleman depends on a number of factors. The Dell example shows that the cost of the products, transportation costs, and the degree of the customer's desire to try before they buy are some of the considerations. We should be suspicious, therefore, of any sweeping claims about the benefits of cutting out the middleman.

In many ways, the Internet is a middleman's ally. Thanks to the Internet, middlemen who used to do business in person—a position that limited their geographic reach—can attract customers from all over and can share information with them more quickly and easily than ever. At the same time, the chapters on Certifiers and Enforcers showed that as people began doing business with people they didn't know, they came to need trusted third parties to guarantee the quality of goods and services sold. The Internet also creates such an abundance of information that, as the Concierge chapter showed, buyers need help navigating through it all. Sellers, for their part, need help "cutting through the clutter," as marketers put it, to get the attention of buyers. And as Internet-based tools have matured, it's become more efficient to hire specialists to use them on our behalf; middlemen who take the hassle out of selling used cars and clothes are benefiting from this development. The Internet has also made it cheaper and easier to start a software business, a trend that, as we saw in the chapter on Risk Bearers, gave rise to micro-VCs, those middlemen who sift through thousands of business ideas each year to pick the ones most likely to bring impressive returns to investors.

Several middleman roles are timeless. The chapter on Risk Bearers showed that we have always relied on middlemen to even out ups and downs of uncertain demand and supply; today's "Uber of" this or that is just the latest technological application of this basic role. The chapters on Certifiers and Enforcers showed how effective middlemen reduce informational asymmetries between buyers and sellers. The Insulator chapter showed how a middleman can act as an equalizer, righting the balance of power between the less experienced players on one side and the experts on the other or enabling the novices to tout their merits and ask for more of what they want than they could comfortably do on their own. In many situations, the middleman gives the less informed, more vulnerable players more knowledge and power, thus serving not as a third wheel in a relationship between two parties but as the indispensable fulcrum between the two sides.

Needing to keep the two sides in balance is a constant for middlemen. Whether they work as talent agents, used-car dealers, or venture capitalists, successful middlemen realize that it is not enough to serve one side; to thrive, they must provide value for both sides, treating both sides well. Jason Horejs, the gallerist we met in the chapter on Risk Bearers, said it well: "As a middleman, you need to realize that your customer is not just the person who is buying the product that you're selling—you've also got to be selling yourself and proving your value to your suppliers. I wouldn't be in business if it weren't for the artists." This dual responsibility is especially true of middleman businesses that have features of a two-sided market, one in which buyers want to be where good sellers are and vice versa. The balancing act can be challenging since the wants of the two sides sometimes conflict, but middlemen who manage it well create a virtuous cycle: by and large, the most admired middlemen attract the best buyers, who in turn attract the best sellers, who attract more of the best buyers, and so on. A two-sided market is not a perpetual-motion machine, though: middlemen must continually work to ensure their policies, attitudes, and prices are serving the needs of both sides.

In general, middlemen who prefer a steady business over a constant hustle take the long view, sacrificing short-term gains for the benefit of larger gains over time. They take the time to become an expert in a specific niche, they swallow the costs of one side's bad actions, and they build relationships of trust over many interactions. During this growth curve, they are patiently investing in their future: such investments are more likely to pay off for a middleman who is in it for the long haul than they would be for an occasional buyer and seller. Initially, it can be tempting to go for the quick gain by accepting a kickback, by skimping on quality, or by vouching for people you don't know well—but that approach is not sustainable. In the long run, shortcuts will cost a middleman more than they are worth, tarnishing the middleman's reputation as a Certifier, Enforcer, or Concierge.

Middlemen get a bad rap. There are many ways to be a good middleman in both senses of the word: good at what you do and good for society. That means being able to deliver what your trading partners expect—and the first step to that is knowing what they expect. A middleman who does a fine job as a Certifier when the customer also expects an Enforcer will fail that customer. So if you are a middleman, I hope you will think about what roles you are good at, which skills your trading partners value, and which ones you would benefit from honing. If you are a buyer or seller, I hope this book has given you the language to express what you're looking for from the middlemen in your life. And if you're an aspiring middleman, I hope you appreciate how challenging middleman work can be—and also see opportunities to do this work well in whatever industry interests you.

ACKNOWLEDGMENTS

EVERY REPORTER IS A MIDDLEMAN: OUR STOCK IN trade is information, and we are only as good as our sources. My ideal sources for this book were busy, successful professionals—accomplished middlemen and scholars—so I could never be sure they would grant me time for an interview. I am grateful that almost everyone did and that they spoke with candor and insight.

Several people not quoted in the book also generously gave of their time and expertise, helping in ways large and small: Max Bazerman of the Harvard Business School, Matthew Bidwell of the Wharton School of Business, Doug Diamond of the University of Chicago Booth School of Business, Matt Jackson of Stanford University, Anna Kovner of the Federal Reserve Bank of New York, Chris Malone of Fidelum Partners, Brian Mittendorf of Ohio State University, Susan Shapiro of the American Bar Foundation, Caroline Tipler of Tulane University, and Steven Wu of Purdue University.

I'd also like to thank a few experts for suggesting leads and making introductions: Joe Liu of Boston College Law School, Heidi Roizen of Draper Fisher Jurvetson (DFJ), Andy Sellars of the Berkman Center for Internet and Society, Stephan Seiler of Stanford University Graduate School of Business, and Monic Sun of Boston University.

Laurie Harting, my editor at Palgrave Macmillan, was a major partner on this project. She really got what I was trying to accomplish, allowed me abundant time to do it, and trusted me to do it right. When the manuscript came in, Laurie knew just what to keep and what to cut and really listened to my opinions. That is the kind of give-and-take an author wants.

Jim Levine, of Levine Greenberg Rostan, has been a virtuoso of an agent. Many people think of literary agents as salespeople or gatekeepers, but Jim shows that the most admirable ones are so much more. Jim masterfully played every one of the six middle-man roles and then some, showing an unparalleled mix of efficiency and care. I am amazed that someone who responds to e-mails within minutes also finds the time to read and provide thoughtful feedback on multiple drafts. Jim exemplifies the joy of matchmaking and the rewards of taking the long view.

I have never met a more astute editor than my colleague, friend, and first reader Ea Macom, who brought her intelligence, erudition, and natural curiosity to every chapter she critiqued. Her thought-provoking questions, her suggestions, and her "middleman sight-ings" made this book immeasurably better.

Where would I be without my writer friends? They listened to my ideas, suggested leads, and proffered encouragement and guidance to help me clamber over various hurdles. I am especially grateful to Jill Adams, Howard Baldwin, Charlotte Huff, Ed Iwata, Debbie Abrams Kaplan, Julia Klein, Roberta Kwok, Jas Lonnquist, Paul McHugh, Kristin Ohlson, and Cynthia Ramnarace.

The ever-gracious Patty Devlin Hart has long been a treasured friend and confidante; our walks always enrich my days.

Other friends who've given practical and moral support over the years include Helen Stavropoulos Sandoval, Leslie Stompor, Krista Willman Formica, Donna Lee, Cynthia Chin-Lee, and Cindy Saenz-Weinand.

For specific help with this project, my thanks also go to Alisa Bowman, Liza Boyd, Kay-Yut Chen, Susan Freinkel, Connie Hale, Laird Harrison, Sonja Lyubomirsky, Jennifer Margulis, Ginny McCormick, Kelly McGonigal, and Philip Yam.

I'd like to call out the biggest influences behind the very existence of this book. I spent the first nine years of my life in the Soviet Union, where my parents opened my eyes to the ways that profit-seeking middlemen relieved some of the dysfunctions of that nation's planned economy. Such early conversations probably explain why *The Merchant of Venice* left such a deep impression when I encountered it in high school: with its multiple merchants, Shakespeare's most economically oriented play got me thinking more deeply about why some middlemen are admired while others are reviled. Later, living in Silicon Valley during the dot-com boom, I saw my share of headlines about disintermediation—and sensed that the elimination of middlemen was more wishful thinking than economic reality. The rise of companies like Airbnb and Uber in recent years has made it clear to me that the Internet was helping make middlemen more important than ever.

The economist Kay-Yut Chen, with whom I had the privilege to collaborate on *Secrets of the Moneylab*, was an inspiration as well. Kay-Yut has an infectious enthusiasm for economic modeling, economic experiments, and operations research: he is the sort of person who can make supply chains sound interesting. Although some of the most important questions about supply chains are clearly beyond the scope of this book (don't ask me about the double marginalization problem!), talking with Kay-Yut made me see that most of a supply chain is just a series of middlemen in which each link plays a special role—and in which the links aren't always pulling in the same direction. Not long after our book came out, and I was casting about for my next big project, I heard a memorable episode of one of my favorite podcasts, Econtalk. The topic was middlemen, of course, and one point of discussion between host Russ Roberts and frequent guest Mike Munger was the story of Radford's POW camp, which I had somehow never heard until then. I was captivated— but was my fascination with middlemen just a geeky obsession or a topic worthy of a commercial book? I might have talked myself into the former had the wonderfully wise Marla Beck not convinced me otherwise. This book has been such a pleasure to research and write and so satisfying to have completed: I thank Marla for nudging me to take the first step and thank my readers for staying with me until the end.

My deepest and most enduring appreciation is for my family. My multitalented, hard-working, and loving husband made me coffee every morning and tipped me off to one of my favorite stories in this book. By nature a skeptic, he always has faith in me. We (and our children) are fortunate not only to live near our parents and our in-laws but also to enjoy a close relationship with them; they have always supported our endeavors. Of course, I must gush about our sweet, bright, enthusiastic children. Through everything they do and everything they are, they bring immense joy, love, pride, and meaning to our lives. In what is a long list of blessings, the two of them are number one.

NOTES

INTRODUCTION: NOBODY LIKES A MIDDLEMAN, BUT MOST OF US ARE MIDDLEMEN

1. Mike Lee, "Senator Mike Lee's Response to the State of the Union Address," January 29, 2014, retrieved from http://www.lee.senate.gov/public/index.cfm /speeches?ID=46dfc240-026d-4825-a9bd-b876bc0e7a4d on December 10, 2014.
2. Perhaps he was alluding to the insurance companies whose revenues rose from the Affordable Care Act.
3. The share of Americans who consider themselves middle class has fallen from 53 percent in 2008 to 44 percent in 2014 according to survey data from the Pew Research Center. See Rakesh Kochnar and Rich Morin, "Despite Recovery, Fewer Americans Identify as Middle Class" (Pew Research Center, January 27, 2014, retrieved from http://www.pewresearch.org/fact-tank/2014/01/27 /despite-recovery-fewer-americans-identify-as-middle-class/).
4. Why do I use the sexist word "middleman"? Unfortunately, English has no gender-neutral version of this word, and any alternative I considered fails for other reasons. "Middleperson" is too clunky. "Matchmaker" is too narrow, as are "broker," "liaison," and "go-between." "Intermediary" is probably closest in meaning to "middleman," but it doesn't have the same connotations, the cultural baggage around middlemen that I aim to unpack in this book. (When was the last time you heard someone talk of "cutting out the *intermediary*"?) Throughout the book, you will meet both female and male middlemen, and though the word "middlemen" will continue to evoke images of men more than of women (as sexist words tend to do), I tried to maintain a gender balance in my text by using female pronouns where appropriate; for example, if a headhunter in this book is a *he*, a hiring manager is a *she*.
5. The *Oxford English Dictionary* makes this derogatory connotation explicit when defining the middleman as "a person standing in an intermediate relation to two parties (often with unfavourable connotations, as implying that direct relations between these parties would be preferable); an intermediary, a go-between; a person who deals in stolen goods." The currently predominant use, the dictionary notes, is "a trader, company, etc., that handles a commodity between its producer and its consumer." Though that sounds neutral enough, several of the examples cited under that entry suggest a negative attitude toward middlemen, such as this advertisement dating from 1921: "Two wonderful Susquehanna Broadcloth Flannel Shirts only $3.69. Direct from factory. No middlemen's profits." See *OED Online*, September 2014. Oxford University Press, retrieved from http://www.oed.com/view/Entry/118156?rskey=a6DVRh&result=1.

6. Bill Gates, *The Road Ahead* (New York: Viking, 1995), 182. Although some of his predictions proved incorrect, Gates did accurately predict that those middlemen who continue to add value will thrive.

7. LinkedIn currently has three revenue streams: Talent Solutions (services specifically for recruiters), Premium Subscriptions (the paid advanced-search service for job searchers and others), and Marketing Solutions (paid ads). For the second quarter of 2014, the most recent period for which data is available, Talent Solutions revenue totaled $322 million while revenue from Premium Subscriptions was $105 million, and revenue from Marketing Solutions was $106 million. See "LinkedIn Announces Second Quarter 2014 Results," LinkedIn press release, July 31, 2014, retrieved from http://investors.linked in.com/releasedetail.cfm?ReleaseID=863494). This is no accident: the company understands that it is operating in a multisided market, where offering low-price or even free entry to one side (in this case, job seekers) will attract plenty of high-paying participants on the other side (recruiters whose livelihood depends on finding the right job seekers).

8. Joe Light, "In Zillow-Trulia Deal, Making Room for Brokers," *Wall Street Journal*, July 28, 2014. For a deeper look at the business models of the real estate sites, see Brad Stone, "Why Redfin, Zillow, and Trulia Haven't Killed Off Real-Estate Brokers," *Bloomberg Businessweek*, March 7, 2013.

9. This is the figure for the most recent year available, 2013, according to the National Association of Realtors, which reports that 9 percent of houses were listed for sale by owner. See "Home Buyers and Sellers Survey Shows Lingering Impact of Tight Credit" (National Association of Realtors, press release, November 13, 2013).

10. Brooks Barnes and Hunter Atkins, "Hollywood's Old-Time Star Makers Are Swooping In on YouTube's Party," *New York Times*, September 15, 2014; and Katherine Rosman, "Grumpy Cat Has an Agent, and Now a Movie Deal," *Wall Street Journal*, May 31, 2013.

11. Noam Cohen, "When Stars Twitter, a Ghost May Be Lurking," *New York Times*, March 26, 2009; and Evan Dashevsky, "Who's Writing Your Favorite Celebrity's Tweets," *PC World*, November 2013.

12. Daniel F. Spulber, *Market Microstructure: Intermediaries and the Theory of the Firm* (New York: Cambridge University Press, 1999), 21.

13. E-mail correspondence with Daniel Spulber, September 28, 2011. See also Daniel F. Spulber, "Should Business Method Inventions Be Patentable?" *Journal of Legal Analysis* 3, no. 1(2011): 279.

14. Interview with Mike Maples Jr., September 17, 2014.

15. The notion that middlemen accelerate connections might be called the catalyst view of middlemen. (In fact, an early book about two-sided markets—an increasingly common type of middleman business we look at in later chapters—is called *Catalyst Code*.) Other scholars reserve "catalyst" for the type of middleman who creates new connections between individuals, as opposed to the type of middleman who facilitates the flow of goods and ideas without actually introducing the two sides of the exchange. For details about this distinction, see Katherine Stovel and Lynette Shaw, "Brokerage," *Annual Review of Sociology* (2012): 139–58.

16. In a review of the scholarly research on entrepreneurship, the sociologist Patricia Thornton sums up the VC's accelerating function this way: "Because they sit at the center of extended networks linking financiers, entrepreneurs, corporate executives, headhunters and consultants, venture capitalists

have a propulsive effect on the rates of business formations." See Patricia H. Thornton, "The Sociology of Entrepreneurship," *Annual Review of Sociology* (1999): 29.

17. Scholars in various fields have proposed many different ways of classifying middleman roles. One pair of sociologists have suggested the roles of coordinator, liaison, representative, gatekeeper, and itinerant broker. See Roger V. Gould and Roberto M. Fernandez, "Structures of Mediation: a Formal Approach to Brokerage in Transaction Networks," *Sociological Methodology* 19 (1989): 89–126. Marketing scholars have long catalogued middlemen's functions, such as sharing risk, transporting goods, and others; for an overview, see Eric H. Shaw and D. G. Brian Jones, "A History of Schools of Marketing Thought," *Marketing Theory* 5, no. 3 (2005): 239–81. My approach, which organizes middlemen's roles by the type of problems they alleviate, combines elements from theories of marketing, economics, and sociology.

18. The economist Stefan W. Schmitz has described this mistake as "the main fallacy of the Threatened Intermediaries Hypothesis." See Stefan W. Schmitz, "The Effects of Electronic Commerce on the Structure of Intermediation," *Journal of Computer-Mediated Communication* 5, no. 3 (March 2000), http://onlinelibrary.wiley.com/doi/10.1111/j.1083-6101.2000.tb00343.x/full.

19. A good explanation of this counterargument is Mitra Barun Sarkar, Brian Butler, and Charles Steinfield, "Intermediaries and Cybermediaries: A Continuing Role for Mediating Players in the Electronic Marketplace," *Journal of Computer-Mediated Communication* 1, no. 3 (December 1995).

20. For a discussion of this point, see Charles Steinfield, "Dispelling Common Misperceptions about the Effects of Electronic Commerce on Market Structure," Presentation to the 35th Anniversary Conference of the Chinese University of Hong Kong, July 24–26, 2000.

21. Nancy Trejos, "Travelers Turn Back to Travel Agents," *Washington Post*, April 25, 2011.

22. Interview with Ellison Poe, June 20, 2014.

23. Thomas Petzinger Jr., *The New Pioneers: The Men and Women Who Are Transforming the Workplace and Marketplace* (New York: Simon & Schuster, 1999): 61.

24. Susan T. Fiske, Amy J. C. Cuddy, and Peter Glick, "Universal Dimensions of Social Cognition: Warmth and Competence," *TRENDS in Cognitive Sciences* 11, no. 2 (2007): 77–84.

25. Consider this headline from a newspaper in the United Kingdom: "Time to ditch the blood-sucking social media gurus," the story accompanied by a Dracula look-alike.

26. Caroline Tipler and Janet B. Ruscher, "Agency's Role in Dehumanization: Non-Human Metaphors of Out-Groups," *Social and Personality Psychology Compass* 8, no. 5 (2014): 214–28.

27. Robert L. Steiner, "The Prejudice against Marketing," *Journal of Marketing* 40 (July 1976): 2–9.

28. Edna Bonacich, "A Theory of Middleman Minorities," *American Sociological Review* 38, no. 5 (October 1973): 583–94.

29. Matt Taibbi, "The Great American Bubble Machine," *Rolling Stone*, July 2009.

30. Other brands in this quadrant were AIG (bailed out by taxpayers), BP (following the fatal explosion and oil spill in the Gulf of Mexico), and Marlboro (the cigarette brand). See Nicolas Kervyn, Susan T. Fiske, and Chris Malone,

"Brands As Intentional Agents Framework: How Perceived Intentions and Ability Can Map Brand Perception," *Journal of Consumer Psychology* 22, no. 2 (2012): 166–76.

31. Eugene F. Fama and Kenneth R. French, "Luck versus Skill in the Cross-Section of Mutual Fund Returns," *The Journal of Finance* 65, no. 5 (October 2010): 1915–47.

32. Stephen R. Foerster, Juhani T. Linnainmaa, Brian T. Melzer, and Alessandro Previtero, "Retail Financial Advice: Does One Size Fit All?" *Chicago Booth Research Paper,* no. 14–38 (November 2014).

33. Paul Solman, "Are You Getting Ripped Off by Money Management Fees?" PBS, *The Rundown* (blog), January 11, 2013.

34. Stephanie Mencimer, "Why You Can't Buy a New Car Online," *Mother Jones*, February 10, 2009.

35. Amy Cuddy, Susan Fiske, and Peter Glick, "Warmth and Competence as Universal Dimensions of Social Perception: The Stereotype Content Model and the BIAS Map," *Advances in Experimental Social Psychology* 40 (2008): 61–149.

36. Julia Moskin, "Helping the Third World One Banana at a Time," *New York Times*, May 5, 2004.

37. Sibylla Brodzinsky, "Central American Farmers Stay One Step Ahead of Profit-hungry 'Coyotes,'" *The Guardian*, June 25, 2013.

38. Steve Stecklow and Erin White, "At Some Retailers, 'Fair Trade' Carries a Very High Cost," *Wall Street Journal*, June 8, 2004; and Jennifer Alsever, "Fair Prices for Farmers: Simple Idea, Complex Reality," *New York Times*, March 19, 2006.

39. Ellen E. Schultz and Theo Francis, "High-Interest Lenders Tap Elderly, Disabled," *Wall Street Journal,* February 12, 2008.

40. Edward Wyatt, "Inventive, At Least in Court," *New York Times*, July 16, 2013; and Andrei Hagiu and David B. Yoffie, "The New Patent Intermediaries: Platforms: Defensive Aggregators, and Super-Aggregators," *Journal of Economic Perspectives* 27, no. 1 (Winter 2013): 45–66.

41. Gina Kolata, "Scientific Articles Accepted (Personal Checks, Too)," *New York Times*, April 7, 2013.

42. Amy Cuddy, Susan Fiske, and Peter Glick, "The BIAS Map: Behaviors from Intergroup Affect and Stereotypes," *Journal of Personality and Social Psychology* 92, no. 4 (2007): 631–48.

1 THE BRIDGE: SPANNING THE CHASM

1. Zero-sum thinking is an example of what has been called "folk economics," incorrect intuitions about economic behavior shared by many noneconomists. See Paul H. Rubin, "Folk Economics," *Southern Economic Journal* 30, no. 1 (July 2003).

2. R. A. Radford, "The Economic Organisation of a P.O.W. Camp," *Economica* 12, no. 14 (November 1945): 189–201

3. "Unfortunately," Radford writes, "the writer knows little of the workings of these people: public opinion was hostile and the professionals were usually of a retiring disposition."

4. Victoria Barret, "Dropbox: The Inside Story of Tech's Hottest Startup," *Forbes*, November 7, 2011.

5. Nicole Perlroth, "Venture Capital Firms, Once Discreet, Learn the Promotional Game," *New York Times*, July 22, 2012.

6. Interview with Pejman Nozad, February 27, 2014.

7. Tiziana Casciaro, Francesca Gino, and Maryam Kouchaki, "The Contaminating Effects of Building Instrumental Ties: How Networking Can Make Us Feel Dirty," *Administrative Science Quarterly* 59, no. 4(2014): 705–35.

8. Kent Grayson, "Friendship Versus Business in Marketing Relationships," *Journal of Marketing* 71 (October 2007): 121–39.

9. Victoria Barret, "7 Networking Secrets from Silicon Valley's Greatest Connector," *Forbes*, March 21, 2012.

10. Interview with Pejman Nozad, February 13, 2014.

11. This is the principle of "indirect reciprocity": I help you and somebody else helps me. See Martin A. Nowak and Karl Sigmund, "Evolution of Indirect Reciprocity," *Nature* 437 (2005): 1291–98.

12. Differences in terminology stem from the fact that social network analysis comes from different fields. For example, graph theory in computer science uses the term "edge" for what social scientists call a "tie."

13. For example, see Nathan Eagle, Sandy Pentland, and David Lazer, "Inferring Friendship Network Structure by Using Mobile Phone Data," *Proceedings of the National Academy of Sciences* 106, no. 36 (2009): 15274–78.

14. Sociologists also use the term "sociogram," whereas computer scientists favor "social graph." Both refer to a network diagram.

15. See, for example, Anatol Rapoport and William J. Horvath, "A Study of a Large Sociogram," *Behavioral Science* 6, no. 4 (October 1961): 279–91, and Carlo Morselli, *Inside Criminal Networks* (New York: Springer, 2009).

16. This is the principle of homophily: birds of a feather flock together.

17. Mark Granovetter, *Getting A Job: A Study of Contacts and Careers* (Cambridge, MA: Harvard University Press, 1974) and "The Strength of Weak Ties," *American Journal of Sociology* 78, no. 6 (May 1973): 1360–1380.

18. Ronald Burt, *Structural Holes: The Social Structure of Competition* (Harvard University Press, 1992).

19. Sociologists most often use the term "network broker" or simply "broker" to describe this person. I prefer the term "bridge" because it seems like the most concrete and neutral metaphor for that which spans a hole. Ron Burt has called this person an "entrepreneur" to emphasize the betweenness (*entre*) and the profit from unique opportunities as well as *tertius* (third), from sociologist Georg Simmel's notion of the *tertius gaudens*, or the rejoicing third, the third party who benefits from conflict between the other two. Because both "entre-preneur" and "broker" have other meanings, and the Latin *tertius* sounds aca-demic, I opt for Bridge. Note, though, that although the word "bridge" might suggest a link, I am thinking of it more as a node. Finally, note that Georg Simmel described another middleman, one without the sinister overtones of *tertius gaudens*—this is Simmel's *tertius iungens* (the third who joins).

20. Ron Burt, "Structural Holes and Good Ideas," *American Journal of Sociology* 110, no. 2 (September 2004): 349–399.

21. Victoria Barret, "Silicon Valley Cinderella," *Forbes*, March 21, 2012.

22. Ronald Burt, *Structural Holes: The Social Structure of Competition* (Harvard University Press, 1992), 28.

23. Burt used the word "bridge" to refer to the relationship, whereas I am using it to refer to the person.

24. Fortune Editors, "The Real Way to Build a Social Network," *Fortune*, January 24, 2012.

25. Interview with Ron Burt, February 10, 2014.

26. This research is described in Ron Burt, *Neighbor Networks* (New York: Oxford University Press, 2010).

27. Interview with LaJuan Stoxstill-Diggs, January 31, 2014.

28. See, for example, "Maureen Orth, "Killer@Craigslist," *Vanity Fair*, October 2009.

29. Buyers of classified ads saved $5 billion between 2000 and 2007 as a result of Craigslist entering the market. See Robert Seamans and Feng Zhu, "Responses to Entry in Multi-Sided Markets: The Impact of Craigslist on Local Newspapers," *Management Science* 60, no. 2 (February 2014): 476–493.

30. He is selling it online as an e-book. See LaJuan Stoxstill-Diggs, *The Craigslist Hustle* (LSD Publishing, 2009).

31. Interview with Jim Angel, February 3, 2014.

32. Anil K. Kashyap, Raghuram Rajan, and Jeremy C. Stein, "Banks as Liquidity Providers: An Explanation for the Coexistence of Lending and Deposit Taking," *The Journal of Finance* 57, no. 1 (February 2002): 33–73.

33. Interview with Genevieve Thiers, January 27, 2014.

34. Libby Kane, "Entrepreneurship 101: Interview with Genevieve Thiers," *LearnVest*, September 12, 2012.

35. Interview with Marc Rysman, January 31, 2014. Rysman's contribution to the literature is Marc Rysman, "The Economics of Two-Sided Markets," *Journal of Economic Perspectives* 23, no. 3 (2009). Another survey paper is Jean-Charles Rochet and Jean Tirole, "Two-sided Markets: A Progress Report," *RAND Journal of Economics* 37, no. 3 (September 2006): 646–67. The classic paper describing increasing returns to scale is W. Brian Arthur, "Competing Technologies, Increasing Returns, and Lock-In By Historical Events," *The Economic Journal* 99, no. 394 (March 1989). A less academic account of these ideas by the same author is W. Brian Arthur, "Increasing Returns and the New World of Business," *Harvard Business Review* 74, no. 4 (July/August 1996): 100–109.

36. These are called "indirect" because they refer to what is happening on the other side; direct network effects occur if users care how many other users are on the same side as they are. In addition, not all two-sided markets produce positive indirect network effects, and growth on one side can actually be a turnoff to the other side. For example, advertisers want to be where many readers in their target audience are, but readers aren't nearly as eager to see ads, so a media company can often attract a larger audience if it doesn't show ads. Whether the media company makes more money that way, though, is another story: the company might be better off taking ads, investing the ad revenue into higher quality, which can attract more readers.

37. For one discussion of this challenge, see David S. Evans and Richard Schmalensee, "Failure to Launch: Critical Mass in Platform Businesses," *Review of Network Economics* 9, no. 4 (December 2010).

38. Chris Anderson, *Free: The Future of a Radical Price* (New York: Hyperion, 2009), 3.

39. Scholars talk about multi-homing versus single-homing: under multi-homing, a user can belong to multiple networks at once; under single-homing, a user must belong to one network exclusively. See Mark Armstrong, "Competition in Two-sided Markets." *RAND Journal of Economics* 37, no. 3 (September 2006): 668–91.

40. Adam Grant, *Give and Take: A Revolutionary Approach to Success* (New York: Viking, 2013), 43–46.

41. According to Relational Models Theory, this assumes that buyers (parents looking for sitters) agree that SitterCity is a market and therefore seeking profits is appropriate. See Alan Fiske, "The Four Elementary Forms of Sociality: Framework for a Unified Theory of Social Relations," *Psychological Review* 99, no. 4 (1992): 689–723.

42. Thiers is using the term "tipping point" in Malcolm Gladwell's sense—the moment at which something suddenly starts to spread like wildfire. Scholars of two-sided networks also talk about tipping (although not tipping points), but they mean something rather different: "the tendency of one system to pull away from its rivals in popularity once it has gained an initial edge," according to a seminal paper on network effects. See Michael L. Katz and Carl Shapiro, "Systems Competition and Network Effects," *Journal of Economic Perspectives* 8, no. 2 (Spring 1994): 106. This kind of tipping doesn't always occur. For example, when users can simultaneously be on two or more platforms (multihoming), a single platform need not prevail—so while SitterCity may have reached a tipping point, the matchmaking between parents and babysitters hasn't tipped toward any one platform.

43. This statement is a corollary of the so-called Metcalfe's Law, which postulates that the value of a network is proportional to the square of the number of users of the network. We shouldn't take this formula literally, and Bob Metcalfe himself has said that his point was to show a crossover point of cost and value, the critical mass of users before which a network doesn't pay, rather than to tout the wondrous value of a large network. Regardless of the exact relationship, the basic idea that the value of a network grows at a faster rate than its size is well accepted. And if it is true, then the larger the network, the more attractive it becomes to new users. See Bob Briscoe, Andrew Odlyzko, and Benjamin Tilly, "Metcalfe's Law Is Wrong," *IEEE Spectrum* July 2006.

44. In Tennessee, where Stoxstill-Diggs works, anyone 18 or older with a high-school diploma can get a license by passing an exam after 60 hours of coursework. To affiliate with a brokerage, candidates need to take 30 more hours of classes.

45. The 90th percentile is $98,090, and the 75th is $65,100. These numbers come from the latest estimates from the Bureau of Labor Statistics for May 2013. Retrieved from http://www.bls.gov/oes/current/oes419022.htm.

46. Panle Jia Barwick and Parag A. Pathak, "The Costs of Free Entry: An Empirical Study of Real Estate Agents in Greater Boston," *Rand Journal of Economics* 46, no. 1 (Spring 2015): 103–45.

47. Chang-Tai Hsieh and Enrico Moretti, "Can Free Entry be Inefficient? Fixed Commissions and Social Waste in the Real Estate Industry," *Journal of Political Economy* 111, no. 5 (2003): 1076–122.

2 THE CERTIFIER: APPLYING THE SEAL OF APPROVAL

1. *American Pickers, Too Hot to Handle,* season 2, episode 18, 2011.

2. Libby Callaway with Mike Wolfe, Frank Fritz, and Danielle Colby, *American Pickers Guide to Picking* (New York: Hyperion, 2011), 11.

3. Libby Callaway with Mike Wolfe, Frank Fritz, and Danielle Colby, *American Pickers Guide to Picking,* 107.

4. Loren Feldman, "Goldman Sachs and the $580 Million Black Hole," *New York Times*, July 14, 2012.

5. Ruchika Tulshyan, "$100,000 Matchmaker, Make Me a Match," *Time*, August 2, 2010.

6. This is the International Marriage Broker Regulation Act of 2005, also known as IMBRA. Government intervention was necessary because there wasn't enough of a market incentive for these brokers to screen the men, who were the buyers in these transactions. For an account of one of the murders that led to IMBRA, see http://www.washingtonpost.com/wp-dyn/articles /A61168-2004Nov18.html.

7. Paul Hawkinson, "Why Recruiters Are Worth What They Charge," *The Fordyce Letter*, November 1, 2005.

8. Ben Fox Rubin, "LinkedIn Reaches 300 Million Members Globally," *Wall Street Journal*, April 18, 2014.

9. LinkedIn, "LinkedIn Announces Second Quarter 2014 Results," LinkedIn press release, July 31, 2014, retrieved from http://investors.linkedin.com /releasedetail.cfm?ReleaseID=863494.

10. Interview with Howard Robboy, May 24, 2012.

11. Decision scientists call this a sequential-search problem, the classic version of which is the secretary problem: candidates must be seen one at a time, and must be either accepted or rejected with no going back. The challenge is to find the optimal stopping rule. See, for example, Thomas S. Ferguson, "Who Solved the Secretary Problem?" *Statistical Science* 4, no. 3 (August 1989): 282–89.

12. Gary Biglaiser, "Middlemen as Experts," *Rand Journal of Economics* 24, no. 2 (Summer 1993).

13. The more expensive the good, the more it's worth spending to learn something about evaluating it, but even with expensive goods, it is usually more efficient to hire someone who you know already has the expertise rather than trying to acquire this expertise yourself.

14. The few times people have asked her to come "cherry-pick their closets" have taught her to avoid the practice, since seeing what she thinks will sell makes people reconsider parting with their clothes.

15. Jonathan Berr, "Mike Wolfe of *American Pickers*: 'It's Rough Out There Finding Good Stuff,'" *Daily Finance*, February 14, 2011.

16. Bronze PowerSellers must have a minimum of $1000 in sales each month. To achieve Silver level, sellers must have at least $3000 in monthly sales. The number rises to $10,000 for Gold, $25,000 for Platinum, and an astounding $150,000 per month for Titanium.

17. You must also get consistently high feedback scores from your buyers: fall anywhere below 98 percent positive feedback, and you lose your PowerSeller status.

18. Interview with Ann Whitley Wood, September 24, 2013.

19. Along the same lines, a recent article pointed out that large players also dominate the Prosper Marketplace (where two-thirds of the lenders are hedge funds and other large institutions) and that nearly half of the hosts on Airbnb had at least three listings on the site, suggesting these hosts weren't just renting out a spare bedroom. See William Alden, "The Business Tycoons of Airbnb," *New York Times Magazine*, November 25, 2014.

20. Paul Resnick, Richard Zeckhauser, John Swanson, and Kate Lockwood, "The Value of Reputation on eBay: A Controlled Experiment," *Experimental Economics* 9, no. 2 (2006): 79–101.

21. Nira Yacouel and Aliza Fleischer, "The Role of Cybermediaries in Reputation Building and Price Premiums in the Online Hotel Market," *Journal of Travel Research* 51, no. 2 (2012): 219–26.

22. Michael Anderson and Jeremy Magruder, "Learning from the Crowd: Regression Discontinuity Estimates of the Effects of an Online Review Database," *The Economic Journal* 122, no. 563 (September 2012): 957–89.

23. Michael Luca, "Reviews, Reputation, and Revenue: The Case of Yelp.com," Harvard Business School Working Paper, No. 12–016.

24. Carl Shapiro, "Premiums for High Quality Products as Returns to Reputation," *The Quarterly Journal of Economics* (November 1983): 659–79.

25. Investing in a storefront is one of several ways sellers can elicit trust among buyers. See Patricia M. Doney and Joseph P. Cannon, "An Examination of the Nature of Trust in Buyer-Seller Relationships," *Journal of Marketing* 61, no. 2 (April 1997): 35–51.

26. In insurance contexts, the vicious cycle is sometimes called the death spiral. See David M. Cutler and Richard J. Zeckhauser, "Adverse Selection in Health Insurance," *Forum for Health Economics & Policy* (1998).

27. George A. Akerlof, "The Market for 'Lemons': Quality Uncertainty and the Market Mechanism," *The Quarterly Journal of Economics* 84, no. 3 (August 1970): 488–500.

28. Joel Grover and Matt Goldberg, "False Claims, Lies Caught on Tape at Farmers Markets," NBC Los Angeles, September 23, 2010.

29. Shoshana Walter, "Farm Fakes: A History of Fraudulent Food," *Modern Farmer*, May 3, 2013.

30. Specifically, the bill created a way for the markets to tax vendors at farmers' markets to fund these outside inspectors. See David Karp, "New California Law Aims to Rid Farmers Markets of Cheaters," *Los Angeles Times*, September 29, 2014.

31. David Karp, "Produce Inspectors Keep Farmers Markets Honest," *Los Angeles Times*, December 26, 2013.

32. Interview with Carol Shamon, April 2, 2014.

33. Michael Neff, "Poise, Tenacity, and Clancy: An Interview with Deborah Grosvenor," Algonkian Writer Conferences, retrieved from http://webdelsol.com/Algonkian/interview-dgrosvenor.htm.

34. Michael Neff, "A View from the Top: An Interview with Robert Gottlieb, Chairman of Trident Media Group," Algonkian Writer Conferences, retrieved from http://webdelsol.com/Algonkian/interview-rgottlieb.htm.

35. Richard Whately, quoted in Richard S. Howey, *The Rise of the Marginal Utility School*, 1870–1889 (New York: Columbia University Press, 1989), 4.

36. Richard Whately, *Introductory Lectures on Political Economy* (London: B. Fellowes, 1831), 253.

3   THE ENFORCER: KEEPING EVERYONE HONEST

1. This term comes from the economist Kenneth Arrow. Hidden information can lead to the problem of adverse selection (the lemons problem), while hidden action can lead to moral hazard. For a discussion of hidden information (also called hidden characteristics) and hidden action, see Mark Bergen, Shantanu Dutta, and Orville C. Walker Jr., "Agency Relationships in Marketing: A Review of the Implications and Applications of Agency," *Journal of Marketing* 56, no. 3 (July 1992): 1–24.

2. Avinash Dixit, "Governance Institutions and Economic Activity (AEA Presidential Address)," *American Economic Review* 99, no. 1 (March 2009): 5–24.

3. One cattle breeder in Palermo told Gambetta, "When the butcher comes to me to buy an animal, he knows that I want to cheat him. But I know that he wants to cheat me." This mutual distrust would prevent the two from doing business. "Thus we need, say, Peppe [that is, a third party] to make us agree. And we both pay Peppe a percentage of the deal." Peppe acts as the Enforcer. See Diego Gambetta, *The Sicilian Mafia: The Business of Private Protection* (Cambridge, MA: Harvard University Press, 1993), 15.

4. M. Gysels, R. Pool, and K. Bwanika, "Truck Drivers, Middlemen, and Commercial Sex Workers: AIDS and the Mediation of Sex in Southwest Uganda," *AIDS Care* 13, no. 3 (2001): 373–85.

5. Terence C. Burnham and Brian Hare, "Engineering Human Cooperation," *Human Nature* 18, no. 2 (June 2007): 88–108.

6. Melissa Bateson, Daniel Nettle, and Gilbert Roberts, "Cues of Being Watched Increase Cooperation in a Real-World Setting," *Biology Letters* 2, no. 3 (September 2006): 412–14.

7. The most complete discussion of this argument is by Ara Norenzayan, *Big Gods: How Religion Transformed Cooperation and Conflict* (Princeton: Princeton University Press, 2013).

8. Interview with Chuck Templeton, March 12, 2014.

9. Some middlemen businesses are trying to change that: it seems easier for highly popular restaurants to get away with asking for deposits. But even so, many customers balk. See Marshall Heyman, "New Services to Score Prime Reservations," *Wall Street Journal*, April 15, 2014.

10. Andrei Hagiu, "Quantity vs. Quality: Exclusion by Platforms with Network Effects," Harvard Business School Working Paper, 11–125.

11. Julia Angwin, "Putting Your Best Faces Forward," *Wall Street Journal*, March 28, 2009.

12. Note the difference between pseudonymity and anonymity; by giving users the opportunity to establish a track record under a given pseudonym, a system that allows pseudonyms combines the best features of anonymity with the best features of real names. For a discussion of some of the economics of pseudonyms, see Eric J. Friedman and Paul Resnick, "The Social Cost of Cheap Pseudonyms," *Journal of Economics and Management Strategy* 10, no. 2 (Summer 2001): 173–99.

13. Airbnb does something similar. See Itay Fainmesser, "Exclusive Intermediation," SSRN Working Paper, March 17, 2014.

14. Julie Weed, "For Uber, Airbnb and Other Companies, Customer Ratings Go Both Ways," *New York Times*, December 1, 2014.

15. Gary Bolton, Ben Greiner, and Axel Ockenfels, "Engineering Trust: Reciprocity in the Production of Reputation Information," *Management Science* 59, no. 2: 265–85.

16. For example, compare TripAdvisor (which enables anyone to post a review) with Expedia (where only customers can post a review): although someone can post a fake review on either site, it is much more costly to do so on Expedia. See Dina Mayzlin, Yaniv Dover, and Judith Chevalier, "Promotional Reviews: An Empirical Investigation of Online Review Manipulation," *American Economic Review* 104, no. 8: 2421–55.

17. This is a central argument of a book chapter that examines enforcement activities by middlemen as seemingly varied as the Roppongi Hills shopping center in Tokyo and the Harvard Business School. See Kevin J. Boudreau and Andrei Hagiu, "Platform Rules: Multi-Sided Platforms as Regulators," in Annabelle Gawer (ed.), *Platforms, Markets and Innovation* (Northampton, MA: Edward Elgar Publishing, 2009).

18. Hongbin Cai, Ginger Zhe Jin, Chong Liu, Li-an Zhou, "Seller Reputation: From Word-of-Mouth to Centralized Feedback," *International Journal of Industrial Organization* 34 (May 2014): 51–65.

19. Interview with Ginger Jin, November 20, 2013.

20. W. Scott Frame, Aruna Srinivasan, and Lynn Woosley, "The Effect of Credit Scoring on Small-Business Lending," *Journal of Money, Credit and Banking* 33, no. 3 (August 2001): 813–25.

21. The Prisoner's Dilemma, dealing with situations in which both sides have reasons to distrust the other, is probably the most common game for studying trust. I focus on the Investment Game because it is a much simpler game, dealing with decisions by just one side.

22. For a description of the first experiments using the Investment Game, see Joyce Berg, John Dickhaut, and Kevin McCabe, "Trust, Reciprocity, and Social History," *Games and Economic Behavior* 10, no. 1 (1995): 122–42.

23. Gary Charness, Ramón Cobo-Reyes, and Natalia Jiménez, "An Investment Game with Third-Party Intervention," *Journal of Economic Behavior and Organization* 68 (2008): 18–28.

24. Interview with Gary Charness, March 17, 2014.

25. This result is actually quite remarkable if you think about how the game is set up. Like the original Investment Game, this third-party variation was a one-shot, anonymous game; therefore, players couldn't see whether the third-party watchdog actually had ever punished anyone. The third party hadn't developed a reputation. It was possible, you might say, that the watchdog's bark was bigger than his bite. Also, the watchdog had no material incentive to punish—and, in fact, third parties who chose to punish Trustees were doing it at a cost to themselves. In the language of social scientists, the third parties were given an opportunity to engage in costly punishment, for which the only reward is altruism, such as the satisfaction of administering justice. Yet, some third parties did choose to punish, even though nobody was watching to make sure they did. That finding suggests a couple things: first, that some watchdogs were indeed willing to pay to punish Trustees, and second, that Trustees weren't perfect at anticipating the watchdogs' actions. (If Trustees knew that their greed would surely elicit punishment, they would have been more generous.)

26. This argument was originally laid out in a 1974 paper by Gary Becker and George Stigler. See Gary S. Becker and George J. Stigler, "Law Enforcement, Malfeasance, and the Compensation of Enforcers," *Journal of Legal Studies* 3, no. 1 (January 1974): 1–18. For an empirical test of this theory, see Caroline Van Rijckeghem and Beatrice Weder, "Bureaucratic Corruption and the Rate of Temptation: Do Wages in the Civil Service Affect Corruption, and By How Much?" *Journal of Development Economics* 65, no. 2 (August 2001): 307–31.

27. See, for example, Kevin Krause, "Former Texas Resident Charged with Extortion for Threatening to Destroy Client's Online Reputation." *Dallas Morning News Crime Blog*, March 27, 2014.

28. Many sellers say the company could do more to protect them from dishonest buyers, though. It is always hard for middlemen businesses to make both sides equally happy.

29. See Andrew Parker, "Spawn of Craigslist," *The Gong Show* (blog), January 21, 2010, retrieved from http://thegongshow.tumblr.com/post/345941486/the -spawn-of-craigslist-like-most-vcs-that-focus.

30. Jason Tanz, "How Airbnb and Lyft Finally Got Americans to Trust Each Other," *Wired*, April 2014.

31. Maureen Farrell, "HomeAway and Vacation Rentals By Owner's Confusing Review Policy," *Forbes*, January 20, 2011.

32. VRBO is just one example, and examples of weak enforcement exist in other industries. Floral-delivery middlemen usually don't check whether the florists they contract with make bouquets that actually resemble the ones in the catalog that customers order from. Also relatively useless as watchdog Enforcers are the sites with real estate agent listings that have no negative reviews whatsoever. A middleman that refuses to take any action against a bad apple damages his or her credibility as an Enforcer, and whatever value the middleman has must then come from something else.

33. Ann Levin, "When Renting Vacation Homes, Ask Lots of Questions," *Associated Press*, March 20, 2010.

34. Retrieved from http://www.consumeraffairs.com/online/vrbo.html.

35. This is the notion of a "psychological contract violation." Research on such violations in online marketplaces finds that when a seller lets down a buyer, the buyer tends to sever the relationship not only with that buyer but also with the marketplace as a whole. See Paul A. Pavlou and David Gefen, "Psychological Contract Violation in Online Marketplaces: Antecedents, Consequences, and Moderating Role," *Information Systems Research* 16, no. 4 (2005): 272–99.

36. There are exceptions to the protective power of Section 230. For one thing, the government can prosecute a website under federal criminal law. Section 230 also doesn't cover intellectual property claims. Also, another legal scholar, James Grimmelmann of the University of Maryland, told me that other enforcers, such as the FTC and attorney generals, can go after websites for making misleading statements—"promises that get taken away by the fine print." Interview with James Grimmelmann, December 22, 2014.

37. François Cochard, Phu Nguyen Van, and Marc Willinger, "Trusting Behavior in a Repeated Investment Game," *Journal of Economic Behavior and Organization* 55, no. 1 (September 2004): 31–44.

38. The phrase "shadow of the future" was coined by the political scientist Robert Axelrod. See Robert Axelrod, *The Evolution of Cooperation* (New York: Basic Books, 1984).

39. Interview with Julie McKenney, April 9, 2014.

40. This is the 2012 national median, which means that in that year half of the weddings in the United States cost less than that. People in the wedding industry sometimes cite the average, which for 2012 was $27,427, but that figure is misleading because it is heavily skewed by a relatively small number of extremely expensive weddings. See Will Oremus, "The Wedding Industry's Pricey Little Secret," *Slate.com*, June 12, 2013.

41. Dropping a vendor is the most common way for an Enforcer to handle disappointing service from a seller. Unless there are very few alternative vendors, there is little incentive to take the time to coach the vendor—it is easier to just switch to a different vendor—and McKenney says that when she gets a

call from a sales rep trying to win back business, she doesn't go into why she stopped referring brides their way.

42. Matthew Bidwell and Isabel Fernandez-Mateo, "Relationship Duration and Returns to Brokerage in the Staffing Sector," *Organization Science* (2010).

43. Interview with Riccardo Boero, March 10, 2014.

44. Riccardo Boero, Giangiacomo Bravo, Marco Castellani, Francesco Laganà, and Flaminio Squazzoni, "Pillars of Trust: An Experimental Study on Reputation and Its Effects," *Sociological Research Online* 14, no. 5 (2009).

45. Oliver E. Williamson, "Transaction-Cost Economics: The Governance of Contractual Relations," *Journal of Law and Economics* 22, no. 2 (October 1979): 234.

46. We are not even talking about the worst agencies, predatory ones that take money from hopeful talent without ever booking any jobs for them.

47. This is essentially a version of "Never attribute to malice that which is adequately explained by stupidity," a principle sometimes called Hanlon's Razor.

4   THE RISK BEARER: REDUCING UNCERTAINTY

1. Matthew Karnitschnig, Deborah Solomon, Liam Pleven and Jon E. Hilsenrath, "U.S. to Take Over AIG in $85 Billion Bailout; Central Banks Inject Cash as Credit Dries Up," *Wall Street Journal*, September 16, 2008.

2. Nicolas Kervyn, Susan T. Fiske, and Chris Malone, "Brands As Intentional Agents Framework: How Perceived Intentions and Ability Can Map Brand Perception," *Journal of Consumer Psychology* 22, no. 2 (2012): 166–176.

3. Michael Lewis, *Flash Boys: A Wall Street Revolt* (New York: Norton, 2014).

4. Margie Alsbrook, "Contracting Away an Honest Day's Pay: An Examination of Conditional Payment Clauses in Construction Contracts," *Arkansas Law Review* 58: 2005–2006.

5. Charles Duhigg, "Aged, Frail and Denied Care by Their Insurers," *New York Times*, March 26, 2007.

6. Interview with Jason Horejs, September 25, 2014.

7. Amanda Lee Myers, "The Art of a Recession: Gallery Owners Struggling," *Associated Press*, July 25, 2009.

8. This insight comes from Jerker Denrell, "Vicarious Learning, Undersampling of Failure, and the Myths of Management," *Organization Science* 14, no. 2 (2003): 227–43.

9. Patrick McGeehan, "When the Home Team Stinks, So Does the Scalping Business," *New York Times*, December 3, 2009.

10. Failure to correct for this bias has been called "selection neglect." See Jonathan J. Koehler and Molly Mercer, "Selection Neglect in Mutual Fund Advertisements," *Management Science* 55, no. 7 (2009): 1107–121.

11. Horejs takes a less contemptuous view of pay-to-play galleries than you might expect of a traditional gallerist and believes more galleries may switch to this model—not to prey on the artist's vanity or naiveté, but because gallerists rightly don't want to bear the expense of displaying an artist's work if buyers who see the work in a traditional gallery try to cut the gallery out by contacting the artist directly. For a thoughtful discussion of this argument, see Jason Horejs, "Should Artists Show Their Art in 'Vanity' Galleries?" *Red Dot Blog*, September 25, 2013, retrieved from http://reddotblog.com/artists-show-art -vanity-gallery/.

12. Kenneth Brower, "Bluefin Tuna," *National Geographic*, March 2014. The first tuna auctioned in Tsukiji each year typically fetches a lot more: in January 2013, the publicity-seeking owner of a chain of sushi restaurants successfully bid $1.76 million for a 222-kilogram tuna. Anna Mukai and Yuki Yamaguchi, "Japan Sushi Chain Pays Record $1.76 Million for Tuna at Auction," *Bloomberg*, January 7, 2013.

13. Theodore C. Bestor, *Tsukiji: the Fish Market at the Center of the World* (Berkeley: University of California Press, 2004), 257.

14. Notice that the tuna court functions as a private Enforcer. The key question the tuna court must decide is whether the wholesaler should have known, from what was visible, that the tuna was likely to be of poor quality. For more information about how the tuna court works as an institution for private enforcement, see Eric A. Feldman, "The Tuna Court: Law and Norms in the World's Premier Fish Market," *California Law Review* 94, no. 2 (2006).

15. So-called acts of God are events outside human control. In contract law, an "act of God" clause means that if an event outside a party's control prevented the party from fulfilling her contractual obligations, she cannot be held responsible. Similarly, in tort law, acts of God can reduce a person's liability for negligence.

16. The literary agent Eric Simonoff quipped in a *New York Times* interview, "Now we see advance amounts being paid in thirds, fourths and even fifths. For a writer dependent on those funds, that's not an advance, it's a retreat." See Michael Meyer, "About That Book Advance...," *New York Times*, April 10, 2009.

17. Alan Finder, "The Joys and Hazards of Self-Publishing on the Web," *New York Times*, August 15, 2012.

18. Kathleen M. Eisenhardt, "Agency- and Institutional-Theory Explanations: The Case of Retail Sales Compensation," *Academy of Management Journal* 31, no. 3 (September 1988): 488–511.

19. For more on this trade-off, see Bengt Holmstrom, "Moral Hazard and Observability," *Bell Journal of Economics* 10, no. 1 (Spring 1979): 74–91. For a more nuanced view, see Canice Prendergast, "The Tenuous Trade-off Between Risk and Incentives," *Journal of Political Economy* 110, no. 5 (October 2002): 1071–102).

20. Mark Koba, "No Job? Can't Refinance? How to Talk to Your Bank." *CNBC*, March 9, 2009.

21. Schuyler Velasco, "Zuckerberg's 1 Percent Mortgage: Why Does a Billionaire Need a Loan?" *Christian Science Monitor*, July 17, 2012.

22. Susan Ladika, "Will a Health Condition Kill Your Life Insurance Options?" *Fox Business*, July 8, 2011.

23. John K. Booth, "The Image Crisis and the Actuary: Understanding Public Misunderstanding," *Record of Society of Actuaries* 17, no. 4B (1991): 2389–2419

24. According to CrunchBase as of February 4, 2014.

25. The Floodgate name is another metaphor getting at the same idea: Maples talks about being "at the headwaters of the capitalist system" and looking for special companies that will be worth more than $500 million, "hoping to help those companies open the floodgates to these massive wins." See Irina Patterson and Candice Arnold, "Seed Capital from Angel Investors: Mike Maples, Founder and Managing Partner, Floodgate (Part 3)," *One Million by One Million Blog*, July 14, 2010, retrieved from http://www.sramanamitra

.com/2010/07/14/seed-capital-from-angel-investors-mike-maples-founder
-and-managing-partner-floodgate-part-3/.

26. Interview with Mike Maples Jr., September 17, 2014.

27. Paul Graham, "A Unified Theory of VC Suckage," *PaulGraham.com*, March 2005, retrieved from http://www.paulgraham.com/venturecapital.html.

28. Russ Roberts, "Marc Andreessen on Venture Capital and the Digital Future," *EconTalk*, May 19, 2014, retrieved from http://www.econtalk.org/archives /2014/05/marc_andreessen.html.

29. Ben Horowitz mentions Rachleff's influence in an interview with Stanford engineering professor Tom Byers, "Disrupting the Venture Capital Industry," Stanford Technology Ventures Program, *Entrepreneurial Thought Leaders Series*, November 19, 2014, retrieved from http://ecorner.stanford.edu/authorMate rialInfo.html?mid=3438.

30. Andy Rachleff, "Demystifying Venture Capital Economics, Part I," *Wealthfront Blog*, June 19, 2014, retrieved from https://blog.wealthfront.com/venture -capital-economics/.

31. "Marc Andreessen on Breakthrough Ideas and Courageous Entrepreneurs," interview at Stanford Graduate School of Business, March 8, 2014, retrieved from https://www.youtube.com/watch?v=JYYsXzt1VDc&feature=youtu.be.

32. Nassim Nicholas Taleb, *Antifragile: Things That Gain from Disorder* (New York: Random House, 2012).

33. Nassim Nicholas Taleb, "Learning to Love Volatility," *Wall Street Journal*, November 16, 2012.

34. For an overview of power-law distributions and some of the many phenomena governed by them, see M. E. J. Newman, "Power Laws, Pareto Distributions and Zipf's Law," *Contemporary Physics* 46 (2005): 323–51.

35. Patricia Cohen, "Richest 1% Likely to Control Half of Global by Wealth by 2016, Study Finds," *New York Times*, January 19, 2015.

36. Taleb wrote that "In Extremistan, inequalities are such that one single observation can disproportionately impact the aggregate, or the total." See Nassim Nicholas Taleb, *The Black Swan: The Impact of the Highly Improbable* (New York: Random House, 2007), 33.

37. Peter Thiel, *Zero to One: Notes on Startups, or How to Build the Future* (New York: Crown Business, 2014), 86.

38. Julianne Pepitone and Stacy Cowley, "Facebook's First Big Investor, Peter Thiel, Cashes Out," *CNNMoney*, August 20, 2012.

39. In the introduction to their book of interviews with 35 top VCs and angel investors (including Maples), Tarang Shah and Sheetal Shah observe that entrepreneurs who had founded successful companies "had a very strong intuition and access to asymmetric information" that enabled them to tap emerging opportunities. See Tarang Shah and Sheetal Shah, *Venture Capitalists at Work: How VCs Identify and Build Billion-Dollar Successes* (Berkeley: Apress, 2011), xvii.

40. This is in part to allow publishers to offset the loss of sales due to the used-textbooks market, as publishers and students have long been locked in a predator-prey arms race on pricing.

41. Maples's comment about VCs' response to the Chegg pitch reminds me of magazine writers' observations about editors who seem to see the world only through the narrow lens of a jaded Manhattanite, loving or hating story ideas based on their own experience alone.

42. Adam D. Galinsky, Joe C. Magee, M. Ena Inesi, and Deborah H Gruenfeld, "Power and Perspectives Not Taken," *Psychological Science* 17, no. 12 (2006): 1068–74.

43. Alison Wood Brooks, Laura Huang, Sarah Wood Kearney, and Fiona E. Murray, "Investors Prefer Entrepreneurial Ventures Pitched by Attractive Men," *Proceedings of the National Academy of Sciences* 111, no. 12 (March 2014): 4427–31.

44. Carmel Deamicis, "Mike Maples on Why So Many Female Founders Pitch Floodgate," *Pando Daily*, May 9, 2014.

45. David H. Hsu, "What Do Entrepreneurs Pay for Venture Capital Affiliation?" *Journal of Finance* 59, no. 4 (August 2004): 1805–844.

46. Interview with Josh Lerner, January 26, 2014.

47. Ernest E. O'Boyle Jr. and Herman Aguinis, "The Best and the Rest: Revisiting the Norm of Normality of Individual Performance," *Personnel Psychology* 65, no. 1 (Spring 2012).

48. Clay Shirky, "Power Laws, Weblogs, and Inequality," *Shirky.com*, February 8, 2003, retrieved from http://shirky.com/writings/powerlaw_weblog.html.

49. Haewoon Kwak, Changhyun Lee, Hosung Park, and Sue Moon, "What is Twitter, a Social Network or a News Media?" *Proceedings of the 19th International Conference on the World Wide Web* (2010): 591–600.

50. Meeyoung Cha, Haewoon Kwak, Pablo Rodriguez, Yong-Yeol Ahn, and Sue Moon, "I Tube, You Tube, Everybody Tubes: Analyzing the World's Largest User Generated Content Video System," *Proceedings of the 7th ACM SIGCOMM Conference on Internet Measurement* (2007): 1–14.

51. Chris Anderson, *The Long Tail: Why the Future of Business Is Selling Less of More* (New York: Hyperion, 2006), 53.

52. Anita Elberse, *Blockbusters: Hit-making, Risk-taking, and the Big Business of Entertainment* (New York: Henry Holt, 2003).

53. Interview with Sunil Chopra, September 23, 2014.

54. A brief review of the research appears in Matthew Bidwell and Isabel Fernandez-Mateo, "Three's a Crowd? Triadic Employment Relationships," in Peter Capelli (ed.), *Employment Relationships: New Models of White Collar Work* (New York: Cambridge University Press, 2008), 147.

55. On the other hand, middlemen can increase demand to create a market at a time of day when in the past it hasn't been efficient to provide one. DoorDash, for example, aggregates orders from many customers and has spurred so much demand that some of its participating restaurants have begun offering food during the traditional lull between lunch and dinner.

56. Ian Urbina and Keith Bradsher, "Linking Factories to the Malls, Middleman Pushes Low Costs," *New York Times*, August 7, 2013.

57. William Feller, *An Introduction to Probability Theory and Its Applications*, vol. 1, 3rd ed. (New York: Wiley, 1968), 466.

5 THE CONCIERGE: MAKING LIFE EASIER

1. This is the "Sarah Hall case," named after the lead plaintiff, a travel agent named Sarah Futch Hall.

2. Interview with Ellison Poe, June 20, 2014.

3. Nina Eberlijn, "Will the Role of the Hotel Concierge Become Obsolete?" *The Quintessential Concierge* (blog), September 27, 2011, retrieved from http://

www.thequintessentialconcierge.com/2011/09/will-the-role-of-the-hotel-concierge-become-obsolete/.

4. Daniel Edward Craig, "Is the Role of the Hotel Concierge Going Obsolete?" *Reknown* (blog), July 26, 2010), retrieved from http://reknown.com/2010/07/is-role-of-hotel-concierge-going/.

5. Tracy You, "Are Hotel Concierges Becoming Obsolete?" *CNN.com*, August 16, 2012.

6. Interview with David Autor, October 1, 2014. See also David Autor, "Polanyi's Paradox and the Shape of Employment Growth," NBER Working Paper No. 20485, September 2014.

7. This comment is widely attributed to the technical writer Alfred Glossbrenner though the original quotation may not have been as pithy. In a 1995 book, Glossbrenner and a coauthor write, "Your opponent is the vast quantity of information that's out there. That's why we've suggested the commando motif. With so much information now online, if you don't know what you're doing, it is exceptionally easy to simply dive in—and drown." See Alfred Glossbrenner and John Rosenberg, Online *Resources for Business: Getting the Information Your Business Needs to Stay Competitive* (New York: Wiley, 1995).

8. Lisa Miller, "Mommy Is Busy Right Now," *Newsweek*, February 6, 2011.

9. Herbert A. Simon, "Designing Organizations for an Information-Rich World," in Martin Greenberger (ed.), *Computers, Communications, and the Public Interest* (Baltimore: Johns Hopkins University Press, 1971), 40–41.

10. Interview with Benjamin Scheibehenne, August 25, 2014.

11. Interview with Barry Schwartz, June 3, 2011.

12. Interview with Duncan Watts, February 24, 2011.

13. Interview with Glenn Ellison, September 19, 2014.

14. Marketing scholars have found that customers interpret higher prices as an implicit promise of a higher level of service quality, hence the dissatisfaction from paying a high price to get a relatively low level of service. See Valerie A. Zeithaml, Leonard L. Berry, and A. Parasuraman, "The Nature and Determinants of Customer Expectations of Service," *Journal of the Academy of Marketing Science* 21, no. 1 (1993): 1–12.

15. The National Association of Realtors is the largest trade group in the United States. See Glen Justice, "Lobbying to Sell Your House," *New York Times*, January 12, 2006.

16. Interview with Jon Levin, June 23, 2011.

17. However, at least one study examining the relationship between real estate commissions and home sales finds no effect of a commission on the sale price of a house. See Panle Jia and Parag A. Pathak, "The Impact of Commissions on Home Sales in Greater Boston," *American Economic Review* (May 2010): 475–79.

18. Interview with Mike Bor, June 30, 2014.

19. This is an echo of a statement by a character in Ayn Rand's *The Fountainhead*, a salesman named Kent Lansing, though Lansing was describing his role as a Certifier for the novel's protagonist, the architect Howard Roark. "You could tell them why they should hire you so very much better than I could. But they won't listen to you and they'll listen to me. Because I'm the middleman. The shortest distance between two points is not a straight line—it's a middleman" (p. 321 in 1994 Plume edition).

20. Patrick Spenner and Karen Freeman, "To Keep Your Customers, Keep It Simple," *Harvard Business Review*, May 2012.

6 THE INSULATOR: TAKING THE HEAT

1. "The Player," *60 Minutes*, October 9, 2011.
2. Neeru Paharia, Karim S. Kassam, Joshua D. Greene, and Max Bazerman, "Dirty Work, Clean Hands: The Moral Psychology of Indirect Agency," *Organizational Behavior and Human Decision Processes* 109 (2009): 134–41.
3. Gabriel Rossman, "Obfuscatory Relational Work and Disreputable Exchange," *Sociological Theory* 32, no. 1 (May 2014): 43–63.
4. Mikhail Drugov, John Hamman, and Danila Serra, "Intermediaries in Corruption: An Experiment," *Experimental Economics* 17, no. 1 (March 2014): 78–99.
5. For a review, see Neeru Paharia, Lucas C. Coffman, and Max Bazerman, "Intermediation and Diffusion of Responsibility in Negotiation: A Case of Bounded Ethicality," in Gary E. Bolton and Rachel T. A. Croson (eds.), *The Oxford Handbook of Economic Conflict Resolution* (New York: Oxford University Press, 2012), 37–46.
6. William Finlay and James E. Coverdill, *Headhunters: Matchmaking in the Labor Market* (Ithaca, NY: Cornell University Press, 2002), 33.
7. Interview with Al Roth, July 25, 2011.
8. Jeffrey Pfeffer, Christina T. Fong, Robert B. Cialdini, "Overcoming the Self-promotion Dilemma: Interpersonal Attraction and Extra Help as a Consequence of Who Sings One's Praises," *Personality and Social Psychology Bulletin* 32, no. 10 (November 2006): 362–74.
9. David Fucillo, "Michael Crabtree: Man, We're Talking About Practice!" *Niners Nation*, October 7, 2009, retrieved from http://www.ninersnation .com/2009/10/7/1075558/michael-crabtree-man-were-talking.
10. Bryan Goldberg, "Michael Crabtree's Agent Has Gone Too Far, Betraying His 'Brother,'" *Bleacher Report*, September 12, 2009.
11. Lauren Shehadi interview with Pete Prisco, "Michael Crabtree Signs with 49ers," *CBSSports.com*, October 7, 2009.
12. Interview with Lucas Coffman, July 22, 2011.
13. Björn Bartling and Urs Fischbacher, "Shifting the Blame: On Delegation and Responsibility," *Review of Economic Studies* 79, no. 1 (2012): 67–87.
14. Chaim Fershtman and Uri Gneezy, "Strategic Delegation: An Experiment," *RAND Journal of Economics* 32, no. 2 (Summer 2001): 352–68.
15. Interview with Uri Gneezy, February 12, 2015.
16. These metaphors suggest a middleman more Predator than Partner: fans blame this kind of agent for raising ticket prices, and they may be right. As long as the agent continues to be valued by players and team owners alike, though, those two groups will continue to admire the agent.
17. Julie Ferrari-Adler, "Agents & Editors: a Q&A with Agent Lynn Nesbit," *Poets and Writers*, January/February 2008.
18. Interview with Kenneth Shropshire, July 18, 2011.
19. Interview with Robert Boland, July 18, 2011.
20. Interviews with Jeff Scott, October 25 and 31, 2012.
21. Interview with Hubert Willman, July 26, 2011.
22. An excellent discussion of how gender norms for communal behavior hamper women in negotiation appears in the book by Linda Babcock and Sara Laschever, *Women Don't Ask: Negotiation and the Gender Divide* (Princeton: Princeton University Press, 2003).
23. Hannah Riley Bowles, Linda Babcock, and Kathleen M. McGinn, "Constraints and Triggers: Situational Mechanics of Gender in Negotiation,"

Journal of Personality and Social Psychology 89, no. 6 (2005): 951–65 and Emily T. Amanatullah and Michael W. Morris, "Negotiating Gender Roles: Gender Differences in Assertive Negotiating are Mediated by Women's Fear of Backlash and Attenuated when Negotiating on Behalf of Others," *Journal of Personality and Social Psychology* 98, no. 2 (2010): 256–67.

24. Vicki Slavina, "Why Women Must Ask (The Right Way): Negotiation Advice from Stanford's Margaret A. Neale," *TheMuse.com*, May 27, 2013.
25. Scott Wiltermuth, "Cheating More When the Spoils Are Split," *Organizational Behavior and Human Decision Processes*115, no. 2 (July 2011): 157–68
26. Website of Rocky Mountain Home Staging, retrieved from http://rmhome staging.com/agents.

CONCLUSION: THE MIDDLEMAN ECONOMY

1. Michael Dell, *Direct from Dell* (New York: HarperCollins, 1999).
2. Matt Richtel, "Dell, in Shift, Will Offer PCs at Wal-Mart," *New York Times*, May 25, 2007; Kathy Shwiff, "Dell Adds Best Buy To Its Retail Push," *Wall Street Journal*, December 7, 2007; and Kathy Shwiff, "Dell Closing US Kiosks For Shift to Store Sales," *Wall Street Journal*, January 31, 2008.
3. Northwestern University, "Sunil Chopra: A New Channel Strategy for Dell," interview video, May 26, 2010, retrieved from https://www.youtube.com /watch?v=81awuyDhfA8.
4. Sharon Gaudin, "Dell Closes Kiosks to Chase HP in Retail Sales," *Computerworld*, January 30, 2008.

INDEX